Born to English parents in Melbourne, Australia, April has always maintained a strong passion for history and the written word. She possesses a deep interest in the spiritual and psychic sciences, and combines these interests to convey her Past-Life Memories.

April has travelled widely around the world, having resided in both Australia and Britain, and likes to think of herself as a "space traveller of the Earth". Currently, she lives with her family in an 18th century cottage in a quiet little village in Lincolnshire.

Dedication

This book is dedicated to my late, good friend, Rowena Brown, for her encouragement and support—and to my Muse, my dearly departed little Manx cat, Morgana. May they both be reborn.

AND TO GAIUS JULIUS CAECINIANUS,
WHOEVER AND WHEREVER HE MAY BE

April E. Claridge

A ROMAN AND A CELT – MEMOIRS OF A PAST-LIFE

AUSTIN MACAULEY PUBLISHERS™

LONDON • CAMBRIDGE • NEW YORK • SHARJAH

A CIP catalogue record for this title is available from the British Library.

ISBN 9781787103566 (Paperback)
ISBN 9781787103573 (Hardback)
ISBN 9781787103580 (E-Book)

www.austinmacauley.com

First Published (2018)
Austin Macauley Publishers Ltd.
25 Canada Square
Canary Wharf
London
E14 5LQ

Acknowledgements

With grateful thanks to the North Somerset Museum Service for their help in compiling historical and archaeological data; and to the Gorhambury Estate for allowing access to the actual site of the Roman villa.

"Man will come into being many times, yet he knows nothing of his past lives, except some dream or thought may carry him back to some circumstances of a previous incarnation. In the end, however, all his various pasts will reveal themselves.

Read, ye who shall find in the days unborn, if your gods have given you the skill. Read, O children of the future, and learn the secrets of the past."

Pharaoh Seti I (c1320 BC)

Britannia

Prequel

Autumn, AD 47
Worlebury Hill-Fort,
North Somerset

Intense cold. Swirls of sea mist upon this chilly autumn eve. The sound of the waves breaking steadily against the shore far below our proud fortress-home. I recall how impregnable our hill-fort always seemed. Bordered by sea and continually flooded grasslands, there being but one safe pathway leading up to the mighty ramparts, it stood defiantly above the surrounding landscape. Many a time the war-like Silures of Southern Cambria would attack from across the channel in an effort to steal food, attempting to scale the mighty stone walls that towered above the sands, and every time they would fail in their attempt. Our magnificent hill-fort remained impervious to attack... or so we of the Dobunni tribe believed.

While not a powerful tribe by any means and posing no great threat to the Roman invaders, we had nevertheless become a rather painful thorn that had caused enough of an irritation to warrant our complete extermination. While our northern brothers and sisters acquiesced to Roman rule, we Dobunni of the south fought fiercely for the lands we farmed and the seas we fished, for our freedom and independence. Our failure to understand the Roman "war machine" would not only result in the destruction of our hill-fort but was to bring about the annihilation of most of my people.

Silence now, and as the moon crept steadily above the horizon, the evening shadows stepped graciously aside before her.

The dank October air felt clammy against one's skin as we settled in for the night, and then, suddenly, out of nowhere, there came screams of pain, fire and rocks falling from the sky… sheer pandemonium.

Scrambling from my bed, half-dazed, I made it out into the open air just in time before my home was hit. I fell to my knees, trying to comprehend what was happening as the house collapsed behind me.

I have but little memory of the events that took place this night, other than they were swift, brutal and merciless. What I do recall, and quite vividly at that, were the feelings of terror, anguish, and the sheer helplessness as I watched my friends and family perish.

The first volley of artillery fire—the flaming fireballs which had torn our homes apart—had caused widespread death and devastation. In an instant, the main gateway had been set aflame. The second and third volleys saw our previously impregnable ramparts begin to crumble as huge chunks of stone were blasted away.

The ensuing panic that followed only added to the confusion that had erupted from the surprise attack. I escaped within an inch of my life, but my family… my father, the chief of our tribe, was most cruelly slain.

The Romans were to massacre everyone in sight: men, women, and even children. No one was spared. This was retribution in its purest form. There would be no pity.

And so, I ran, amidst my rage and tears of anguish in the scramble to escape, until suddenly I collided with something solid. I can still feel the cold condensation on the Roman shield. It pushed me backwards and I stumbled onto the ground. In an instant, the Roman soldier was upon me, pushing me onto my back and pinning me down against the damp earth. I struggled in vain, but his strength was too much for me, and then, just as swiftly, he himself was slain. The Roman legionary rolling awkwardly onto his side, a Dobunnic spear protruding from his back.

All, save seven of us, perished that night. Having fled through the western gateway and down to the beach, we had edged our way carefully northward along the shoreline, dodging in and out of the shadows like hunted animals, not daring to stop until finally we came to rest at a nearby rock shelter.

There, we had remained, cold and afraid, for what seemed an eternity yet in reality was perhaps but half the night. We could see the fire and smoke from across the bay and waited for the silence to return.

Slowly and cautiously, we then made our way back in the vain hope of locating more survivors. None were found. The retreating Roman Army was now nowhere to be seen. In one night, they had taken everything from us: our homes, our families, and our honour. They had left behind a desolate wasteland in the form of our once proud and mighty hill-fort, now reduced to so much rubble amidst the smoking remains of our homes. We would not forget.

Hurriedly now, we buried what dead we could as a final mark of respect before the wolves came scavenging, the bodies being interred into previously dug storage pits, and in many cases, some three or four to a pit. We then salvaged what little food remained and headed mournfully across the plains towards our only surviving settlement upon the Mendip Hills. Our little group walked in silence together beneath the clear, starlit sky. A full moon shone brightly overhead—the "Hunter's Moon"—and we, the hunted. A time when the moon was known to stay longer above the horizon, turning night into day. An obvious reason why the Romans had chosen to attack this very night, instead of, as was their usual practice, by day.

The Hunter's Moon had fallen late in the October this year. No one would have ever expected an attack after nightfall, especially given the swamp-lands that surrounded our fortress, but the Romans had been clever. They had sailed up the coastline from the south, with rafts bearing their mighty war-machines upon them. Our people atop the Mendip had not noticed their arrival until the fireballs had been unleashed, so no warning could be given.

A fair-haired young warrior, and my childhood friend, Anturiaethus, was leading the way. It was he who had got us all to safety and who had struck down the soldier who had pinioned me. I followed closely behind, a rebellious young girl of some sixteen years.

Next to me walked a woman. We were both rugged up against the bitter night air, the chill foretelling a frost this night. Shivering from both the cold and shock, I tugged my shawl closer around my face. We both wore our heavy woollen shawls pulled up and over our heads, and carried an earthenware jar each containing the last remnants of our food. All our possessions were what we now carried or wore on our backs.

Behind us walked two more warriors. The first bore a small boy of four upon his shoulders, the warrior's reddish-brown hair shining like burnished copper as it caught the light of the moon. The remaining warrior was carrying a girl of not more than six. They were this warrior's children and that of the woman. The little family of four all shared the same shiny, black hair, a trait of our tribe, the father sporting a long moustache.

Together, we headed off sadly into the night, frightened and alone.

Romano/Celtic era

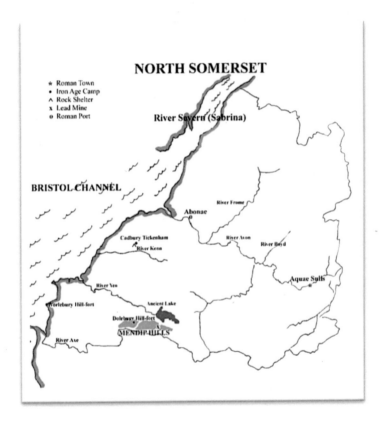

NORTH SOMERSET

* Roman Town
• Iron Age Camp
∧ Rock Shelter
x Lead Mine
o Roman Port

River Severn (Sabrina)

BRISTOL CHANNEL

River Frome

Abonae
o

Cadbury Tickenham
∧ River Kenn

River Avon

River Boyd

River Yeo

Aquae Sulis
*

Worlebury Hill-fort

Ancient Lake

Dolebury Hill-fort
∧
MENDIP HILLS

River Axe

Chapter One
Spring, AD 48
Mendip Hills,
North Somerset

Springtime and the Mendip came alive with wildflowers that spread from the grassy tops to the flood plains below. The sun was shining brightly overhead, although there remained a slight chill to the air. The winter snows had departed late this year, leaving the rivers in full flood.

I was running merrily across the top of a low hill, laughing and happy with the sheer pleasure of springtime and the simple joy of being young and alive. I felt free and unrestrained, my long, dark hair left loose and flowing, like the mane of a wild horse. Behind me ran a man, a little older than myself. We tripped in the long grass, rolling over and over together in a tangle of arms and legs, relaxed and happy in one another's company.

Our large, white pony was tethered a little way up the hill. He tossed his long mane about in the afternoon sun, watching our exuberance as if he wished to join in.

Finally, we came to a halt, breathless and dishevelled. 'Come on,' my companion said once we'd managed to catch our breath, his short, dark hair still quite neat despite the tumble down the hill. He stood up and dusted himself off, his white, woollen robe now besmirched with grass stains. 'We've gathered enough herbs and wildflowers for one day. It's time we were getting back. It'll be dark soon enough.'

'Oh, not yet, Dafydd,' I complained with a sigh. 'It's still quite early.'

Not now! Not while I was enjoying my freedom so very much. The mere thought of returning to the restrictions of hill-fort life was almost more than I could bear on such a sunny, carefree day as this. The winter snows had penned us in for so long that I had almost forgotten how it felt to have fresh grass beneath my feet.

I flung my long hair off my face. It was tangled up with bits of grass, so I sat there for a moment, deliberately taking my time as I carefully picked them out.

Dafydd gave me an exasperated look. 'I'll get the horse,' he stated flatly, and he began to walk back up the hill.

'Spoilsport!' I berated him teasingly as he strolled off.

Rolling over and onto my stomach, I gazed out across the flood plains below, taking in every detail as I scanned the horizon. The land seemed to stretch to infinity, the long grass waving gently in the breeze. The swollen riverbanks were abundant with wild birds and I watched them for a moment as a large flock took off towards the coast, and then I turned my gaze downwards, following the steep contour of the hill upon which I lay, to the flat land below. A small lake had formed off one of the flooded streams. It sparkled and glinted in the late afternoon sun. There were always floods at this time of year.

My eyes swept closer to the edge of the hill and suddenly I caught sight of someone below.

I drew in a sharp breath as I recognised a Roman soldier camped immediately beneath us. My heart was pounding wildly in my chest as I peered cautiously over the edge. Fear welled up in the pit of my stomach. For a moment, I was unable to move, afraid that he might see me.

'Dafydd!' I cried out urgently, as loudly as I dare. 'Get back here, quickly!'

Dafydd looked back over his shoulder, immediately turning about as he registered the look upon my face.

Desperately, I scanned the Roman's campsite, yet strangely the soldier seemed to be alone, having pitched a tent far below the fall of the hill. Why he should choose to venture into enemy territory alone, I had no idea, neither at this point did I care, but he was very foolish in doing so. The soldier had set up a small campfire by the side of the lake, where he was now busily involved in cooking some freshly caught fish.

Dafydd came running back down the hill and I signalled for him to stay low and keep silent.

'What is it, Dana?' he whispered.

'Look!' I said, pointing downwards to where the Roman was barely visible.

Dafydd frowned. 'We'd best get back and warn the others,' he remarked, sensible as always. If there was only the one Roman, our warriors would soon send him to his gods—but then, I thought again.

'Why?' I replied, as a wild plan was beginning to form in my mind. 'There is only one of them.' Now was an ideal time to strike, and I would have my revenge against their kind!

'You can't be serious!' Dafydd exclaimed, seemingly reading my thoughts. He was good at that was Dafydd.

'Why not? I can kill him easily,' I boasted in a huff. 'I have my sword.'

For a moment I thought Dafydd was going to laugh. 'You have your father's sword,' he corrected me patiently, his lips curling into a half-smile.

'Mine now!' My temper was beginning to rise.

'And do you know how to fight with it?' he taunted.

'I've had a few practice lessons,' I bluffed, grabbing hold of the hilt firmly for emphasis.

'Oh yes? Slashing at trees and playing at mock-battles with children?' he snapped sarcastically. 'No-one will teach you. You're just a girl!'

'Keep your voice down or he'll hear!'

Dafydd pursed his lips, his patience now beginning to wear thin. 'Our tribe doesn't permit its women to fight, let alone learn the sword. You know that, Dana,' he continued, lowering his voice somewhat. 'You shouldn't even be carrying that… that thing!'

That was it! My temper had now flown completely out of my control. Dafydd's continued sarcasm combined with my own burning desire for revenge having only added to my fury. He could be so irritating sometimes. 'Are you with me or not?' I snapped hotly.

'What do you think?' Dafydd retorted. 'Besides, you know I never carry weapons. I want no part of this. On your own head be it!' And with that, he turned his back on me and stormed off up the hill, obviously expecting me to follow.

'Coward!' I cursed under my breath, together with a few other choice words.

I scrambled to my feet. Nervously, I drew my sword, salvaged from the aftermath of Worlebury. Struggling to hold it proudly aloft, and with nothing but revenge in my heart, I began to run at full pelt down the hill, recklessly waving the heavy sword above my head in a fit of rage.

Although the Roman had his back to me he heard my approach from above him well in advance, for I was anything but stealthy. In an instant, he whirled about, instinctively reaching for his own sword and withdrawing it from its scabbard in one fluid movement.

The Roman "*gladius*" was a short, stabbing sword, extremely effective and lethal, deceptive for its size. I skidded to a halt a short distance before him, bracing myself for the first blow that must surely come.

Yet, to my utter surprise, and annoyance, the Roman actually lowered his sword. Perhaps it was the sight of a young woman that had stopped him? I was certainly not what he had expected. Whatever the reason, his refusal to fight me only served to raise my temper further. My anger and hatred remained intense as I raised my sword high once more. 'Fight me!' I yelled.

'I don't want to hurt you,' he said in very good Celtic, which I did not expect to hear… the words, nor the language.

Nevertheless, I began to run straight at him, bringing the sword down upon the soldier in one, angry blow as soon as I was within striking range, but the Roman merely stepped aside. The weight of the weapon combined with the gentle slope of the hill propelled me forward, and the heavy sword, which was somewhat longer than the Roman *gladius*, thudded into the ground before me as I over-balanced. The vibration of the impact ran up along the length of the blade and into my arm, stunning me for a moment.

'Leave it be, Dana.'

I turned my head slightly to see Dafydd, casually sauntering down the hillside, leading the pony. He stopped when he reached the bottom and sat down on the grass, looking on dispassionately. Ignoring Dafydd's remark, I returned my attention to the Roman.

'Come on and fight me!' I screamed angrily and struck out at him again, the rage inside me spurring me on.

Our swords made contact this time, metal upon metal, as he blocked my attack with ease while at the same time pushing me backwards. My clumsy attack had once more left me out of balance, and I stumbled to regain my feet.

'I'm not going to fight you,' the Roman officer stated calmly, and as if to emphasise his words, he casually turned his back on me.

Crouching down beside his campfire, he then stabbed his sword into the soft earth, and to my continued annoyance, and amazement, he not only totally ignored my presence, but returned to preparing his meal.

The impudence of the man! How dare he treat my attack so lightly, as if I posed no threat to him at all! Enraged, and seeing the perfect opportunity to strike him down at last, I ran at him. It was a coward's attack, I knew, but he was foolish to turn his back on me, was he not?

Obviously, although feigning disinterest, he was acutely aware of my every movement, and the Roman instantly spun about, retrieving his sword with great swiftness. Our swords came together once more with a deafening clang. It was quite apparent from the look upon his face that he was now becoming ever so slightly annoyed by this headstrong young Briton who would not take no for an answer.

He fought back hard this time, striking at my sword again and again, forcing me backwards one step at a time. Again he struck, and again, until a sharp pain suddenly seared my left shoulder. At this point, the Roman immediately ceased his attack.

Despite his claim for not wishing to hurt me, the move had been a deliberate one, fully intending to draw blood. Shocked and surprised, I stood transfixed for a moment glimpsing the wet blood upon my shoulder and feeling its warmth trickle slowly down my arm, then, taking a step or two backwards, I stumbled over a branch that was jutting out from beneath a fallen tree.

The soldier advanced towards me, a determined look in his eyes. My death was close at hand, of this, I was certain.

Dafydd instantly shot to his feet, the first sign of concern he'd shown. For all his aloofness and occasional sarcasm, I knew that deep down inside somewhere, he did actually care. In fact, he was one of the few close friends I had made since our relocation to Dolebury.

As the Roman moved in closer, fear and panic overcame me. There was no escape. Instinctively, I covered my head with my arms and closed my eyes tightly, waiting for the final moment. I felt the Roman grasp me firmly about the arms and waist, his hold upon me strong as he lifted me bodily off the ground.

All of a sudden, I was flying high into the air, and moments later I was completely enveloped in the icy waters of the lake. Coughing and spluttering, I struggled to sit up once I realised that where I had landed was really quite shallow. The sudden shock of the freezing water however had completely dampened my fighting spirit, leaving me dithering and feeling quite sorry for myself. Slowly, it began to dawn on me just how close to dying I'd actually been. The Roman soldier could just have easily decided to kill me.

I recalled my life as a child, how often as I strolled through the woods near my birthplace home at Tickenham I would play a little game to help pass the time. I would pretend there was some enemy or wolf perhaps close by and pre-determine my escape route should they give chase and attack. It was just five years ago, that I had encountered my first Roman.

On this day, my little game was to save my life, or at the very least, my freedom. Having only just decided in which direction I would flee should an enemy approach, there had been the sudden snap of a twig behind me and I'd taken off, heading down the hill to my right, at the bottom of which lay a river.

My heart was pounding wildly as I'd leapt into action, running down the slope as fast as I could, dodging trees and bushes as I went. In-between my footsteps I could hear those of another, also running, but becoming more distant.

I leapt over a fallen tree and ducked down behind it in order to catch a glimpse of my pursuer, my feet skidding upon the dampened earth. Peering out from behind the log, I saw a flash of red between the trees. I was not to know it at the time, but this was to be my first glimpse of the Roman invader. The man was strong and broad-shouldered, wearing metal body armour and with a large red plume upon his helmet. He caught sight of me peering out at him in astonishment and had allowed himself a wry smile before resuming his pursuit.

Instantly, I was on my feet. My only escape then, ironically, I thought as I stood there now dripping wet, was to be the river. Frantically, I had thrown myself across the remaining bushes and into its murky depths.

The water then had been cool but not unbearably so, though it was thick with silt from the riverbed and laden with twigs and fallen leaves. Distasteful though this was, the river had saved my life. My pursuer had given up the chase. He had watched me swim across safely to the opposite bank where I dragged myself ashore. Standing silently, he gazed upon me as I sat to catch my breath.

For some time, we continued to stare across at one another. I must have looked a sight, my eyes wide with fear, my long hair matted with twigs and mud. I tossed it across my right shoulder and wrung the excess water out, not for one moment taking my eyes off this strange warrior. Then, slowly he merely turned and walked away.

Most of my people had not believed the incredible description I had given them of this stranger who wore metal clothing and a large red plume, yet there were a few I think who remembered the stories of our grandparents, and how during the time that Caesar had arrived upon our shores he had set up camp briefly at Worlebury before moving on. They must have suspected what was to come. It was only shortly after my encounter with this stranger that there came the first raid upon the Dobunni.

Although unable to penetrate our hill-fort home, those caught outside had been either killed or taken as slaves. My only brother, yet still a babe in arms, had been one of them.

Sold into slavery or perhaps for adoption by some wealthy, childless Roman couple, and to be brought up in Roman ways, I was never to see him again. Thus, was planted the seed of my hatred.

Now, as I gazed towards the grassy bank, I saw Dafydd standing there, arms folded across his chest and giving me his *"I told you so"* look. I always hated it when he was right! He would never let me hear the end of this, I was sure.

Carefully, I attempted to stand. Although the water was not even waist high, the mud beneath my feet felt slippery, and they were beginning to slide.

Despite the flight through the air and the sudden drenching, I had still retained my grasp on my sword; however, the weight of the weapon now only served to hamper my efforts. I took a tentative step forward. My feet went from under me, and down I went beneath the water once more!

Again, I managed to stand, balancing as best I could. I dared not move for my feet would surely slip anew. It was then that I noticed the Roman, watching my plight from the water's edge. He smiled and stepped forward, placing one foot in the water as he offered me an outstretched hand.

'I don't want to hurt you,' he reiterated once again.

Hesitating, I began to shiver as the breeze suddenly grew in strength, blowing upon my wet garments and chilling me to the very bone. Reluctantly, I reached out with my free hand, realising that I had very little choice but to accept his assistance. He clasped it firmly, pulling me swiftly up onto dry land, while at the same time grasping my sword and twisting it out of my other hand before I had time to complain. He then casually tossed the sword aside, our eyes locked together in silent battle.

I hardly even noticed when Dafydd placed his cloak about my shoulders for my attention was firmly focused upon the Roman who still had a tight hold of my hand. I stood transfixed as I gazed up at him, his complexion unusually fair, I thought, for that of a Roman. He returned my look with a hint of amusement in his eyes.

'So tell me,' he said at length, 'are you as passionate in bed as you are in battle?'

Angrily, I snatched my hand away from his grasp. 'Typical Roman!' I snapped. 'First you try to drown me, then you want me in your bed!'

I stormed over to the fallen tree and sat down upon it in a huff. Whether I was shaking from anger or the cold I could not tell.

'It's your own fault.'

I looked up. Dafydd had followed me over.

'I hate to say "I told you so",' he added, 'but…'

'Don't then!' I retorted hotly. 'In any case, I didn't see you offering any assistance!'

Dafydd sighed. It was that weary sort of sigh that always got on my nerves. He was such a placid, even tempered man that sometimes I found it quite hard to believe he was of full Dobunni blood.

'Coward!' I accused him once again, turning my head away.

The Roman, I noticed, stood watching us both in obvious amusement, arms folded across his chest in a relaxed sort of manner, clearly enjoying the entertainment. Smiling, he walked across slowly to stand before me.

'I wasn't trying to drown you,' he stated plainly. 'Throwing you into the lake was the only way I could think of to stop you from fighting me, without actually killing you.' His gaze didn't falter as he looked down upon me, studying me with a piercing intensity, yet with the trace of a smile still playing upon his lips.

I felt the blood rush to my cheeks and I turned away quickly. The Roman, too, then turned away. He strolled back over to the water's edge and I watched him surreptitiously as he began to search amongst the reeds for something. It did not take him long to find what he was looking for. He bent down to retrieve my discarded sword.

My eyes were fixed upon him without expression as he turned it over idly in his hands. He seemed deep in thought, thoroughly admiring the details of its workmanship with a keen eye and taking particular interest in the highly decorated hilt with its design of swirls and patterns: A gift from the Atrebates, Antur's people. He turned it over yet again in his hands, continuing to admire the decoration, and then held it out straight before him looking along the full length of the blade for any sign of imperfection.

I suddenly felt fiercely possessive of this weapon—this sword—which was after all, all that I had left of my home and family at Worlebury. I looked upon it almost as a symbol of our people, of all we stood for, and now it was in the hands of the enemy!

The Roman officer was expertly testing the sword out for weight and balance as he began to stroll back over towards us. He halted in his stride, looking across at me with a steady gaze.

'You shouldn't carry one of these if you don't know how to use it,' he commented drily. At this I felt somewhat embarrassed, and I lowered my eyes, suddenly feeling ashamed of both my behaviour and lack of skill. He then approached nearer. Standing directly in front of me, and to my surprise, he held the sword out before him, offering its return.

Shyly, I looked up at him and carefully took the sword, returning it to its scabbard with all due reverence.

A warm smile crept across his face. 'Why don't we see if we can't find you something dry to wear?' he entreated amiably, offering me his hand.

I hesitated for a moment and he gestured towards a small tent. It was more or less square in shape and seemed just about high enough for a person to stand up in. He had positioned it hard up against the base of the hill so that it was well concealed from any prying eyes.

I arose slowly, if a little shakily, refusing his assistance and began to walk towards it with as much dignity as I could muster. The Roman was following close behind.

He reached across in front of me as we neared the tent, holding the flap aside for me to enter. I stepped inside and halted in astonishment, for the tent was filled with all manner of things. I had to wonder how they ever managed to transport so many items across the length and breadth of the country, or why they should even want to bother.

There was a heavy woollen blanket lying on the ground to the left atop some fur skins, obviously for sleeping on, while along the opposite wall lay a variety of bowls, urns and cooking pots, all neatly aligned. Beside these stood a pitcher of water, and in the far corner to my right were hung a few robes. Lastly, below these lay some writing instruments and rolled up pieces of parchment that had been carefully positioned to one side. The Roman eased his way past me and walked over to where the robes were hanging.

'I've no clothing for a woman,' he said softly, 'but perhaps you can do something with one of these?' He held out a garment for me to inspect.

I stepped forward and slowly took it from him, feeling the quality of the cloth beneath my fingertips. My fingers

27

accidentally brushed against his in the process and I blushed suddenly. He pulled his hand away swiftly, seemingly a little embarrassed himself. I couldn't help noticing that he was standing somewhat closer than necessary, even given the size of the tent and the number of items in it. I could feel his hot breath upon my shoulder, making it extremely hard for me to concentrate.

'Yes, well,' he murmured uneasily. 'I'll just wait outside.'

I wondered if he was perhaps embarrassed by the sudden close proximity between us, as he turned swiftly about and abruptly left the tent.

Returning my attention to the few garments that hung before me, I tried to regain my composure myself, browsing idly. Presumably these were worn when the soldier was off-duty. I came across one that seemed suitable and began to remove my wet clothing, wrapping the robe around myself and securing it with my own, coarse, rope belt, complete with scabbard and sword attached. Although the rope was also soaking wet, it would have to suffice, and at least I now had dry clothes to wear until my own had dried out. With darkness soon to fall, there would be no chance of doing so until the following day.

The rope belt still had plenty of length left, so I brought the end pieces up and across my shoulders to ensure that the loose-fitting robe would not slip, and knotted it well behind my back. My injured shoulder began to sting as the rope began to chafe upon it, making me wince. I gave it a cursory glance. The wound seemed but a minor one and was not half as deep as I had expected. At least it had been washed clean by the water, or so I thought, and the bleeding seemed to be coming to a halt. I pulled the cloth back over it, easing the rope to one side a little, and thought no more about it.

Ready now to venture outside, I halted in my stride, my hand upon the tent flap, as I overheard Dafydd and the Roman soldier laughing and chatting amiably, as if they were old friends. For a moment, I angered, thinking that they had been laughing at me, but no. Curiously, as I continued to listen, they seemed to be discussing everything from Roman Army food to tactics and regulations, and generally comparing the differences, and similarities I realised with some surprise, between our peoples.

I braved a peek through the tent flap. Dafydd was happily engaged in munching on some of the baked fish that the soldier had been cooking earlier.

'You speak our language well,' he remarked between mouthfuls.

'Thank you,' the Roman replied courteously. 'I spent some time in Gaul,' he went on to explain. 'Many of us did. Actually, my grandfather's grandfather was a Gaul. He served alongside the great Caesar himself...' pausing in mid-conversation as I stepped from without the tent, 'and obtained Roman citizenship when he retired,' he finished off, gazing across at me and smiling admiringly. 'That looks much better,' he remarked. He arose and walked towards me. 'Come! Have something to eat and drink.'

He offered me an arm, which this time I accepted meekly, and I returned with him to the fireside. I declined his offer of food, however, and took only a little of the wine.

The Roman introduced himself as Gaius Julius Caecinianus, and then went on to explain the reason for having the three names. Ever since his great, great grandfather had acquired citizenship, the first two names had been repeatedly handed down throughout the generations. One always took the first name, or names, of the emperor who had granted the citizenship, apparently; in this case, Gaius Julius Caesar himself. The last name could be either inherited, or adopted as a personal distinction.

I found this to be most confusing, but at least his Gallic ancestry explained his fair complexion. 'So, which name do we call you by?' I enquired boldly, adding somewhat cheekily. 'Or do you prefer all three?'

'Gaius will suffice, thank-you,' he replied with a smile as he noticed the perplexed look upon our faces while totally failing to respond to my taunt.

'I am Dafydd, and this is Dana,' Dafydd stated matter-of-factly. 'Actually, that's the shortened version of her name,' he added in his teasing manner that never failed to irritate me. 'It's really *Danamanadera*, but shortening it makes it simpler.' Dafydd gave me a wink and a wry grin, which I ignored.

'Well, shortening it certainly makes it easier to remember!' Gaius Julius commented with a laugh. 'You Celts have such long names!'

'We're *not* Celts!' I declared haughtily. How dare he insult our names, our heritage, and he himself claiming Gallic ancestry! 'At least we only have the one name, and our names all have meanings too you know!'

'I know that,' he answered patiently, as if talking to a child. 'I also know that your ancestors were as Celtic as my Gallic grandfather.'

I could not believe the impudence of this man! How could he possibly presume to know the ancestry of my people? No one, other than a Dobunni knew this. I was about to dispute his last remark with him further when Dafydd interrupted.

'You'll have to excuse my friend,' Dafydd apologised sincerely as I gave him an icy look.

What did he think he was doing?

'Not so long ago your Roman Army destroyed Dana's home,' he went on to explain. 'She lost all her family.'

'The hill-fort by the coast?' queried the Roman, and Dafydd nodded. 'I know of it.' He scratched at his chin thoughtfully.

Dafydd gave a sardonic sort of smile. 'Caesar's Camp, they sometimes called it,' he added in disdain. 'It is said that he once paid visit to our fortress atop the Worle.'

Dafydd knew all the tales of our people but hearing him recall the attack had now made me feel quite sad.

The Roman smiled gently. 'So, now you both reside, where?' He raised a questioning eyebrow and Dafydd pointed in the general direction where Dolebury Hill-fort lay. 'Atop the hills?' Gaius Julius asked, and Dafydd nodded once more. 'Ah!' he remarked knowingly, as if there were more he could add.

I began to wonder what it was, what he was thinking, what the Roman's plans were? A shiver of fear ran through me.

Swiftly he changed the subject. ''Tis beautiful country around here,' he said, gazing all about. 'I can see why you defend it so vigorously.'

With thoughts of Worlebury still spinning in my mind, and now this newfound fear, it took all my effort to hold back my tears—tears that I had never cried, not even after Worlebury's destruction, tears that I had been holding back for months and months. Not since that dreadful night had I shed a single one. I clenched my fists and rose abruptly, letting the wine cup fall to the ground as I ran to the water's edge. One stray tear had managed to escape, wending its way down my cheek and I wiped it away angrily with the back of my hand. I heard the two men approaching. They halted not far behind me.

'Are there many left of your tribe?' Gaius asked me softly.

I swallowed hard. 'Not many,' I replied, regaining my composure as I turned to face him. 'Our tribe consists mostly of women and children now. We've only a handful or warriors left.'

The centurion took a step nearer. 'All right, I accept what we've done in battle,' he remarked sincerely, 'but invasion is never pleasant.'

'This land belongs to us!' I snapped furiously, my temper rising to a pique once more.

'You? Does it?' The soldier laughed suddenly. 'Why, you're no more native to this land than we Romans are! Centuries ago, your ancestors—the Celts—did exactly the same thing. They invaded this country, and other races did so before them...'

Infuriated, I interrupted sharply. 'Perhaps my ancestors did, but we wouldn't have done so by wiping out entire settlements, slaughtering innocent women and children!' I could feel the

31

tension gripping my entire body as I debated hotly with this Roman.

'How do you know?' Gaius argued back just as sharply. 'No invasion is ever carried out without resistance!'

He had spoken quite harshly and I turned my back on him, bitter and angry. I too knew the tales and origins of our people quite well, and he had got it wrong on at least a couple of points… important points, at least they were to me. How dare he presume to know more about my people than I?

Gaius took a deep breath to calm him down, and then I felt him touch my arm lightly as he turned me around to face him once more.

'Nevertheless,' he began, softer now. 'I am sorry for what we've done to your people.' He smiled sympathetically, tenderly brushing his fingers across the moist trail left by the rebel tear that had escaped.

I remember thinking that he must be the first Roman soldier in history to ever apologise for such a thing. I could not imagine Caesar ever doing so.

'Come, have something to eat now,' he entreated.

I shook my head vigorously. 'I'm not hungry.'

'Please,' he added sincerely. 'How long is it since you last ate?'

'I don't know… midday perhaps.'

'Then, please?' he implored, a genuine look of concern upon his face. He smiled a smile which held such warmth that I found it quite impossible to resist.

I followed him lamely back to the campfire where I nibbled quietly on some of the bread while he told us more about himself.

We talked quite a bit as we sat around the fire, discovering that our Roman was not only an excellent swordsman, but also a *"militaris peritus"*, or tactician, previously with Legion XIIII Gemina, and was now a *"Prefect"* in charge of an Auxiliary cohort aligned to the Fourteenth, having taken command when the invasion first began, replacing a soldier who had fallen in battle.

Gaius was also a *"duplicarius"*, or an officer who receives double pay, and was fluent in three languages: Latin, Greek and the Celtic tongue. Added to this, he was learned in history and qualified in Roman Law before enlisting, being forced to do so by his father who had also paid for him to be enlisted directly into the rank of centurion without having to work his way up. In the Roman world, apparently, one's father's wishes must be obeyed; there was no other choice.

'Julius Caesar was my father's hero,' he continued on, finishing the last of his bread. 'He used to listen to tales of bravery and valour that *his* father... *my grandfather*... would tell about *his* grandfather, fighting alongside Caesar. I think my father envisioned me becoming a great General, like Caesar, but I've no ambition in that direction. He had me schooled in Roman Law, as Caesar himself was, precisely for that reason, but there my interest stops.'

So, here we had a Roman officer who was more interested in justice than he was in conquest. I had to smile at this, finding it quite amusing. And yet here I was being totally antagonistic towards him, when he had shown us nothing but courtesy and kindness, strange though this may seem. I had to admit I was beginning to warm to this Roman, and I laughed at myself in spite of it all. But why was he here?

'I know nothing of your Roman Law,' I stated plainly, 'and I've yet to see evidence of any true Roman justice, if such a thing exists. In our world, it is the druids who make and uphold the laws of our tribes.'

'Druids?' Gaius echoed, looking thoughtful. 'Ah, yes. Caesar had much to say on those.'

Again, I felt that he could have said more but was holding back. 'Dafydd is learning to become one,' I added. 'Did he tell you?'

The Roman shook his head. 'No.'

'He's already a Bard. He knows all the tales of our people, and more.' I continued proudly. 'Soon he will be travelling to the Isle of Mona to join the druids there. That's where the seat of their power is.'

The centurion's gaze was intense. He smiled thinly.

'But... you already knew that.' I leaned back casually, flicking my long hair over my right shoulder and smoothing it down somewhat.

He was watching me with a steady gaze, my every movement, my every expression. He was good at watching, I realised. Reading people like the druids would read the weather, or the future... The future. Would there even be one?

'There is much that we know,' Gaius replied softly. 'We Romans make it our business to know. There is not much that we miss.'

A chill wind began to blow across the flats so I wrapped Dafydd's cloak tighter about me. I couldn't help feeling that this was slowly becoming a battle of wits.

'So, tell me,' our Roman continued, 'do you speak or understand much of our Roman language?' For whatever reason, he seemed genuinely interested in all we had to say.

'We speak enough so as to be understood,' Dafydd answered promptly. He gave a contented stretch and placed his hands behind his head. 'T'was necessary for trade purposes, in the early days,' he added, 'well before our time.' He brought his arms down and folded them across his chest. Both men eyed each other up thoughtfully for a moment, locked in silent battle. Yet again, I had the feeling I was missing something.

Then there came an awkward lull in the conversation. There was one subject that nobody had broached. All this amiable chatter, yet the subject had been continually skirted around. It was Dafydd who finally broke the silence, abruptly voicing the question that no one had yet dared to mention.

'So, what are you doing out here on your own?'

There was a slight pause before the tactician answered, as if he was trying to formulate exactly the right words to say. He smiled knowingly, then, leaning forward, he placed his hands upon his knees.

'Oh, I'm just scouting ahead for the rest of the Army,' he replied nonchalantly.

Dafydd was beginning to look a little apprehensive at this reply. He sat up straight, his attention focused on the Roman Commander. 'So, just how many men would you have in this Army?' he queried slowly, trying to sound calm yet totally failing to keep the concern from his voice.

The air became tense, the joviality from any previous conversations long since forgotten. Time seemed to stand still as we anxiously awaited his reply.

'Only the two Legions,' Gaius Julius replied casually, as if it were nothing. He paused for maximum impact. 'About ten thousand men.'

'How many?' I declared, aghast, although I'd heard him perfectly well.

'And, exactly how far ahead of your Army are you?' Dafydd persisted, as if trying to piece together a puzzle yet giving the distinct impression that he really didn't want to see the result.

'About two days march,' Gaius answered truthfully. He appeared calm and relaxed, although he watched us intensely, I realised, poised like a coiled viper.

I could feel a sense of panic rising inside me. We Dobunni panicked easily. The words came forth from my lips before I knew what it was I was saying. 'And... how many days have you been camped here?' I tensed, dreading what the answer might be.

The answer came.

'About two days.'

'What!' I exclaimed, jumping to my feet in alarm. One didn't have to be a mathematician to work it out. The Roman Army could be descending upon us at any moment!

'I was wondering how long it would be before someone worked that one out,' Gaius commented drily, showing little or no concern for our apparent consternation.

'We've got to warn the others!' I announced, beginning to run towards our awaiting pony. Dafydd too leapt to his feet and swiftly began to follow me. All I could think of was the massacre of Worlebury happening all over again. I couldn't let

35

it happen a second time! I had to prevent it somehow! I was oblivious to all else.

Suddenly, our Roman friend was before us. To this day I do now know how he managed to move so swiftly; one moment behind us, the next, standing directly in front, blocking our way, sword in hand. His reaction had been an automatic one, ingrained by years of training and experience with the Roman Army. Dafydd immediately seized my arm and we skidded to a halt. Startled out of our wits, we discovered that I'd almost run full force upon the deadly blade that was less than a hand-span before me.

Even Gaius himself looked somewhat stunned by his own instinctive reaction. He swallowed hard

'You're not going anywhere,' he commanded sternly. 'No-one's warning anyone.'

It was a strange turn of events. We'd all been chatting so amiably all afternoon that we'd forgotten, for the briefest of moments, that we were mortal enemies. Even I, so determined at first on avenging my people, found that I no longer hated the Roman with the intensity I originally felt.

Yet now, as the tension remained, all my fears were beginning to return. 'Please!' I cried out passionately.

'You forget,' Gaius Julius stated coldly, his military mind snapping into action. 'I'm still a soldier with the Roman Army.'

'But… my people,' I pleaded desperately. 'They'll all be killed!'

The centurion gazed upon me without any hint of compassion, any trace of his previous warmth well concealed.

'And I have my men to consider,' he retaliated sharply. 'I cannot risk leading them into a trap!'

If this Army of ten thousand men were to attack our remaining settlement it would mean the total annihilation of the Southern Dobunni tribe. What trap could a handful of natives provide that could possibly harm those numbers? What could I say to convince him? What could I do? I took a deep breath to steady my nerves.

'At least let us get the women and children away to the hills?' I implored earnestly, holding his gaze. 'Please?'

The Roman officer sighed, then, against his better judgment, and to my sheer amazement, he relented. 'Very well,' he said. 'He can go,' indicating Dafydd. 'You, stay!'

Letting either one of us leave was going to lose the Romans their element of surprise that they had obviously hoped to maintain, yet how could they fail? They outnumbered us one hundred to one at least.

I nodded my agreement to Dafydd. Somewhat reluctantly, he began to walk across to our restlessly awaiting pony. It tossed its mane and whinnied at his approach.

'And Dafydd,' Gaius called out to him just as Dafydd was about to mount. 'Only the women and children.'

There was the subtle hint of a threat behind his words, just enough to remind Dafydd that my life was in Roman hands. He would need me as insurance of course, else our warriors could easily come and kill the Roman seeing as he was alone and an easy target, something I had failed to accomplish. Dafydd nodded his understanding, and then with one last glance towards me, he rode off along the track that led between the fourth and the fifth western most hill upon which Dolebury lay.

The setting sun had painted the sky above the floodplains a glorious mixture of red and orange. I stood now in silence as I watched my friend ride off towards that sunset.

So peaceful now, but what would the daybreak bring? So many of our people had died these past years, so many battles, so much sadness.

'I wish we weren't enemies,' I muttered absently, voicing my thoughts aloud as Dafydd disappeared from view. Another tear reluctantly began to descend down my cheek as I defiantly considered the safety of my people.

I heard Gaius walking up behind me, slowly replacing his sword within its scabbard.

'You're free to go too,' he said softly.

Surprised, I turned to face him. He took a step nearer, and then reaching out towards me he gently wiped away my tear with the palm of his hand. 'If you wish,' he added in a whisper, slipping his left hand firmly about my waist and drawing me in closer.

I gazed up at him, a nervous smile playing upon my lips as I idly traced the outline of his face with my fingertips; his golden eyebrows and greenish-blue eyes, the smoothness of his white skin. I noted particularly the high cheekbones that gave his face a softer look, all framed by golden, wavy hair brought forward onto his forehead in typical Roman fashion.

His smile was warm and tender as he pulled me into his embrace, kissing me with such an intensity of passion that it left me quite breathless. His arms felt warm and protective against the cold night air. Trembling somewhat, I clung onto him tightly.

'It's all right,' he whispered gently.

The small oil lamp within the tent flickered slightly. The breeze outside was beginning to strengthen. It played mischievously around the Roman tent, tugging at the flaps for all it was worth.

Gaius kissed me once more, tenderly this time. I felt curiously safe somehow, for the first time in a long while, his attentive, caring nature, for a moment, sweeping away everything that had ever made me afraid.

He unfastened his sword belt, carefully placing it upon the ground nearby, the *gladius* glinting softly in the pale light. I tensed slightly as my gaze fell upon it.

'Don't worry,' he said, noticing my expression and sensing my unease. 'Everything will be all right.'

Holding me close, he kissed me once again, his kisses becoming more and more passionate, more demanding, as his fingers began to fumble with the knotted cord about my waist.

And then abruptly, he released me. 'How on earth does one undo this thing?' he declared in exasperation.

Laughing, I teasingly backed away, untying the knot myself and letting the garment slip slowly to the floor. I gave myself to him there and then. We lay contentedly together, blissfully unaware of the world beyond the confines of the tent.

I was to learn that my centurion had not, in fact, set out alone on his journey southward as Dafydd and I had previously thought, but that he had been accompanied by three of his best men—soldiers of the VIth Thracian. They had come under attack from the Silures of Southern Cambria, extremely fierce fighters, and a common enemy of both our peoples. His soldiers slain, Gaius had then been reluctantly forced to flee for his life.

We talked much that night, and embraced, and made love. 'Ah, so I was right!' Gaius remarked at length as we lay back for a moment in order to catch our breath. 'You are as passionate in bed as you are in battle!'

Playfully feigning offence, I retaliated swiftly as I boldly leapt upon him, pinning him down in mock-battle.

'All right, all right, I surrender!' he laughed, taken completely by surprise. 'I may have vanquished you in battle, but you've certainly vanquished me in bed!'

Then, suddenly, unexpectedly, the situation was reversed. He somehow managed to twist his ankle around mine and in so doing flung me off him and onto my back.

I was totally unprepared for such a move, an immediate panic beginning to spring up inside of me as I was reminded of the assault I'd suffered at Roman hands during that dreadful night when Worlebury was destroyed. His grasp was firm about my wrists, pressing me down onto the bed so that I was unable to move. I began to struggle fiercely against him as my deepest fears arose.

'Easy, easy,' Gaius whispered softly, as if trying to soothe a wild horse, easing back a little when he realised my distress. I ceased my struggling and concentrated instead on fighting back the fear that was welling up within me. Slowly, Gaius released his grip on my wrist. He laughed softly. 'My little warrior,' he said, gently brushing my hair back from off my face.

Such was his manner and concern that I could not help but laugh with him for a moment before modestly turning my head aside when I began to blush a little.

'You like that name?' he enquired, and I nodded shyly.

Gaius smiled. He kissed my neck, then my shoulder, halting only when he noticed the sword cut. He sat back.

'I'm sorry I had to hurt you,' he apologised sincerely. 'I'll never hurt you again, I promise.' He bent over and kissed my wounded shoulder gently.

We could have been the only two people in the entire world as we lay there in the darkness and the silence, a silence that would all too soon be broken by the sound of marching feet of the advancing Roman Army.

Gaius held me closer, and closer still. Such a passion I had never known before. It tore at my very soul and wrenched at my heart. How could I be feeling like this about a Roman—our enemy? What was I thinking of? What was I doing? His compatriots had slaughtered and killed over half of my tribe, yet admittedly this Roman had shown me nothing but kindness and compassion. My thoughts were in turmoil. I felt both happy and afraid at the same time. I was helpless to stop the confusion that reigned in my mind. Memories of the massacre of my people, my family, the destruction of my home, came flooding back, returning to haunt me again and again, and with these memories came all the feelings that went with them... hatred, fear, panic, and sorrow... while simultaneously I could also feel an intensity of passion, warmth and joy.

The confusion suddenly became too much to bear. The torrents of tears that I had been holding back for months suddenly began to pour down my face in endless streams. Until this day, I had not shed a single one—for anything.

Not even after our initial escape from our burning fortress, when we had reached the safety of the Rock Shelter, having made our way slowly, painfully, northwards along the coastline, fearful with every step that we had been followed, had I allowed myself to cry. I had felt cold and afraid, my mind numb, yet I had never cried. Antur had kindly given me his cloak, but he had offered no other means of comfort. He was not one for showing affection. That was Antur for you—hot tempered and cold hearted, although, in reality, I knew that he really did care—of course he did, but in his own way.

Now, no matter how hard I tried, it seemed impossible to stop the tears from flowing. Past, present and future—all pleasure, all pain, was combined into one tempestuous storm.

Gaius held me gently, stroking my hair.

'I'm sorry,' I said shakily between sobs, tears still cascading down my cheeks.

'It's all right,' he replied soothingly, kissing my forehead gently.

'I'm so confused,' I wept. I wiped my tears away as best I could. 'The thought of your Army arriving here tomorrow, it… it terrifies me.' I felt annoyed with myself for sobbing such. This was not the behaviour of a bold warrior, of what I aspired to be.

'I know it does,' he smiled reassuringly. 'They won't hurt you,' he added. 'Not if I tell them you belong to me.'

My heart sank. I sat up. 'You mean as your slave,' I stated blandly. Was this to become the fate of the remainder of my tribe too, those that were permitted to live? Many had already become so, my own brother amongst them. Surely, death would be a more honourable way out?

The Roman gazed keenly at me, his expression giving nothing away. 'That is one way of putting it, yes,' he replied matter-of-factly. 'But I was thinking more along the lines of, my wife.'

'Wife?' I declared in astonishment. 'That's ridiculous!' I added with a laugh. Surely, he must be jesting?

Gaius turned aside, and for a moment he seemed shy and embarrassed. It had never occurred to me for one moment that his proposal might be a serious one. I certainly had no wish to hurt his feelings, and I suddenly felt rather awkward. Perhaps I had been wrong to laugh as I did? I began to feel quite bad for doing so. Slowly, I reached out toward him and placed my hand on his.

'You… you know nothing about me, hmm?' I remarked, by way of explanation. He looked up at me and I smiled apologetically, relieved to see him return my smile with the same warmth.

'Oh, I think I've seen enough for one day to know what you're like,' he teased, his gaze full of wickedness and delight.

Now it was I who felt abashed. It was true, in these times of rapid change, one had to grasp what happiness one could, for one never knew what tomorrow might bring. There may not even be one. Life could be short. The attack on Worlebury had taught me that, if nothing else.

'When… when we first met,' I stammered, my eyes downcast. 'I didn't mean, to be rude,' I finished off, as apologetically as I could.

'I know you didn't.' Gently, Gaius tilted my chin up and smiled. He placed an arm about my shoulders and hugged me close. 'I must admit, I quite enjoyed our little battle,' he added with a grin. 'You weren't that bad with the sword.'

At this I laughed! 'Liar!' I was hopeless, and I knew it.

'Well, at least you had plenty of courage!' he concluded with a smile.

'That wasn't courage,' I admitted sheepishly. 'That was anger.'

'I know,' he whispered. 'It's all right.'

I leaned my head against his shoulder and closed my eyes for a moment, trying to put my muddled thoughts into some sort of order. An idea began to formulate slowly in my mind.

'All right, I'll marry you, on one condition.' I gazed earnestly up at him. Gaius raised an enquiring eyebrow, so I continued on enthusiastically. 'Teach me how to fight with the sword?'

'Oh no!' he replied sharply, rising to his feet, his face set.

I was crestfallen. 'Please?' I urged.

'No!'

'But…'

'Listen,' he rounded on me, beginning to pace up and down as best one could within the confines of the tent. 'You start carrying one of those things about and you become a target!' He swung round to face me, his arm raised high, pointing directly at me for full emphasis.

I cowered away a little, but I was not to be put off, and then I thought if I hadn't had my sword with me this day Dafydd and I would most likely have ridden straight back to Dolebury and given the alert that there was a Roman nearby, and he would now be dead. And then, when the Roman Army does arrive, they would attack us without warning and we would be no more—the worrying thought remained that they may yet decide to do this.

Dobunni women were never taught to fight, and certainly not with a sword, unlike many other British tribes who had their roots in Celtic ancestry and proudly took their place alongside their husbands in battle. I admired those women, proud and strong, who could stand up for themselves.

Still determined to make my point, I continued on, for once I'd got an idea into my head there was no halting me. 'Well, what about self-defence?' I argued back desperately. If I could think of a logical reason, perhaps he would accept this? 'You can't expect me to live amongst you Romans without knowing how to defend myself?' I gazed pleadingly up at him, his expression remaining steadfast and unflinching. 'Hmm?' I ventured a weak smile and Gaius sighed.

'All right, all right,' he relented at last, 'but only for self-defence. And listen, I wouldn't go waving that sword of yours around at any more Romans,' he added emphatically.

This last remark of his made me giggle as I saw now the funny side of our first encounter.

'I'm serious,' Gaius reprimanded me sternly, putting a halt to my merriment. 'If you're going to insist on carrying that sword around, you'd better keep it well hidden. Roman Law can be very severe.'

My moment of triumph had waned and I modestly nodded agreement to his terms.

'Besides,' Gaius continued, sitting back down beside me, 'I don't want anything to happen to you.' He smiled warmly, tenderly stroking my cheek, deep in thought. 'Perhaps, I should not have asked you to marry me.'

My heart skipped a beat. He was not about to change his mind, was he?

'You may not feel comfortable living amongst us Romans,' he said by means of explanation. 'And your people will no doubt look on you as some sort of a traitor. It won't be easy for you, knowing how much you hate us.'

This most certainly was true. It would not be easy and there would most likely be all sorts of unimaginable problems, one of which was the agreement of the Dobunni Chieftain. Although it was not unusual for marriages between tribes to be arranged in a hurry, for trade or other agreements, but to wed a Roman? I mulled his words over carefully before replying.

'If someone would ever have suggested to me previously, that I'd be here like this, right now, with a Roman,' I began in a serious tone, and then I laughed, 'I probably would have hit them!'

That too was true. How much things had changed within the course of a single day. How much more would change in the days to come? I gave him my warmest smile, then holding him close I hugged him with all my heart, and Gaius laughed too. I felt safe now… I was his.

Sleep came in snatches that night, the day's activities leaving me feeling restless, unsettled and overwrought, despite my new-found security. What was to become of my people though was still in question.

Eventually, when at last I did manage to doze off, my mind became filled with a multitude of memories… bad memories, which all began to culminate like a brewing storm into one, horrific nightmare. So deep within this horror was I, that when Gaius awoke me gently I found that I was crying.

'It's just a dream,' he whispered softly, brushing my hair back from off my forehead. 'You're quite safe.'

I took several deep breaths as I tried hard to compose myself, trembling and afraid.

'What were you dreaming?' he asked gently.

I shook my head emphatically. The images had been too vivid, and I had no wish to recall them. I glanced at him briefly and he smiled encouragingly.

'It's all right,' he said, wrapping his warm arms around me.

It took me a few moments to gather my thoughts. Eventually, still trembling, I managed to tell him a little of what I'd dreamt.

'It was our settlement, on the Mendip.' I took another deep breath. 'Everyone was being slaughtered... just like before.' A tear began to form and I blinked it away angrily. Warriors didn't cry.

I had seen them all fall, in my mind, in my dreaming. I had watched the last of my tribe perish before my eyes.

The Roman forces had broken through our defences. People were running with nowhere to run to, then, one by one they fell. Roisin, my best friend and sister of Dafydd, and Dafydd himself were both slain. They had been the ones who had got me through those terrible first weeks after the destruction of Worlebury, for I did not speak nor eat for days. Anturiaethus—Antur for short—had been the next to perish in this nightmare. I had seen him gesturing towards me, when suddenly he fell, lying at my feet, speared through by a Roman javelin.

I shook my head to clear the image, swallowing hard, reminding myself that we were all still alive, at least for the present.

Gaius squeezed my hand reassuringly. 'It won't happen again,' he stated solemnly. 'I won't let it.'

How, by the gods, he was going to prevent it I was sure even Gaius himself had no idea, for while his advice was valued as a tactician, he was not the commander of his Army.

Although his words were comforting, it was now for the Fates to decide.

Southern Dobunni

Dana at Worlebury Hill-fort

Chapter Two

Spring, AD 48
Mendip Hills,
North Somerset
(The Next Day)

Sunrise promised a fine day ahead, weather-wise at least. I awoke this morning feeling stiff and sore. Every muscle seemed to ache incredibly. It was the sort of pain that seemed to numb one's entire body and it took a moment or two before I could move, stretching tentatively as I did so. A sharp pain suddenly shot through my left shoulder and I winced aloud.

'Are you all right?'

I turned my head slowly to see Gaius peering at me in concern. He looked as if he'd been awake for some time for he was already up and dressed.

'Just a little stiff,' I replied, managing to sit up slowly. Carefully, I began to rub at my injured shoulder. 'Battle fatigue,' I added with a laugh, trying not to sound too concerned.

'Possibly,' he replied. 'Nevertheless, I'd best take a look at that shoulder. I've some ointment that should help.'

He got up and began to rummage in a small, leather satchel, returning a moment later bearing the ointment together with a small bowl of water.

'I should never have wounded you,' he remarked apologetically as he began to bathe the injury. He paused a moment. 'The cut is deeper than I intended. I'm sorry.' He rubbed the ointment in as gently as he could. 'I was trying to teach you a lesson.'

'You did,' I confessed shyly. 'It was my fault, not yours.'

'You'll have a scar,' he pointed out gravely.

'Good!' I exclaimed with a smile, and he raised an eyebrow in surprise. 'Then I'll always have a reminder of how we met,' I explained, laughing. 'Not that I'm ever likely to forget!' I placed my hand upon his. 'The shoulder will be fine.'

Half the day had elapsed before the first sign of the approaching Army came. I knew the sound only too well and I had grown to fear it. That first sound, that continuous rumble, like the distant thunder of an approaching storm—the unmistakable sound of an Army on the move. From our vantage point atop the hill, the sight that now met our eyes was truly awesome.

'How many men did you say were in your Army?' I asked breathlessly, having run all the way up to the summit with Gaius at the first sound of their approach.

'About ten thousand,' he replied absently, gazing in admiration at the vast Army spread out before us. 'Only the two Legions; The Fourteenth, detachments of the Twentieth, and the Auxiliary units of course.'

The dazzling array of armour glinted in the afternoon sun. While Gaius obviously found the sight impressive he was totally oblivious to the effect it was having on me. This same sight had me frozen to the spot in absolute terror.

All I could see was masses and masses of Roman soldiers, my enemy and that of my people, advancing unceasingly across the fenland towards us. My worst nightmare was about to come true… again.

After a moment, Gaius glanced toward me. 'Are you all right?' he asked, for the second time that day. Judging by the expression on his face I must have looked quite pale. He reached out and gently took hold of my wrist. I was trembling with fear.

Sheer panic was taking hold of my very being, my every instinct telling me, screaming at me, to flee.

'I… was just wondering… why, I wasn't… running… away,' I stammered helplessly, swallowing hard.

Gaius laughed softly with amusement, and then suddenly he began to realise just how terrified I actually was.

'Don't be frightened,' he whispered, and I threw myself into his arms, clinging to him desperately like a terrified child. I closed my eyes tightly, shutting out the vision below.

'Nothing will happen to you, or your people,' he stated earnestly, easing me away a little and gently stroking my cheek. 'I promise.' His gaze was steadfast. 'Trust me,' he added with a smile.

I managed a weak smile in return, the knot of fear still tight within the pit of my stomach.

'You've still time to run away if you want,' he said. 'I won't stop you. Go and join your people, hide away in the hills…'

'And return to what?' I interrupted. 'To be captured and enslaved upon my return, or even killed?' I trembled at the thought.

'I won't allow that to happen,' he assured me.

'But you cannot guarantee it?'

Gaius paused for a moment, looking thoughtful. 'No.'

'Then I shall stay with you,' I said decidedly, and he smiled broadly.

'Let's go freshen up then, before they arrive,' he suggested. 'We have a few moments to spare.'

Gaius had taken but a mouthful of water before beginning to put on his full armour, securing his *gladius* with a strap that came across his right shoulder, then his "*pugio*", a long, ornate dagger, that hung from a belt around his waist. Finally, he fastened his cloak. As an officer, this was worn over his left shoulder.

I glanced down at my own apparel only to realise that I was still wearing the centurion's robe he had loaned me yesterday.

Quickly, I dashed outside to retrieve my clothing which had been drying across a low branch in the sun all morning. It felt dry enough, except for the woollen overdress that was still a little damp.

The sound of the Army approaching was becoming more noticeable. They could not be far away now, I reasoned. My heartbeat quickened as I re-entered the tent and began to disrobe, quickly throwing my dress over my head, straightening it out as best I could, and leaving the over-dress to one side to dry a little longer. I was just securing my sword about my waist when Gaius frowned at me.

'I'd leave that here if I were you,' he said. 'At least for the present,' adding quickly before I had time to object. 'It'll be quite safe.'

Stubbornly however, I refused, and continued to sling the rope belt about my waist. Although I had come to trust Gaius, I certainly did not trust the ten thousand Romans that were soon to arrive here.

Gaius sighed in exasperation. 'Well, if you're going to insist on wearing it, at least use a better belt than that impossible rope!' he suggested with a wry grin. He grabbed something from amongst his robes and tossed it to me. 'Here,' he said. 'Try this, it's a spare.'

I caught it deftly with one hand. 'Thanks.' The leather belt felt so much better than my course rope one, so I sat down and began to secure my scabbard upon it.

'And keep that sword well hidden,' he warned, tossing me Dafydd's cloak.

Reluctantly, I flung the over-dress on, despite the dampness and the fact that it was a little stained, concealing the sword beneath it, and then secured Dafydd's cloak about my waist for added security.

Gaius nodded his approval and poured me a cupful of the water. He then groomed his hair quickly before sitting down on the edge of the bed.

'Don't worry,' he said, smiling encouragingly. 'Everything will be fine, you'll see.'

Somehow, I still had my doubts. I took a gulp of water. 'Just the two of us to stop an entire Army of three Legions?'

'Two Legions,' he corrected me. 'And I am their best tactical advisor. They will listen to my advice.'

'And what if my people refuse to surrender?' I asked nervously. Gaius refrained to answer. He didn't have to. His silence spoke for itself. 'I'd be lying if I said I wasn't frightened.'

'I know,' he said plainly. 'We can do it, but I shall need your help to convince the governor not to attack. That was true, what you said, about the numbers of your tribe?'

I nodded sadly. Gaius took my hand and kissed it lightly, meanwhile the sound of the approaching Army was becoming louder and louder.

'They're here,' Gaius remarked. He arose slowly and peered out of the tent. The noise was now quite deafening. There came the sound of horses being reined to a halt outside.

Gaius turned toward me. 'Stay in the tent until I call for you, all right?' he said. 'Just watch what you say, and don't let them see you're afraid.'

That was easy for him to say! What made him think I even wanted to talk to them at all?

The marching feet became more of a shuffle, and with it came the sound of many voices, some of them louder than the rest, shouting out orders. My feet, meanwhile, wished to run the other way.

Gaius picked up his helmet and, tucking it neatly under one arm, strode outside into the bright daylight.

Instantly, I leapt to my feet and cautiously peered through the tent flap at the assembled Legions. I was careful to stand to one side so that I could not be seen. I watched transfixed as Gaius approached two officers mounted on horseback. He marched over to them and saluted smartly. I strained to hear what was being said, only just making out the general gist of the conversation.

He reported that the element of surprise had been lost when one of his two captives had "escaped", but that he didn't see that as a problem seeing as the tribe had neither the strength nor numbers to defend themselves, let alone fight a full-scale battle.

I knew my people well, and it would be no exaggeration to say that we would far sooner go down fighting than surrender to an enemy, even if it meant we would be completely wiped out. This thought nagged at me continually.

He also reported the loss of his men en-route to Dobunni lands.

Gaius then suggested that the General ought to try to talk with the tribal leader in an attempt to come to some agreement. But would our chief agree to such a meeting?

'Perhaps,' one officer replied, scratching his chin thoughtfully. He seemed a little older than his comrade who had now begun to dismount, and I deduced that he must be the new Governor of Britannia, the much-hated General Ostorius Scapula. He had already gained a reputation for bluntness that was second to none and had insulted many a tribal chieftain. Not an ideal leader to forge the *"Pax Romana"*.

'What then of your other prisoner?' the General asked abruptly. 'Where is he?'

'She,' Gaius corrected quietly, 'is still here, General. I wish to take her as my wife,' he added in a whisper.

There was a stunned silence followed by a murmur among a few of the men who had overheard this last remark. I froze, wishing that I was anywhere but here. To my surprise, the General let out a hearty laugh that echoed around the campsite.

'Ha! And to think that all this time we were in fear for your life.' Obviously, he was amused by this latest piece of information. 'You'd better bring her over then. I would ask a few questions of her myself.'

'Yes, sir.' Gaius saluted promptly. Turning about, he then marched swiftly over to the tent to fetch me. He pulled the tent flap back abruptly. I leapt back.

'Come on,' he said, extending his hand towards me.'

I hesitated, and Gaius reached into the tent and grabbed hold of my hand. I shook my head vehemently and tried to pull away.

'It's all right,' he whispered, dragging me outside into the daylight and under the full gaze of any nearby soldiers.

I had taken no more than a few steps when I came to an abrupt halt, the size of the surrounding Army totally overwhelming me. As far as the eye could see there were Roman troupers: legionaries, cavalry, archers, and soldiers in charge of massive slingshot machines, the likes of which I had never seen before. They stretched from the edge of the lake to far across the plains.

I stood, rooted to the spot, petrified as I imagined ten thousand pairs of eyes upon me. In truth, most had probably not even noticed me, or were too far away to see.

'Dana? Dana, it's all right,' Gaius said softly, trying to coax me forward. He tugged on my hand and my feet skidded a little in the soft earth as I tried to pull away. 'Come on, you'll be all right,' he added sincerely. 'Trust me.' Again, that steadfast gaze.

I swallowed hard, my mouth dry with fear, then, taking a deep breath I let him lead me over to where the General remained seated upon his horse, like a king upon his throne, I thought. Perhaps it made him feel more superior somehow, sitting up there where he could look down upon us all?

'This is the new Governor of Britannia, General Publius Ostorius Scapula,' Gaius introduced formally. 'This is Dana, of the Southern Dobunni.'

Gaius ushered me forward a little and I gripped his hand tightly. General Ostorius gazed down at me with piercing intensity. 'You are from the *oppidum* on the Mendip?' he asked bluntly, switching to my native tongue.

'Yes,' standing my ground firmly. 'I *was* from the hill-fort by the sea,' I added coldly.

General Ostorius nodded thoughtfully, his gaze unfaltering. 'Your people have only themselves to blame for their own destruction,' he retorted sharply. 'They should not have stood against us by joining in the rebellion last autumn!'

I pursed my lips together, my fury quelling any fear I had previously felt. Although it was the Second Legion that had been responsible for the destruction of Worlebury, Ostorius must have given the order.

True, we had continued in our efforts to repel the Roman invaders, but why shouldn't we? This was our land, our homes we were defending, and so we had joined in the rebellion that had broken out upon Ostorius Scapula's arrival in Britannia. In my mind, Scapula had it coming. He had no sooner set foot upon these shores than he had the audacity to place a ban upon all the weapons held within the tribes—any tribe—even those that were friendly to Rome, and had set about confiscating them all. They didn't get ours. The Romans couldn't get close enough without a fight breaking out.

Throughout the recent winter we had kept up our endless attacks upon their forts and garrisons, having joined forces with our neighbours and allies, the Durotriges. Their hill-fort at Maiden Castle had now also been decimated, like that of Worlebury, ruthlessly, for their continued rebellion.

'Is it true that most of your warriors have been slain?' Ostorius asked abruptly.

I hesitated a moment, seeing the dead again in my mind's eye. 'Only a few remain,' I stammered. I felt my blood boil. Oh, how I wished that I could strike him down and knock him off that horse of his!

General Ostorius then turned his attention back toward Gaius. 'Your estimate of their number, does it agree with what the girl claims?' he asked, switching back to Latin.

'Yes, sir,' Gaius confirmed, also in the Latin tongue. 'I've not seen more than fifty or so warriors together at any one time.'

So, he had been spying on us while he was here! I supposed it made sense, but I felt rather irritated by the thought.

'So, does *she* think her people will now agree to a surrender?' Scapula continued as if I wasn't even there. How infuriating the man was! Probably thinks I cannot understand their ridiculous language.

Gaius replied somewhat cautiously I thought. 'Actually, sir, they could take some convincing.'

'Convince them then!' he snapped brusquely. 'You don't sound too sure of that, soldier!'

'Yes, sir!' Gaius replied, coming to attention.

'If they fail to surrender totally to Roman rule, then my original plan still stands!' he paused, running a hand through his short, dark hair. 'I don't suppose *she* has any influence with the chief of the tribe? Perhaps *she* ...'

'The name is Dana!' I interrupted hotly in the very best Latin I could manage. I gritted my teeth and glared angrily up at him, taking a step forward in defiance. 'So use it... Roman!' I almost spat that last word out. There were a few choice names I'd liked to have called him, and I cursed him in the name of our gods, but after my initial outburst I held my stance and kept silent. Gaius was trying to pull me back behind him, but to no avail.

A deathly silence fell. Time seemed to stand still. I was rooted to the spot as General Publius Ostorius Scapula stared down at me coldly, his face an unreadable mask. He drew in a deep breath. 'There is hatred in those eyes,' he remarked at length, holding my gaze. He paused and turned back toward Gaius. 'Are you sure she can become loyal to Rome?'

I had overstepped the line, and I knew it. Suddenly, I felt afraid. I averted my gaze, my eyes downcast.

'Oh, she'll never be loyal to Rome,' Gaius replied casually, and to my horror he released his grip on my hand.

Panic overcame me suddenly. I couldn't believe what I was hearing! What was he doing? He took a few steps closer to the General, leaving me standing there alone and defenceless. 'She doesn't need to be,' he added abruptly. 'She is loyal... *to me*.' He held out a hand towards me. For a moment I couldn't move, then throwing myself into his arms, I buried my face in his shoulder in a feeble attempt to hide.

'Aha! And you are loyal to Rome,' Ostorius reasoned. Gaius responded with a respectful nod of his head. Ostorius suddenly let out a raucous laugh. 'Ha! Good answer!' he added in amusement. 'Very well then, but mind, I shall hold you totally responsible for her, and her actions.' He scratched at his chin thoughtfully again. 'We'll discuss our plans in detail once we've had a chance to set up camp proper. Shall we say over dinner?' It was a command, not a request. Gaius saluted obediently. 'You may go,' Ostorius remarked, waving us away arrogantly with a flick of his hand.

I breathed a sigh of relief and we began to head back towards Gaius' tent.

'One moment!' the General called after us. I stiffened visibly. Gaius turned about to face him. 'Bring...' pausing for a moment, '*Dana*,' he added graciously.

Slowly, I peered at him over my shoulder, and to my surprise, Ostorius actually smiled! I'd insulted him in front of his men, and he had actually smiled! And, what was more, he'd called me by name, almost I thought, apologetically.

Gaius merely indicated his understanding with a curt nod of his head. Dazed, we returned to the sanctuary of his tent, my mind in a spin.

'Are you all right?' Gaius asked yet again. 'Dana?' He touched my arm gently in concern and I rounded on him sharply as the full impact of my encounter with the General began to hit home.

'Don't you ever, do that, to me again!' I was absolutely furious, and trembling with fear and rage at the same time.

'I am sorry,' he apologised with heart-felt sincerity, 'but I had to make an impression, especially after what you said.' He pulled me towards him, wrapping his arms about me. Overcome with the day's events, I found I couldn't stop shaking.

'I'm sorry,' I stammered helplessly. How by the gods was I ever going to manage to live amongst these people? What was

I doing here? I was a rebel, of a rebel tribe. I would never agree to be "civilised", as the Romans would put it. I didn't even fit in with my own people sometimes and had frequent arguments with Antur and Dafydd, and even once or twice with the chieftain himself!

'It's all right,' he replied, 'but I wouldn't push Scapula too far, that's all.' How I hated the arrogance of that Roman General! 'Actually,' Gaius added, 'you were lucky. None of our soldiers would ever dare speak back to him the way you did!'

'Gaius Julius! Are you in there?' A booming voice suddenly called from outside making us both jump.

Gaius gave me a wink and a wry smile before pulling the tent flap aside. A handsome, dark-haired man stuck his head through, looking quite comical.

'I'd have knocked but it's difficult to do so on a tent!' he jested, grinning broadly.

Gaius smiled. 'Come in, come in my friend, before you alarm every tribe from here to Camulodunum!' He clasped arms with the dark-haired soldier as he entered.

'This is my good friend Marcus Petronius,' Gaius introduced. 'An old friend from way back.'

Marcus coughed. 'Not so much of the old, thank-you,' he replied in jest. 'I'm younger than you, remember!'

Gaius took my hand. 'This is Dana. She's to be my wife.'

Marcus raised an eyebrow in surprise, and then he smiled amiably. 'Wife, eh? Well, you didn't waste any time. And all the while we thought you in peril for your life, captured by barbaric tribesmen, tortured and goodness knows what! Ha!' He bent down and kissed my hand, his azure eyes sparkling mischievously against his olive complexion. I had never seen eyes so blue. 'Pleased to meet you, Diana,' he added.

I blushed shyly. 'It's Dana, actually.'

'Ah, you mean you're not named after a goddess?' he teased. 'You ought to be!'

Gaius placed an arm about me, possessively, playfully. He seemed a little embarrassed by his brazen friend. 'Dana was from the coastal *oppidum*, the one that was destroyed by our valiant Second, and now she resides on the Mendip,' he said.

'Aha, so that explains it then,' Marcus responded.

'Explains what?' Gaius queried, curious.

'The talk that was going around the camp as I rode up, about a native girl who stood up to old Ostorius!' He grinned, his eyes full of mischief. 'Well, I'd never have believed it!'

Embarrassed, I averted my eyes and withdrew a step or two backwards.

'No, no, no, it's all right,' Marcus apologised quickly. 'You must forgive my brashness. I'm only sorry that I missed it all.' His manner was so amiable that I could do little else but laugh.

Late afternoon came and the Roman encampment had been erected properly now. Tents were pitched in neat, orderly rows, and defensive ditches had been dug. Earth ramparts encircled the camp and guards had been posted around it.

One side was hard up against the hill where Gaius' tent lay. They had worked extremely hard and fast. The military precision with which the soldiers had accomplished their tasks had been phenomenal. Every man knew exactly what he should be doing and how he should be doing it.

The size of the encampment was absolutely awesome. It stretched from beneath the Mendip to far across the valley, skirting around the edge of the lake and with some troops even stationed on the opposite bank of the adjoining stream.

Gaius took me by the hand as I stood idly by watching all the activity. 'Come and meet my soldiers,' he announced cheerfully. He began to lead me a short distance between the multitude of tents and men. We stopped at the edge of the stream where his soldiers were encamped.

'These are my men,' he pointed out rather proudly with a wave of his hand. 'The VIth Thracian Cohort.'

'The what?' I asked.

Some of them nodded or waved in return as they busied themselves. They seemed amiable enough, I thought.

He laughed lightly. 'A Cohort of Auxiliary soldiers, that's about five-hundred men, sometimes a thousand, non-Roman troops.'

'They're not Roman?' I was a little surprised at this.

'They're from Thrace, that's why they're called a "Thracian Cohort",' he explained patiently, stating what should have been obvious. 'This particular Cohort is a *Cohors Equitata*, which means they're made up of both cavalry and infantry.'

'Right,' I replied, still none the wiser. 'So, where is this 'Thrace'?'

Gaius laughed. 'Never mind,' he said. 'It's a long way from here.' He placed an arm about me. 'I see I've much to teach you, my love!'

One of the Thracians was signalling to Gaius. 'Rufus!' he called out, raising an arm in acknowledgement. 'Wait here,' he said to me. 'I'll be back in a moment.' He strolled across to speak with the red-haired Thracian, leaving me to stand alone beneath a large tree.

Becoming bored, I wandered over to inspect some of the massive catapult machines that stood in a straight row to one side of the Thracian encampment. My people too were adept with the catapult, but ours were small and mostly hand-held weapons, nothing like these monsters. The Roman catapults stood upright, being mounted on carts with which to move them, and were as high as the tree under which I had been standing moments earlier. They were both fascinating and terrifying. An involuntary shiver ran down my spine as I remembered the flaming fireballs that had hurtled down upon us at Worlebury that dreadful night not more than six months hence, and I realised that it must have been machines like these that had propelled them.

Gaius walked up behind me, startling me a little.

'We call them *catapultae* and *ballistae*,' he said. 'They're really just very large catapults.' I spun around. The red-haired Thracian was standing beside him. 'This is Rufus Sita,' he introduced, 'my best cavalry man.'

Rufus bowed slightly in greeting, his red curly hair bobbing about as he did so. 'Enchanted,' he said, and smiled, his accent strange to my ears. I guessed him to be about mid-thirties, and certainly one of the older soldiers there for many appeared to be quite young.

'Rufus, this is Dana,' Gaius added, and Rufus smiled again. 'I'll speak with you later, and the rest of the men. Tell them to relax for the present.'

With another curt bow, Rufus Sita walked off. He indeed seemed very different to the Romans. At least these Thracians, wherever they were from, had manners.

I gazed absently upwards at the large catapult that we stood alongside. 'Have you ever...' I began hesitantly. 'Have your men, your Thracians, have they ever used these catapults on... on the tribes of this land?' Visions of the fireballs raining down on the Worle filled my mind. Would they use them on Dolebury too?

'Only once,' he replied earnestly. 'Many of the tribes pledged their allegiance to Rome straight away without so much as a fight, so it was unnecessary to use any sort of force.'

He paused a moment, seeming a little uneasy, then gazing out across the plains he recalled an incident. 'We launched an attack upon the Cornovii Tribe to the north of here, at a place they call "*The Wrekin*",' he continued. 'They were showing some initial resistance. It was a token gesture, nothing more, a show of strength. They surrendered after just two volleys. We then built a vexillation fort nearby to house my men, a sort of long-term fortress, whereby we could keep an eye on things and ensure that peace was established in the area.'

Gaius turned to face me, stroking my cheek gently. He smiled. 'I'm not in the habit of raining fireballs down upon people, if that's what you mean,' he added, a warmth of compassion in his voice. He truly did seem disturbed by recounting this memory. 'I don't enjoy making war.'

'I know,' I replied, relieved.

'Come and meet the rest of my cavalry,' he announced suddenly, changing the subject and cheering a little. 'You'll like them. Well, you'll like the horses anyway!'

I giggled in amusement, but Gaius was right. The cavalry horses were magnificent. I couldn't help but admire them, stroke their muzzles and talk to them softly.

Gaius laughed at me. 'You see, I told you you'd like the horses,' he said, 'but I didn't expect you to strike up a conversation with them!'

I smiled modestly. 'They are beautiful animals,' I agreed, stroking the mane of one huge stallion. 'I've never seen any the like before, and so much larger than our horses. The horse is sacred to the Dobunni, did you know?'

'They are to many of the Celtic Tribes I've encountered. They come from Germania,' he added, pausing thoughtfully for a moment. 'No doubt your tribe would like to acquire horses such as these?'

'Are you jesting?' I laughed. 'Of course they would!'

'We'll see then,' he said mysteriously. Perhaps he was planning to bribe us with these fine creatures, or trade at least? 'Actually, Marcus began his career tending the horses,' he continued, 'and now he commands the entire Cavalry of the Fourteenth. Did I tell you? He's what we call a "Prefect of Horse". If you wish to know anything about our horses, just ask Marcus. He's a veritable expert!'

The sun became lower over the Mendip as the time I had been dreading arrived, the finalising of the Roman military plans, and with it came dinner amongst the Army's elite, something to which I was definitely not looking forward to and, understandably, I had little appetite.

I stood outside a very large tent that had been set up as a temporary *"principia"*, or headquarters, alongside Gaius, gazing out across the Roman encampment. The sheer numbers of men, horses and equipment was incalculable. If this massive Army were to launch an attack on my people then we would be entirely wiped out—forever. It was too horrific to think about.

Our proud, and sometimes foolish warriors, often preferring to fight to the very last. An "honourable death" they called it. Convincing them to talk, let alone listen, was not going to be an easy task, and getting them to surrender would be even harder.

Gaius and I entered. Several of the officers were already there and General Ostorius was awaiting our arrival impatiently, tapping his fingers upon the arm of his chair. He arose as we walked in, Gaius carrying some rolled up maps that he'd been working on.

Military plans and tactics were discussed briefly before dinner. Every now and then the General would nod his head gravely in agreement. I was made to sit to one side while the soldiers worked out their strategy. I was wondering about the original plan Ostorius had mentioned earlier, and what it might be. I confess, it wouldn't have been too hard to guess and I hoped he didn't need to resort to it.

Dinner itself was pleasant enough although I ate sparingly. I concentrated on looking at the various array of foods, my head bowed, too nervous to speak. Although General Ostorius seemed to be making a deliberate effort to be pleasant, I sensed that my comments would not be welcome.

As the evening drew to a close, General Ostorius summed up his conclusions. 'Well, either we give the *"Pax Romana"* one last try, or...' he tailed off ominously, looking directly towards me. 'Do you think Dana's chieftain will speak with us? What do you think, Caecinianus?'

'Well, sir,' Gaius began, 'I think that we perhaps need to offer them something other than the sword. An incentive,' he said practically. 'Perhaps some goods and maybe some of the horses to begin with, then, once we can all sit down and talk, we can hopefully come to certain agreements.'

'Such as?' Ostorius asked bluntly.

'Well, perhaps an agreement that no slaves should be taken from their tribe, together with a policy of non-intervention in their way of life, nor intrusion into their lands,' Gaius suggested, 'saving for the lead mine of course,' he added in afterthought, running a finger around the rim of the cup of wine that lay before him. 'After all, that is what we really want from their territory. Once we have them sitting down and listening,' he waved an arm for emphasis, 'then, and only then, can we begin to negotiate.'

General Ostorius mulled this over for a moment, his expression impossible to interpret. 'We'd have to retain access to the ports and rivers,' he remarked at length, 'but I suppose we needn't litter the area with a multitude of forts and villas, at least not for the present—so long as they remain peaceable. Should they break any agreement however, we would be free to do as we wish.'

He paused, picking at a piece of bread as he seemed to ponder the matter. 'Of course, they will need to agree to discuss this in the first place, otherwise we shall merely do as we please, with or without their consent,' he added brusquely.

Didn't they always do this, I thought.

'They should think themselves lucky then,' he continued arrogantly, 'that we are even giving them this chance to discuss anything instead of just annihilating the whole damn tribe, but should they not agree to at least discuss the matter then I really see no alternative.'

'I can!' I spoke out in haste and in anger, and without really thinking.

All eyes turned towards me as if those present were expecting me to say something wise and profound. I hesitated for a moment, lost for words, and then I spoke but one word; 'Leave!' I demanded brusquely, coming to my feet. I glared directly at Scapula, this time holding his gaze as if daring him to challenge me on this. Gaius paled visibly. He stood up.

'General Ostorius,' he began apologetically, 'I…'

'It's all right, it's all right,' Ostorius responded, hands outstretched before him as he returned my gaze.

My courage failed me. Suddenly terrified of a rebuke, I turned and fled the scene.

'Hadn't you better go after her?' Ostorius added as I ran out of the tent.

I ran on blindly with no idea of where I was going, my mind in a spin, only to find myself moments later atop the hill behind Gaius' tent where Dafydd and I had been only yesterday, our horse tethered to a small tree. Tears rolled down my cheeks and my knees were a tremble. I stood there gasping for breath, gazing out helplessly across the Roman encampment and then turned my head in the direction of my new home at Dolebury. It was dark now, the night illuminated only by the occasional glow from the scattered campfires and a handful of stars. If I stared hard enough I could just make out the outline of the horizon against the black night sky.

Tears rolled down my cheeks. I knew that our warriors, or what was left of them, would be preparing to do battle at this very moment. They would fight until the end, but there was no way that they could ever hope to defeat this vast army of soldiers.

I heard footsteps approaching from behind me. They stopped, halting a short distance away, and I knew that it was Gaius.

'They won't leave,' he stated simply. 'Not now.'

'I know,' I replied weakly. I sniffed involuntarily. 'I'm sorry, I didn't mean to say the wrong thing,' glancing over my shoulder to where Gaius stood leaning casually against the tree.

'On the contrary,' Gaius remarked, as he walked across to stand beside me.

I shivered in the cold breeze and he placed his cloak about my shoulders before turning me around to face him.

'I think you said exactly the right thing.' He paused to tenderly brush away my teardrops. 'I did say it wouldn't be easy,' he continued. 'It will never be easy.' He smiled suddenly at some hidden thought which he then voiced. 'A Roman, and a Celt,' he added in amusement, as if it were the most unlikely of unions. At that time, it probably was, for there had not been many marriages heard of betwixt Romans and Natives, Celts or otherwise, and neither was I about to dispute the fact that he had yet again called me a "Celt". His hand brushed against my cheek as he gently tilted my chin upwards, seeking my lips with his.

Early the next morning, Gaius received his orders from the General.

'Ostorius has decided to send a small detachment to your settlement in an attempt to arrange peace talks.' He informed me. 'He wants me to lead them.'

'You?' I questioned in alarm. 'Why you? Why can't he go himself?'

Gaius smiled sardonically. 'Well now, I should have thought that was obvious,' he stated calmly, then added, 'It was my idea.'

'Then I shall go with you,' I declared steadfastly.

'I don't think so,' Gaius responded promptly, shaking his head.

'But, if any fighting breaks out, you'll be the first target!' I argued back. 'If they see me with you, they won't attack.'

'Aha! If they see you!' Gaius countered. 'Men keyed up for battle often strike at the first sign of movement. They may not realise it's you until it's too late.'

He picked up his helmet and gave it a brief polish.

I opened my mouth to protest his decision once more but he cut me off.

'In any case,' he continued with a wave of his hand, 'I wouldn't want you caught in the middle should any fighting take place, and it's probably bound to,' he added with a shrug.

I thought on this for a moment. 'Then let me go alone,' I suggested. 'I could take a message?'

'No,' he stated firmly and somewhat sharply. 'I will not risk your life!'

I turned away, worried and frustrated.

'I will be coming back,' Gaius remarked sincerely in an attempt to comfort me. 'I promise.' He placed his arms around me lovingly. 'Now that I have something worthwhile to come back to.'

I turned around to face him, hugging him closely and with all my heart. 'Then, take this,' I said, unclipping my brooch pin and handing it to him. Gaius turned the brooch over in his hand and studied the design on the front.

'It's a horse, pictured amongst the stars,' I informed him. 'The wheel beneath represents the Sun. It stands for eternity. My friend, Antur, made it for me shortly after the massacre.'

'Was he from Worlebury too?' he asked.

'Yes,' I replied. 'He's the one who lead us all to safety. Perhaps the brooch will help to identify you as a friend, should you be captured, or, or...' I failed to complete the sentence. The idea that Gaius may be injured or perhaps not even survive at all was too horrible to contemplate.

'Thank you,' he whispered softly. He pinned the brooch to his cape. 'I've seen this horse depicted on the back of some of your coinage.'

'Antur used to help to make the coins, a while ago now. That's where he got the design from.' Native coinage had all but ceased production since the introduction of Roman money.

'Time to go!' It was Marcus, calling from outside the tent.

'I'll be right there,' Gaius replied. He smiled once more and then kissed my forehead lightly before turning to leave.

'There is one other thing,' I said hesitantly. He halted by the entrance and looked back towards me, waiting patiently for me to continue. 'You know how I said there were only a few warriors left?' Gaius nodded. 'They are our strongest and our best warriors.'

'I'd already figured that out,' he replied gently, then turned to leave once more.

'They have a particular way in which they often fight,' I added quickly before he had a chance to step outside. He walked back towards me, showing a little more interest.

I felt as if I was about to betray my own people, but I had to tell him. I couldn't let him walk into a trap.

'Yes?' His gaze steady and alert.

'If they attack, they will attack from the front, drawing you forward with but a few warriors and probably within the gap

68

between the hills. The main force will be waiting atop the rocks and will launch a surprise attack from behind you once you are within range, trapping you in-between.' I took a deep breath, 'You must look to the cliffs above. Remember, the danger will come from behind you.'

'Thank you,' he said gratefully. 'I'll remember.'

'There's just one more thing.'

He raised a quizzical eyebrow.

'You must keep this to yourself,' I entreated. 'Please?'

The centurion looked thoughtful for a moment. To not inform his men of such a ploy could possibly lead to their deaths, but were they to know many of our warriors could be slain. He knew the odds and the consequences.

'I promise,' he replied after some deliberation. 'I know how difficult it must have been for you to tell me that, Dana.' He smiled sympathetically then gave my hand an encouraging squeeze.

'We are both of us caught up in the middle of all this, aren't we?' he continued. 'I won't betray your trust. Don't worry, everything will be all right. You'll see.' He paused. 'Marcus will look after you while I'm away,' he added in afterthought. 'He's not coming along.'

'Gaius?' I gave him a brief smile as he looked back over his shoulder. 'Take care.'

'I will,' he replied softly, and then he walked out.

Lunchtime came and went with still no sign of Gaius' return. There had been the faint sound of distant shouting and yelling some time ago, then nothing. It wasn't hard to guess that some form of an encounter had taken place. Now, we waited. That was the worst part.

Marcus had seen that a splendid lunch was brought out to us but I had little if any appetite. I couldn't help wondering about the skirmish that must have taken place. I felt cold, more from fear than from the weather, so I sat basking outside in the midday sun. A legionary approached and saluted. Marcus returned the salute forthwith.

'What is it my man?' he asked.

'General Ostorius is holding a meeting in the *principia* and bids you attend at once,' the legionary replied promptly.

'Thank you,' Marcus replied amiably. 'I'll be right along.' He stood up and fastened his cloak, adjusting it carefully. 'I'm sorry, but I shall have to go,' he apologised with a shrug of his shoulders. 'It shouldn't take too long.'

It was only after Marcus had gone that I realised there was no fresh drinking water left in either of the urns. While having little appetite for food, the afternoon sun had however left me quite thirsty, so I picked up one of the urns and began to carry it down to the stream, making my way carefully between the tents and small groups of soldiers who were too busily engaged in their own conversations to notice me.

Having filled the vessel to the brim and quenched my thirst a little, I then splashed a small amount of the cool water from the stream upon my face before picking up the urn and beginning to make my way back. The urn had become quite heavy now with the weight of the water, so I was careful to take my time, concentrating on not spilling any of the precious liquid while deliberately averting my gaze from those of the soldiers, whom by now I knew must be watching.

My eyes downcast, I almost bumped straight into a young legionary who had suddenly stepped right out in front of me. Startled, I came to an abrupt halt. A little of the water spilt out onto his boots and I looked up.

'Clumsy savage!' the legionary cursed.

I pursed my lips and said nothing, stepping to one side in order to go around him but he quickly stepped in front of me once more.

'Please, let me pass,' I entreated, as calmly as I could and tried to step around him once again.

The impudent young Roman swiftly followed my movement, deliberately blocking my way. I glared angrily up into his quite astonishingly handsome face. He grinned back at me mischievously, his dark brown eyes teasing, yet with a hidden malice.

'Well, well, well,' he said impudently. 'If it isn't our barbarian whore!'

'Get out of my way!' I snapped, cursing the heavy urn with which I was laden.

A small group of soldiers had moved in closer to watch the spectacle and were beginning to laugh as they murmured amongst themselves.

'I don't really think your lot are worth sparing, do you?' The legionary continued, his lips curling into a sneer. 'I can't see why we're bothering. We should have stuck to our original plan and exterminated the lot of you by now!'

He grinned at me arrogantly as if daring me to make a move. My blood was beginning to boil and I thought about my sword that I had concealed beneath my robe. If only I could reach it quickly enough I would wipe that smile off his face for good!

I shifted the heavy urn onto one hip in readiness as I prepared to reach for the sword hilt, but then I remembered Gaius' warning about drawing my sword on a Roman, and the penalties therein. I *had* promised.

'For the last time, get out of my way!' I warned, my voice beginning to quiver.

'Quite the little savage, aren't we?' The legionary teased, his colleagues nearby jeering and laughing at the free entertainment.

That was it! My temper exploded, like their Roman fireballs that they had hurled at Worlebury. Before I could stop myself, I had thrown the entire urn full of water at him, completely drenching him from head to foot. He fell backwards onto the ground, his face turning red with rage. His tousled brown curls were wet and bedraggled. Raucous laughter surrounded us, but this time they weren't laughing at me.

I looked down upon him with satisfaction. The piercing gaze he returned me spoke of pure hatred and I began to fear the consequences of my action. My antagonist arose slowly to his feet. He brushed the droplets of water from his off face.

'I'll kill you for that, bitch!' he swore, immediately lunging towards me.

Swiftly I backed away, yet he managed to strike me viciously across the face. I fell to the ground, clutching my cheek. Silence fell. The laughter stopped as he slowly and deliberately drew his sword.

Abruptly, a voice called out from nearby. 'Hey!' It was Marcus, running speedily towards us. The young legionary hurriedly replaced his sword within its scabbard and took a step backwards. 'What's going on here?' Marcus demanded, giving the legionary an angry glance before kneeling down beside me. He looked at the assembled crowd. 'Get about your business,' he commanded sharply. 'All of you!'

My assailant ambled off, re-joining his friends yet watching us vengefully from nearby. I knew he would not let this rest.

'Are you all right?' Marcus asked me, his voice full of worry and concern.

I nodded and gave him a half smile, which was the best I could manage with the bruise I could now feel developing on my cheek.

'You've made an enemy there I'm afraid. Vecilius is not one to antagonise. He has, shall we say, friends,' he continued. 'I'm sorry I should have been here for you.'

'It's not your fault,' I replied sincerely. 'You got called away. I only wanted some more water.'

Gently, he helped me to my feet. 'Well, I should have made sure you had everything you needed before I left,' he chastised himself. 'It was most remiss of me!'

We began to head back, passing by the young legionary and his friends. Marcus took him aside suddenly, grabbing him by the elbow and swinging him round. 'I'll deal with you later, Vecilius,' he whispered sharply.

After bathing my cheek with some cool stream water that Marcus had brought, I made my way to the top of the hill to watch in silence for Gaius' return, sitting in the shade of the solitary tree. I pushed my long hair back over my shoulder, my hand automatically feeling for the bruise on my swollen cheek. A fine cut ran down the centre of the bruise where the soldier's signet ring had scratched me.

I glimpsed Marcus far below, keeping a watchful eye, albeit at a distance. He saw me look towards him and raised his arm in salute.

It was then that I caught sight of something glinting in the sun, a short way off in the distance. I stood up, raising my hand to shade my eyes. Marcus saw me and ran halfway up the hill before turning to peer across the encampment towards where I was looking.

'They're coming back!' he shouted, pointing into the distance. 'They're coming back!'

It seemed to take forever for the soldiers to wind their way back across the plains, following the little trackway that Dafydd had taken, yet in reality I knew that it wasn't long at all. As they approached nearer, I could see Gaius in the lead. He was all right! I ran down the hill anxious to greet him and learn what had happened, halting beside Marcus, who was also much relieved to see his friend's return.

As Gaius rode into camp, I was about to run over to him but Marcus held me back. 'Wait,' he advised.

Gaius first saluted the General before dismounting from his horse. Obviously, he had to report first. He glanced in our direction briefly and then after a few words with Ostorius Scapula he began to walk across to where we both stood, waiting impatiently.

Before he had a chance to reach us however, I had run eagerly over to greet him, flinging my arms enthusiastically about his neck in sheer relief.

Gaius hugged me closely, stroking my hair and kissing me gently on the forehead. 'Your people have agreed to talk with Ostorius, so that's a start,' he announced, much to my relief, and then he frowned as he noticed the bruise on my cheek. 'What happened here?' he asked in concern, tilting my head up and to one side.

Quickly, I turned my head aside, self-consciously pulling my hair across the offending cheek.

Marcus stepped forward. 'A slight altercation with one of our legionaries,' he stated. 'I'm sorry, Gaius. I was called away.'

Gaius tensed, but nodded to show his understanding. 'Who was it?' he demanded, anxiously peering around the encampment. His gaze fell suspiciously upon Vecilius, who was watching nonchalantly from a short distance away, before slyly turning aside.

'I'll tell you inside,' Marcus said confidentially, then louder. 'Come and freshen up!'

Entering the tent, we found a young slave boy placing some fresh fruit and water upon a small table. Gaius nodded his thanks and the boy began to help him off with his armour while Marcus poured out some water.

Gaius accepted the water with gratitude, drinking thirstily. The slave removed the last of the armour. Gaius winced suddenly.

'Careful,' he remarked, as a wound to Gaius' right shoulder was revealed.

'Sorry, Master,' the boy murmured in alarm.

'You're hurt!' I exclaimed in horror, rushing to his side.

'It's nothing,' Gaius replied casually. 'Believe me, I've had a lot worse.'

I removed the dressing that had been placed upon it—a Dobunnic dressing, and I recognised the handy work of my friend Roisin, Dafydd's sister. The wound looked quite brutal, but it had been well cleaned.

'The ointment's over there,' Gaius remarked to the slave boy, indicating the little jar of ointment he'd used on my shoulder the previous day. The slave boy retrieved the ointment and then began to rub the salve into the wound.

That young boy should have been left with his family, I thought. In any case, a thing such as this was a wife's or healer's duty.

'Here, let me do that,' I offered, taking the ointment from the slave. 'A Dobunni needs no slaves,' I added, and quite proudly at that.

Marcus burst out laughing. 'You'd better watch her, my friend,' he said. 'She'll be freeing all the slaves next!'

Gaius gave a wry smile. He waved the young slave away, and the boy left the tent.

'Here,' Gaius said, handing me back my brooch as I finished rubbing the last of the ointment in. 'It did help to save my life after all, thank you.'

I took the brooch from him and clipped it carefully back into position on my robe.

'You should have told me Antur was your boyfriend,' Gaius added casually. 'He could have killed me out of jealousy.'

I was momentarily stunned. 'He's not my boyfriend!' I retorted sharply.

'He seems to think he is,' Gaius remarked placidly.

'He's just a friend,' I stammered. 'He's been like a brother to me ever since we were small children.'

It was true, we had been brought up together as children, when Antur was fostered by my family, and yes, there was the expectation that we would one day be wed. It was an arranged marriage between us the Dobunni and Antur's people, the Atrebates, the details of which I had tried to ignore my entire life.

In my mind, Antur was but a good friend, and that was all—a brother. A sudden realisation dawned on me as I gazed at Gaius' wound, gently running my fingertips across his injured shoulder.

'He did this to you, didn't he?' I asked, appalled, and Gaius nodded. 'I'm sorry.'

'It's not your fault,' he responded kindly, taking my hand and kissing it gently. 'What about this?' he queried, running his hand lightly down my bruised cheek.

'It was Vecilius Lascivus,' Marcus stated matter-of-factly. 'I can't see what we can really do about him. It's just the way he is, and he's not under our direct command either.'

'I know what I am going to do about him!' Gaius remarked with a determined edge to his voice.

'Just you be careful,' Marcus warned. 'Remember, he has a lot of powerful friends. I don't expect he'll remain a legionary for long before he gains himself a promotion—one way or another. In any case,' he added, 'he's with the Twentieth Augustan. With any luck, they'll be off building towns and roads shortly, and we won't see him again.'

'Good!' I remarked, relieved to learn that this impudent young soldier would not be around for much longer.

Marcus grinned broadly. 'So, Gaius Julius, my good friend,' he said. 'Apart from being attacked by a jealous lover, are you going to tell us what else happened at Diana's settlement or not?'

He folded his arms across his chest and bit into an apple quite noisily. Marcus had insisted on repeatedly calling me "Diana" after the Roman moon goddess, who was also goddess of the wild hunt. A title I kind of liked.

Gaius smiled and then seated himself comfortably on the edge of the bed before he began to fill us in on the day's events.

I sat beside him, wrapping my arms around him, relieved that this day was all but over and he had returned safely.

He had led a small band of legionaries into the gap, leaving a second small group as back-up. These he had positioned at the very entrance to the track itself. He and the first group of legionaries had then come under attack once they reached the middle. Many legionaries were taken completely by surprise as our Dobunni warriors leapt upon them from above, calling out their blood-curdling war cries as they did so.

Gaius had instructed the men beforehand to maim and not kill, taking life only as the last resort. He had kept his word and not informed them of the Dobunnic tactics of decoys and surprise attacks. This had led to the deaths of two of the men but had spared the lives of my people, and for this I was grateful, yet sorry for the soldiers who had perished. By some strange twist of fate, it happened to be Anturiaethus who had leapt down behind Gaius, finding his chosen victim not so easy to take when Gaius had turned to face him even before his feet had touched the ground.

'He's a good swordsman, your friend,' Gaius remarked in admiration. 'He would have killed me too, but for this.' He indicated my brooch. 'Even then, I had difficulty convincing him to halt the fighting and let me speak with your chieftain.'

He laughed suddenly. 'I can see where you get your fighting spirit from!' he teased. 'Tell me, are all your tribe like that?'

I looked down, a little embarrassed. A strand of dark Dobunni hair slipped down across my face. I raked back my long locks, blushing slightly.

'Most,' I admitted shyly, 'except for Dafydd. He's always reminding me that he's a healer, not a fighter. He'll be a druid soon enough.' I smiled as fond memories of Dafydd flooded back. We had teased each other often, but in truth we were, and had been quite close—very close in fact—and I had given myself to him freely that day high upon the Mendip atop Crooke's Peak.

'Actually, Gaius,' I confessed, 'if you're looking for a "boyfriend", I was much closer to Dafydd than I ever was to Antur. He helped me a lot after the massacre of my family and we became quite close—for a while at least.' But that was another story.

Gaius just smiled. 'Well, I did wonder.'

Southern Dobunni

Dafydd

Chapter Three

Spring, AD 48
Dolebury Hill-Fort,
Mendip Hills, North Somerset

Morning came all too swiftly for the few of us who were to accompany General Ostorius to our hill-fort at Dolebury. Although both leaders had agreed to discuss their demands amicably, there was no guarantee as to the outcome.

Our newly appointed chieftain had also insisted that Gaius be in attendance and of course I was expected home safe and well. General Ostorius chose two other centurions, and asked Gaius to select two of his best cavalry officers to join us. Added to these were half a dozen or so legionaries. Before we left, Ostorius addressed the men.

'When we meet these natives, we need to show them that while we are diligent, we can also be friendly and co-operative,' he paused momentarily, as if struggling to find the correct words to use and waved an arm in the air for emphasis. 'Open to discussion and new ideas.'

There was a general murmur amongst the soldiers. I had to smile. The thought of Ostorius and these Romans being "friendly" did not sound right somehow, but I was grateful that he was at least making an effort. I was surprised that our chief had agreed, but then he was young and inexperienced, so perhaps this was an advantage as older leaders often get stuck in their ways.

'And,' he added, holding both hands up in a bid for silence once more. 'No running off with any more native girls and marrying them!'

The soldiers laughed aloud, as did Ostorius, at his all too obvious jest aimed at Gaius and me. He seemed to like a laugh, especially at other's expense. As for us, however, I'm sure Gaius felt as embarrassed as I did, taking a step backwards, our heads lowered. Several of the soldiers came up to Gaius, smiling, and patted him amiably on the shoulder as they passed. There was a time, however, when Gaius had first been enlisted that many a centurion had resented the fact that he had bought his way into the Army instead of having to work his way up through the ranks as they did. As Gaius had said though, it wasn't his decision, and his father coming from quite a wealthy and influential family left him with no choice. Now that he had proved his worth however, he was well thought of and valued amongst all the ranks.

So, with Titus Flaminius, the Eagle Standard Bearer of the Fourteenth leading the way, we headed off with some degree of uncertainty and trepidation towards Dolebury Camp.

We proceeded steadily along the track that runs between the fourth and fifth hill to the west along the Mendip, the most westerly hill being that where Dolebury lay. There were no attacks in the combe today. A lookout posted on high signalled our approach as we turned onto the pathway that led to the fort. He raised his spear high and waved to those guarding the gate.

'Whoa!' General Ostorius reined his mount to a halt at the start of the track. He held one hand aloft, signalling for us to stop.

We pulled our horses up alongside. I peered ahead over Gaius' shoulder, my arms wrapped tightly about his waist. I could see the main entrance up ahead with its huge stone ramparts turning inwards.

Chief Eber was standing nearby with his Council of Elders, watching our approach. Dafydd stood beside him, and to the rear I glimpsed site of Antur.

Eber was a handsome man of slim build with shoulder-length dark brown hair and a well-trimmed but large moustache. Although only in his early-twenties and quite young to become a chieftain, the slaying of my father, our previous chieftain at Worlebury, had left us with little choice.

Despite his lack of years, Eber was thought to be a good option, for he had been head man at Dolebury for quite a few years now having taken over from his own father when he'd died suddenly, his heart having given out, and in any case the majority of the men folk remaining were either warriors needed for fighting or considered to be too old.

'Perhaps you ought to take the lead now?' Ostorius suggested to Gaius, giving the hill-fort an appraising look. It was even more imposing from below.

'Sir!' Gaius saluted respectfully and edged our horse to the front of the little procession. We started off again at a steady pace, winding our way up the steep hill and along the track that led to the gatepost.

Eber raised a hand in greeting as we came to a halt. He smiled cordially, although the lines of tension apparent on his youthful face betrayed his innermost feelings.

'Thank you for receiving us,' Gaius began diplomatically.

The Council of Elders looked on coldly. Some of them even snarled, like the wolves that roam the woods nearby.

Antur marched promptly up to me, his face set. Reaching up, he grabbed my arm and pulled me roughly from the horse. I winced.

'Take it easy, Antur!' Dafydd protested.

'As you can see,' Gaius continued, with a glare towards Antur. 'Dana is returned to you and quite safe.' He nodded greeting to Dafydd.

I felt as if all eyes were upon me and me alone. I was trying to twist my arm free of Antur's grip, but he only held me tighter.

'This is General Ostorius Scapula, Governor of Britannia,' Gaius added be way of introduction as the General reined his horse in behind him.

'Thank you, Gaius Julius,' Eber replied formally. He eyed Ostorius up cautiously. 'I am Eber, Chief of the Dobunni of the South. Please, enter,' he entreated with an expansive wave of his arm.

One by one, the Romans entered our fortress for the first time. We, of the Dobunni, fell in behind. The heavy gates were swung to behind us and barred.

My eyes were upon Gaius. I wanted desperately to stay beside him. I struggled to free myself from Antur. 'Let go of me! Let go!' Finally I succeeded, Dafydd came over and Antur stormed off. I struggled to keep my eyes upon Gaius. Dafydd frowned. Embarrassed, I looked away, shuffling my feet nervously in the dirt.

'Are you all right?' he asked curiously.

'Fine,' I muttered.

He ran his fingers down the side of my bruised cheek. 'Hmm?'

'It's nothing,' I turned away from Dafydd and almost ran to catch up with Gaius.

A small group was gathering up ahead by the Chief's Hut. I glimpsed Antur amongst them, his face set in a deep scowl, his eyes burning with hatred for the Roman invaders. I looked quickly aside, pretending I had not seen him. I was in no mood for one of his lectures.

The Chief's Hut, a large Round House, was the most important of our dwellings, being set well aside from the others. It was often used for meetings and celebrations. The Romans approached the hut. I quickened my step, coming up alongside Gaius.

One of the Elders suddenly thrust an arm across the entrance. He glared at Ostorius quite rudely. Ostorius was taken aback.

'You come in peace?' the Elder asked gruffly.

Broduil was the young chieftain's personal advisor and bodyguard, a huge hulk of a man, with dark wavy hair and a small shaggy beard.

Ostorius glared back at him arrogantly. 'We do,' he replied.

'Then, why do you bring weapons with you?'

There was silence for a moment. Ostorius pondered this question thoughtfully. 'We are Romans,' he stated at length, believing that no further explanation was necessary.

Broduil wrinkled his nose up as if there was a bad smell underneath it. 'Yes,' he sneered. 'So you are!' The two men glared icily at each other, locked in their own private battle.

'General Ostorius,' Eber intervened, 'if we are to talk of peace, then I shall have no man in this hut bearing weapons, my own people included. May I suggest that yours do the same?'

General Ostorius clenched his fist in irritation but nevertheless he conceded and the weapons were discarded, one by one, to the side of the doorway.

'Thank you,' Eber responded graciously. 'Now, we may enter. You may of course have them returned to you upon leaving the hut.' He gestured the Romans inside.

Ostorius led the way with his usual arrogance. I linked arms with Gaius. Eber was staring meaningfully at me.

'Dana,' he said.

'What?' My heart began to pound. 'I'm on your side, remember?' But was I? I wasn't sure anymore, for hadn't I just fallen for a Roman? Yet I wanted my people to be safe and the killing to end.

He raised an eyebrow. 'This is for the menfolk only,' Eber pointed out.

I pursed my lips in annoyance. Everything here was for men! They got to do all the exciting things. It wasn't fair!

Gaius took my hand firmly, sensing my annoyance. 'Dana is very much a part of this,' he remarked practically. 'We wouldn't be here now if it wasn't for her.'

Eber considered this for a moment, and then he smiled. 'Very well,' he relented, stroking his long dark moustache thoughtfully. 'We'll bend the rules, just this once.'

I was beginning to walk through the door, when Eber grabbed my arm gently, pulling me aside. What now? 'You've not got that sword with you per chance, have you Dana?' he whispered.

I didn't answer, and just shrugged dismissively, looking furtive.

'Come on, Dana,' he continued. 'Put it with the others.'

Reluctantly, I obeyed. It took a moment to remove it. 'No one will take it, will they?' I asked in concern. 'You won't let Antur take it?'

'It will be quite safe,' Eber smiled, understandingly. He knew how much just having that sword meant to me. 'Broduil here will guard it with the others. Won't you, Broduil?'

Broduil grunted in disapproval. 'A woman with a sword!'

'Won't you, Broduil?' Eber repeated, and Broduil made a grunt again. I supposed that this meant "yes".

Gaius and I walked inside.

'You'll get us both into trouble if you keep carrying that around with you,' Gaius whispered confidentially, although he knew that I had it concealed beneath the many layers of woollen material, secretly hidden from view. He smiled and took my hand. 'Come on.'

The peace talks were going badly. Half the day had elapsed and there was still no resolution in sight. Progress had been painfully slow. So many grievances, so much pain, so much anger. My tribe had a long memory. Events were passed on by word of mouth, from parents to children, and to their children's children. This was how it had been for generations.

If nothing else, we of the Dobunni were a proud race, hot tempered, yes, and fiercely independent. We didn't suffer fools gladly. If there was one thing we knew how to do well, it was fight! Yet we were also farmers and fishermen too, for those of us who lived near the coast and the rivers.

So far, this meeting had resurrected nothing but bad memories. There had been accusations and counter-accusations. There had even been those seeking recompense dating back to Caesar's first landing here! Ostorius for most part only seemed to make matters worse. His brusque nature and Roman arrogance had led to further insults. His words had been lost in the commotion that ensued. The noise was deafening, until finally Chief Eber stood up and called for an adjournment.

It was so good to walk outside into the open air and to feel the sun on my face once again. I collected my sword and secured it back about my waist, concealing it beneath the folds of my overdress. Meanwhile, some Dobunni warriors were still exiting the hut; while others stood around in groups, muttering angrily amongst themselves. The Romans had been the first to leave the meeting, General Ostorius storming out in exasperation, his face red with rage. No one had dared to get in his way.

Dafydd approached us, a serious look upon his face. He didn't look very pleased.

'So, Gaius, you lost the element of surprise but used Dana here to force negotiations, was that it?' he remarked caustically. Dafydd then smiled sardonically, a sort of half-smile. 'That's clever, that's very clever!' he added. 'But it isn't working, is it? No one's willing to negotiate anything it seems! So much for your precious peace talks!'

Gaius looked Dafydd squarely in the face. 'Come on, Dafydd, you know better than that,' he replied calmly.

'Do I? Hmmm?' Dafydd continued. 'What about this then?' He ran his fingers down the side of my bruised cheek. I flinched.

'That wasn't anything to do with Gaius.' I frowned, 'Why are you being so hostile?'

Dafydd laughed. 'You should talk!' he exclaimed sarcastically, and then paused. He turned to Gaius. 'Antur says that you threatened Dana's life should we not agree to these talks.'

'Antur says a lot of things,' I countered angrily. 'You should know better than to listen to him!'

'Actually, your friend Antur was telling the truth,' Gaius admitted reluctantly.

I was aghast. What was this he was saying?

'I did say something like that,' he confessed. 'I was buying some time, that's all,' he continued with a shrug of his shoulders. 'I had to convince Antur to let me talk with your chief.' He took a step closer to me. 'I told him my men had orders to kill you if I didn't return. It was all a lie,' he added hastily, 'but your friend Antur believed it. You know I'd never really have had you harmed.' He took my hand and squeezed it gently, at which Dafydd raised a quizzical eyebrow.

I admit that it was all a bit beyond me, nevertheless I felt angry yet somewhat stunned for a moment. Yes, he had used me in a way, but it had worked and it was worth it, for it had not only spared Gaius' life but had brought our two leaders together, although at present the peace talks didn't seem to be succeeding.

Dafydd just shook his head, and then he laughed. 'The ploys of war!' he remarked. 'I should have guessed.' He turned to me. 'Is there something you want to tell me?'

Before I had time to reply, a woman's voice called out. 'Dana!' I turned, surprised. Roisin was running across to greet me.

'I thought you'd have left with the others?' I queried, pleased to see the woman who had become like a sister to me. It was obvious that most of the women and all of the children had been removed to a place of safety, probably far up in the Mendip. In fact, I was surprised that Dafydd hadn't gone with them!

'Who, me?' she laughed. 'Then who would tend to the sick and the wounded?'

'We hope there won't be any more wounded!' Gaius put in with a smile. 'Hello, Roisin.'

'How's the shoulder now?' she asked kindly.

'Much better, thanks to you.'

'So, it was you who tended to Gaius' shoulder,' I greeted her. 'I thought it was!' I hugged her warmly. 'Thank you, Ros.'

'Is my little brother being a pain?' she enquired, laughing.

'Hey!' Dafydd complained.

'Oh, no more than usual!' I said, and we all laughed, even Dafydd, restored now to his normal humour.

'It's Antur who's the pain,' Dafydd added with a grin. 'You see this?' he said, tilting his chin up to reveal a rather painful bruise. 'It seems he blames me for leaving you behind.'

'He hit you?' I remarked, shocked, running my hand gently down the side of his cheek. Abruptly, Dafydd stepped back— well out of reach.

I looked across to where Antur was standing, deep in discussion with a couple of other young warriors. He looked up and I turned away in annoyance.

Centurion Flavius Biticus approached and raised an arm, catching Gaius' attention.

'I think I'm needed elsewhere,' he said slowly. 'If you'll excuse me for a moment?' He began to march over to where Flavius awaited, and then followed him across to speak with Ostorius.

'He's very nice, isn't he?' Ros pondered. 'For a Roman I mean,' she added hurriedly in afterthought.

I stared at her in amazement, and ashamedly even admitted to a pang of jealousy towards my friend.

'Is he?' I looked away quickly, feigning disinterest. 'I hadn't noticed,' I lied.

With excellent timing as usual, Dafydd made his excuses. 'If you don't mind, I think I'll get myself some water. It's quite hot in the sun.' He nodded courteously, 'Ladies,' he added, and walked off.

Ros turned towards me. 'I'm sorry,' she said. 'I didn't realise you liked him *that* much.'

I felt embarrassed now. I kicked at the dirt with my foot.

'So, are you going to tell me what happened or not?' she persisted, smiling.

I laughed. 'Of course,' I replied. 'Let's go somewhere we can't be overheard!'

We sat just outside Roisin's hut, refreshing ourselves with a little food and some cool stream water, chatting amiably and whispering in confidence to one another like young children as I informed her of all that had occurred during my absence from Dolebury.

A short while later I noticed that Gaius was looking for me. I could see him searching by where we had previously stood.

'I'd better go,' I said, getting up in a hurry.

'Talk to you later then,' Ros called after me 'You'd best keep on Antur's good side!'

'That will be difficult,' I replied with a laugh as I ran towards Gaius, calling out to Ros over my shoulder. 'He doesn't have one!'

'It's all right,' Gaius said as he saw me approach. 'Ostorius hasn't given up all hope, at least, not yet.' He frowned and scratched his head. 'We just have to get him to sit down with your chief and discuss things amicably.'

I tensed as I saw Antur coming over to us. Gaius must have seen my look as he swung around to face him. Antur halted but a few steps before us, his manner full of menace. He looked us up and down in cold appraisal, his gaze piercing and intense. 'You can't have her!' he sneered. 'She's mine!'

How did he know, I wondered? Had he merely guessed, or had Gaius mentioned something when he was here before?

'I've been watching you the whole time,' he added in disgust, in answer to my unspoken question as if he could read my very thoughts. 'I can see where this is leading, so I'll tell you again, Roman dog!' he almost spat the word, there being no love lost between them. 'Dana belongs to me! Do you hear? You Romans, you think you can come here and just take whatever you want!'

'And does Dana agree to this?' Gaius was not to be put off. He took a step closer. 'Does she agree to being yours?'

'She doesn't have to. We've been betrothed since we were children. She has no choice,' Antur countered sharply, his humour hostile and malevolent. 'You can't have her unless I say so. Dobunnic Law won't let you. And I say you can't have her! You think you can just take without asking?' Gaius paled slightly. 'What's the matter? Didn't she tell you?' He spat rudely at Gaius' feet and he walked off.

Gaius heaved a heavy sigh. 'Is that true?' he asked wearily.

I nodded meekly, my eyes downcast and staring at the spittle on Gaius' left boot. I felt both angry and upset. I couldn't stop shaking.

'Why didn't you tell me all this before?' he enquired gently.

I couldn't face him. I had to turn away. Blinking the tears from my eyes, I swallowed hard. 'You're a Roman,' I reasoned, almost inaudibly over my shoulder. 'You can, you can just take what you want, can't you?' Agreeing somewhat with Antur's comment.

'I'd sooner have you with your chief's blessing than without. I've no wish to provoke another war!'

I turned around sharply and glared at Gaius as if it was all his fault. 'I'll not let Antur ruin my happiness a second time! Not again!' I snapped.

'Dafydd?' Gaius asked perceptively after a moment's pause.

I sighed. 'Dafydd,' I confirmed.

'And so Dafydd becomes a druid?'

'Something like that,' I explained. 'When I first came to the Mendip—to Dolebury—he was there for me, him and Ros. They were so kind, and Dafydd and I, well we were happy together until Antur complained to Chief Eber—told him that I was his—that we were betrothed.'

'And were you?'

'I don't know,' I stammered in frustration. 'I suppose so. Yes.' I shrugged in defeat. 'Antur's father was Chief of the Atrebates, one of our trading partners, so I guess it was only to be expected that Antur be wed to the daughter of a Dobunni Chief.' It was true. It was all true. Damn Dobunnic Law!

Gaius reached out and pulled me in close. 'Wait a minute,' he reasoned suddenly. 'You're the daughter of the previous chief? The one that was slain at Worlebury?'

I nodded sadly. Perhaps I should have mentioned this earlier?

'After our tribe split, our numbers were quite low,' I continued, 'lower than that of our northern brothers and sisters. We needed the Belgae's support, specifically the Atrebates tribe, and my father was elected as the new chief.'

This had all happened some twelve years or so before the Roman Invasion had begun and I was still a babe in arms.

We stood back and watched as the crowd began to disperse. Some people were sitting out in the sun, nibbling on fruit or bread, or just sipping on some water. Others had returned to their own huts.

The Roman entourage had retreated to where their horses had been tethered, standing around listening to Ostorius as he waved his arms dramatically about. We were too far away to hear what was being said.

'It's a wonder he hasn't called for you,' I remarked to Gaius, 'to ask of your expert advice.' I sat down on a nearby boulder. 'This is hopeless,' I sighed.

'No, it's not,' Gaius replied staunchly.

We watched as Chief Eber saw the last of his Council of Elders exit the hut. He patted each one of them warmly on the shoulder, and then after a moment's deliberation both he and Broduil went back inside.

'I guess it's up to us now,' Gaius remarked suddenly. He scratched at his chin, deep in thought.

'What?' I asked, puzzled.

'Come on.' He held out a hand towards me and then nodded his head towards the Chief's Hut, his intentions obvious.

'We can't!' I exclaimed aghast.

Gaius just smiled. He looked at me earnestly, imploring me to accompany him.

Feeling like an errant child, I slowly took his hand. We all but ran across to the hut, halting only briefly at the entrance as we gathered the courage to enter, unannounced.

Eber was deep in conversation with Broduil when we marched boldly inside. Broduil looked up sharply, glaring at me particularly, for I at least should know the ways of my people. Tribal protocol had been breached, and in Broduil's eyes at least, I had clearly committed the worst possible crime.

'What is this!' he roared. 'You dare to interrupt the Chief of the Dobunni, to enter his house unannounced, and in such a manner?' He stood up, clenching his fists.

'Broduil, calm yourself,' Eber commanded practically. He held up a hand for silence. 'Let us hear what they have come here to say, just for the present at least. This meeting is important to us all.' He gestured for us to be seated.

Broduil remained standing a moment until the chief glared at him. 'You too, Broduil,' he said patiently. Reluctantly, the big man sat down again.

'Thank you, sir,' Gaius responded courteously. We approached and seated ourselves opposite.

'We Dobunni are a proud people, Gaius Julius,' Eber remarked. 'You will find me extremely stubborn, but I am not an unreasonable man.' He smiled. 'Now what is it you wish to say? Is it about the peace talks that you wish to speak of?' He gazed meaningfully at us, raising a quizzical eyebrow.

I realised suddenly that I was still holding onto Gaius' hand, and released it quickly, consciously aware of the chief's gaze upon us.

'Sir, I shall be honest with you,' Gaius began. 'Before I met Dana, I was quite prepared to carry out my orders, to prepare for an attack on your settlement here that would have wiped out your people without warning nor even the chance to fight back. I admit, I have been camped here for days, watching you, spying out the land, assessing your strength and numbers in preparation for the attack. Then, when our Legions arrived I reported my findings to General Ostorius who would command the attack. It was only Dana who convinced me otherwise.' He paused momentarily, seeking out the right words. 'And, well, when I noted that your numbers were so low, in truth, when we set out on this campaign, we assumed them to be far greater,' Gaius continued.

'It is only because of Roman hands that our numbers are so few!' Broduil interrupted abruptly.

'Broduil, please,' Eber chastised. 'Please, continue, Gaius Julius.'

'No one imagined your population to be so low. You can pose no possible threat to the Roman Empire now. Even Ostorius should realise that.'

'So, what is it that you suggest?' Eber enquired.

The centurion took a deep breath. 'Well, simply, the fighting has to stop. We have to find another way. Agree to the *Pax Romana*, then that will be an end to it.'

'You want us to agree to what we've been fighting against all these years?' Eber responded, somewhat irritably. 'To give in to your Roman ways and ideals? To help you expand your empire at the expense of our own? You presume too much, Gaius Julius!'

'Look, you at least need to sit down with Ostorius alone in order to come to some form of an agreement,' Gaius suggested sensibly. 'You cannot do so with a room full of angry warriors.'

'This much is true,' Eber agreed with a sigh. 'The disruption they cause does not help.' He thought for a moment. 'But what does this *Pax Romana* of yours mean? What does it do?'

'Chief Eber,' Gaius continued, 'we do not ask that you abandon your ways, nor your gods. The choice would be yours and yours alone to make. You shall all remain free to live your lives the way you wish.'

Broduil was not looking very pleased. He was glaring at Gaius with contempt. 'Ah, and speaking of "free", what of the slaves you have already taken? Are they to be returned to us? Will you take more?'

'Sadly, I cannot return those already taken,' Gaius replied. 'Among other things, it would be impossible to locate their whereabouts.'

'Ha!' Broduil declared triumphant.

'But,' Gaius went on to say, 'we can draw up an agreement to ensure that no further slaves be taken from the Dobunni people. It can form part of your *Pax Romana*. In fact, General Ostorius has already agreed that this be so.'

'Go on,' Eber urged as Gaius halted briefly to gather his thoughts.

'As a further incentive, I can offer you some of our finest Arabian horses, such as the ones we rode in on,' Gaius stated. 'You saw how fine they looked?' he added with a grin of encouragement.

The young chieftain brightened instantly. 'Yes, indeed,' he responded with interest. 'Fine animals. We have not seen their like here about.'

'They hail from Germania. Strong and swift in battle,' Gaius added persuasively. 'No other tribe in this land possesses any.'

'Your General, he has agreed to this?' A look of concern furrowing his tanned brow.

'Actually, no,' Gaius replied swiftly, and then he smiled, 'but he will.' He paused slightly. 'I won't lie to you, sir. Rome will want complete control of the lead mine and there will be taxes to pay, but no more than that, you have my word.'

'Ha! Taxes!' Broduil muttered, only to be ignored.

Gaius gazed earnestly at Chief Eber. 'Please don't let your pride cause the annihilation of your people,' he implored. 'It shouldn't have to come to that, and it doesn't have to. At least give the peace treaty a chance. If it doesn't work out, then I guess we all go back to fighting again!'

Eber was amused by that last remark and smiled thoughtfully. 'You speak with much wisdom, Gaius Julius,' he said. 'I shall consider your words carefully.'

'Thank you for listening, sir,' Gaius replied courteously.

Eber arose, indicating that the interview was at an end. We all stood.

'You may tell your General that I will speak with him,' Chief Eber announced suddenly as we prepared to exit the hut. 'Alone this time I think,' he added with a smile.

Gaius acknowledged his request and we both stepped outside into the afternoon sun breathing a heavy sigh of relief but content in the knowledge that perhaps we had helped to achieve something.

A short time later, discussions began afresh between Eber and Ostorius. The two of them shut themselves away for what seemed like ages. Ostorius Scapula was not a condescending, diplomatic sort of person. There remained a very real possibility that he may do more harm than good. It was almost dark when they finally emerged from the meeting hut. Instantly, a crowd gathered about them.

Eber raised his arms high, calling for silence. 'My people!' he began triumphantly, 'After much deliberation, let it be known that we have reached an amicable agreement of sorts.' He paused a moment, waiting for those objecting to quieten. 'While there are still some details that we will need to go over, as of this moment however, a truce shall now exist between our peoples,' he continued. 'One, I might add, that will retain our freedom and our honour!'

There was a mingled response to this announcement, with some cheers, yet with much muttering from those warriors who did not trust this so called *"Pax Romana"*.

Gaius grabbed hold of me suddenly, picking me up in jubilation and swinging me around. 'Yes!' he cried out merrily.

Abruptly there came a shout and some jeering from Antur and his young warrior friends who were standing close by, their faces defiant. He led the warriors away, muttering and scheming slyly. Antur would never agree to this Roman Peace.

Nevertheless, there were celebrations that night. Most people were in a joyous mood now that there was an end to the hostilities, and with the promise of peace and safety the women and children had returned from the hills. General Ostorius and his entourage had left for the Roman encampment in readiness to move out, with the expectation that Gaius would then re-join them the following morning.

Dafydd was helping out with the entertainment by providing some music on a small flute. Two others and a man who beat out a lively rhythm on a drum accompanied. Oftentimes, when Dafydd would play I would join in, singing along to one of our native folk songs. On this occasion however, I was content just to sit on the grass beside Gaius, leaning back upon my elbows as I surveyed the surrounding scene. Gaius moved in closer.

'You see, I told you it would be all right,' he whispered in my ear before kissing my cheek lightly. 'Come on,' he added. Let's go and find a quiet spot.' He took me by the hand, his touch warm, his smile warmer still.

'Dafydd's music is very good,' Gaius remarked as we strolled along, 'but after today I think we could both do with a little peace and quiet!'

'True,' I agreed with a laugh. 'Even had the druids themselves forecast this day's event, I don't think I would have believed it!'

Arm in arm, we walked slowly around the hill-forts perimeter, but our peace was soon to be short-lived. Upon approaching a scattering of boulders that lay amongst the long grass to the east, we noticed Anturiaethus, sitting gloomily upon one of them as he watched the camps festivities from a "safe" distance. He seemed to be in a pensive mood. It was too late for us to turn away unnoticed, and he frowned as he saw us approach.

'Oh yes, it's Antur,' he remarked coldly, echoing my very thoughts. 'Too late to run away,' he added childishly. 'I've already seen you!'

Gaius released my hand and casually walked towards him. 'Why don't you stop sulking and come and join in the celebrations?' he said cordially.

Antur snapped to attention, instantly grasping the hilt of his sword as he jumped down from the boulder. He glared icily at Gaius. 'The only celebration I intend to enjoy is your death, and that of all other Romans!' he exploded, his cheeks flushed with anger, his muscles tensing like coiled springs. 'And as for you!' he added, turning his attention on me. 'I cannot believe you would want to take off with this, this... Roman pig! Have you forgotten what they did to our home, to our families, and to your own father?'

Antur's last remark definitely hit home, and I stepped forward to confront him. 'Of course I haven't forgotten!' I retaliated sharply. 'Nor shall I ever forget,' I added. 'I only wish I could, but Gaius is a good man. I have seen now that not all Romans are alike, no more than we are.'

Anturiaethus was not to be appeased, however. 'I saved your life on more than one occasion that night,' he countered angrily. 'If I hadn't speared that soldier you so clumsily ran into, you'd be lying at the bottom of one of those pits together with the rest of the corpses! You owe me!' he snarled. 'Never forget that!'

It was true. Antur had saved my life, however, this didn't give him the right to ownership, even though our betrothal did I suppose.

'Understand this,' I stated, fighting to keep my temper in check. 'I don't owe you anything. I'm not yours and I never was!' Angrily, I snatched off the horse brooch he'd made for me, breaking the clasp as I did so, and thrust it into his hands.

He seemed somewhat stunned by my outburst but quickly recovered his composure. Antur reached forward suddenly, taking hold of my chin and roughly turning my head to one side. He glared accusingly at Gaius as he examined the painful bruise.

'You promised me Dana wouldn't be hurt,' he snapped. 'So, what about this?'

I pushed his hand away abruptly, releasing me from his grasp and taking a step backwards. '*One* bad Roman,' I retorted swiftly before Gaius had a chance to explain. 'It wasn't Gaius.'

'And that?' Antur enquired brusquely, pointing to the sword cut beneath my torn tunic, his face set in a deep frown.

'That… that was my fault,' I stammered, pulling my tunic up to cover the wound. 'It is nothing.' Antur was bound to know if I attempted to lie, and in a way, it was my fault.

'I warned you to be careful with that sword of yours,' he reprimanded sharply, apparently satisfied with my brief explanation and assuming the wound to be self-inflicted.

'You should have given that sword to me, or to the new chief. Such things aren't for the likes of girls!'

Antur laughed cruelly, and my temper blew.

'Well, perhaps if someone would just teach me!' I glanced toward Gaius, remembering his promise.

'No one will teach you!' Antur remarked sarcastically. 'Women are not permitted to handle the sword. Swords are for men to wield!'

Gaius Julius then intervened, taking a step forward. 'There, at least, we agree,' he remarked, giving me a cursory glance as he tried to restore some vestige of peace. He patted Antur on the shoulder as if he was an old friend, much to Antur's surprise and disgust. Antur moved aside rapidly. Gaius then turned back towards me.

'Having only just met you, I'm not too keen on losing you at the point of a sword in some battle,' he explained reasonably as he noticed the look of annoyance I was giving him. He held up his hands in surrender. 'I will teach you to fight properly with the sword, as I promised,' he continued pressing a finger to my lips before I had a chance to protest, 'but *only* in self-defence,' he added sternly, then smiled as he gently cupped my face in his hands and kissed me gently. Enthusiastically, I wrapped my arms about him, quite forgetting about Antur who was watching the display with complete disdain.

'Oh, I give in!' Antur snarled abruptly. Gaius and I looked across at him in total surprise. 'I don't know what I ever saw in her,' he added hotly. 'You can have the little wildcat!' Turning on his heel, Antur stormed off, leaving us both bewildered, and relieved.

Antur's words had stung however, and stung hard. I did not love Antur as he would have wished me to, but I didn't want to lose his friendship. A tear slipped silently down one cheek and Gaius gently brushed it aside. Neither did I want Gaius to think of me as a "wildcat", but he merely smiled once more.

'My little warrior,' he whispered softly, and then he kissed me tenderly. Arms intertwined, Gaius was gazing thoughtfully into the distance. 'My only question now is,' he asked with a grin, 'how long before I can marry you? The Army will be moving off very shortly.'

I looked up at him, a worried expression on my face. What if Chief Eber wouldn't permit me to wed a Roman? What if Antur changed his mind?

'Don't worry,' Gaius laughed. 'I'll not leave here without you, I promise. Still, I'd best speak with your chieftain about it. After all, we wouldn't want to upset this truce that now exists by some stupid breach of protocol, now would we?'

Although it was customary to wait for an allotted amount of time to pass from the initial announcement of the intended marriage to the actual ceremony, Dobunnic Law allowing for any other possible suitors to make a formal protest, there had been instances of inter-tribal marriages that had required instant settlements. Would a marriage to a Roman be viewed in a similar fashion, or even permitted at all I wondered? And would Eber be willing to annul the previous agreement for the arranged marriage to Antur?

'I will speak with Chief Eber first thing tomorrow. All will be well, you'll see,' he added confidently. 'But for now, I think we had both better get some sleep.'

I looked around. 'Where?' I asked, my head spinning with the events of the past three days.

Gaius turned his head. 'Here looks pretty good,' he said cheerfully, removing his cloak and laying it down on some soft grass next to one of the boulders. He sat down, using the boulder as a backrest and beckoned me over. I lay down beside him, placing my head upon his lap. We lay there in silence, gazing up at the stars above us until we both drifted off peacefully into a well-earned sleep.

At first light, Gaius awoke and immediately began to head toward the Chief's hut. I stumbled after him, still half asleep. We had to wait a short while until Eber was ready to see us.

Eber had been elected chieftain simply because he was the head man at Dolebury at the time. Even now, seeing as our numbers were so low, there was talk of combining the last of our tribe with that of the Belgae, which included Antur's people, the Atrebates tribe, with whom we had existed peaceably for some time now. Eventually Eber emerged from the hut and greeted us with a broad smile.

Gaius began to explain our wishes to him. Eber just smiled and nodded his head occasionally, giving the distinct impression that he had been expecting this request all along. I suppose that it wouldn't have been difficult to guess, seeing as Gaius and I had hardly been away from one another's company since we arrived here.

'We would have to leave today,' Gaius concluded. 'The Roman Army…' he tailed off with a vague wave of his hand for emphasis.

Eber nodded his understanding. 'As soon as that?' he remarked, scratching his chin thoughtfully. 'Well, I certainly have no objections,' his brow furrowed somewhat, 'but what of Anturiaethus?'

I cringed slightly.

'He has agreed to release Dana to me,' Gaius responded swiftly.

'Has he?' Eber seemed surprised at this news. 'Not that I don't believe you, and I shall have to send word to his people, the Atrebates, regarding the change of plan.' He toyed with his moustache while he deliberated, then added quickly, 'They won't like it, but I'd better hear it from Antur himself. I don't wish to incur his wrath if we've got it wrong!'

And so Antur was summoned to join our early morning meeting. He arrived looking as if he hadn't slept at all. His hair was matted, his face gaunt, and his short, neat beard be-smudged with dirt. He glared harshly at Gaius.

'Anturiaethus,' the Chief began formally, 'is it true that you have relinquished your claim upon Dana, and that you have released her to Gaius Julius here seated?'

Antur was taken aback. He stared at me for some time before answering, and for a moment I thought he would deny his words of the previous evening. I held my breath in anticipation of some stinging denial, but none came.

'She can do as she pleases,' he said simply with a shrug after some deliberation. 'Dana is free to go with whomsoever she wishes.' His voice was bland, his expression harsh and cold as he resigned himself to his fate. Antur then turned his back on us all and walked away. I was stunned.

'He'll be all right,' Gaius remarked softly, catching my worried expression. 'He'll probably go off and sulk somewhere,' he added.

This remark did nothing to ease my torn feelings.

'Well, Dana, I guess you are free to go,' Chief Eber stated simply, 'but I hope you'll both come back and visit us from time to time?'

'We will indeed, sir!' Gaius responded with a smile, 'And thank you for your hospitality.'

'It is we who should be thanking you,' Eber replied. 'I only hope this *Pax Romana* of yours can be maintained. Incidentally,' he added. 'What would you have done if Dana had not been permitted to leave with you?'

Gaius paused, giving the question some thought. 'Well, I wasn't going to leave without her,' and Eber just nodded and smiled.

Wondering what the future would have in store for us all, I said my farewells quickly to Ros and Dafydd, and with tears and hugs, I gazed around fretfully for Antur.

'Go and find him,' Gaius had whispered softly, reading my thoughts, and so I began quickly searching for him.

He wasn't with any of his warrior friends, nor was he in the forge, but it didn't take too long to locate him. He stood alone, high upon the eastern ramparts gazing out across Dolebury and the flood plains beyond towards where Worlebury had once stood. I swallowed hard as painful memories swept across me like the rising tide.

'Antur?' I ventured weakly, pulling my shawl about me as the breeze began to strengthen.

He spun around and jumped down to face me, his manner detached, his face unreadable. I could not tell whether it was from the cold breeze or Antur's cold expression that I shivered, or perhaps the ghosts of Worlebury Hill-fort some six miles or so distant?

'I came to say goodbye,' I continued hesitantly. There was no need to say any more.

Antur smiled wanly and took a step forward. 'This is yours,' he said plainly, holding out the horse brooch. 'I made it for *you.*'

I smiled gently and accepted the return of the brooch gratefully from him. I knew Anturiaethus only too well and knew this to be his only means of an apology.

'I've mended the clasp,' he added with sudden enthusiasm, startling me slightly. 'You see?' pointing eagerly to where a new pin had been fixed into position. 'I was up half the night fixing it, and polishing it for you too.' He stopped short, seeming somewhat embarrassed. 'Here,' pinning the horse brooch into position carefully upon my shawl for me.

We both laughed nervously. Cold, hard Antur. It was so unusual for him to show any sort of emotion other than anger; a true warrior.

I gazed up into his piercing blue eyes and for a moment, a very small moment, they seemed to soften slightly. He smiled, and we hugged each other tightly.

Immediately, he jumped back. 'You're still wearing that darn sword of yours, aren't you?' he accused.

It was a little hard to miss at such close proximity.

'So?' I countered sharply.

'It will get you into trouble one of these days!' he added, 'You mark my words!'

'It already has.' Gaius remarked as he approached, smiling. 'Ready to go?'

'Not really,' I replied, a little sadly. I was becoming nostalgic and gazing out across at Worlebury was not helping any.

He turned to Antur. 'I will take good care of Dana,' he stated sincerely. 'You have my word on that.'

'Ha! A Roman's word?' Antur responded cynically, back in fighting form. 'What is the good of that?'

Gaius merely stepped forward, offering his hand in friendship. 'I only hope, someday, that we can become friends,' he said directly.

Antur looked at Gaius suspiciously, and scowled, and then to my complete surprise and utter astonishment he accepted, and the two men clasped arms firmly if a little awkwardly to begin with.

'See that you do take good care of Dana, else you'll have me to answer to,' Antur snapped, and then he added softly, 'she's all I have left.'

He was right. We were as family. Antur had moved in with my family as soon as we had been betrothed, with the expectation that once we were wed Antur would then become the next chieftain. Over the years we had grown very close, but I had always thought of him as a brother. I had not even given our arranged marriage a second thought. As a child I had never really understood those things. And now, all we really had left from the wreck of our hill-fort home, was each other.

Gaius smiled and nodded to Antur, and then he took me by the hand to where his horse awaited.

'There's one thing I can't quite work out,' Gaius remarked curiously, scratching his head as we walked away. 'The name of your tribe, *Dobunni*.'

'What of it?'

'I can't seem to place it in either the Gallic or British Celtic languages either,' he explained. 'And it means nothing in Latin.'

I laughed aloud. Gaius, the scholar, and here finally was something he didn't know.

'That's because our ancestors were not Celtic. I tried to tell you but you wouldn't listen!' I stated practically. 'Our language, and our people are closer to that of Hibernia, and we are kin to those in Armorica. *"Doo-Boo-Nee"*, means simply "The Dark-Haired People"!' I laughed, flinging my long dark locks over my shoulder for emphasis.

'Dark Celts?' Gaius pondered for a moment. He shrugged and smiled, mounting the horse.

'What?'

'That's what Caesar called "Celts" of your colouring.'

'But we're not Celts!' I retaliated hotly.

'I know that. I do,' he replied, offering me a hand up onto the horse. 'Forgive me, but we tend to call all Britons "Celts". It's nothing personal.'

I smiled and swung myself up behind him. Typical Roman mentality, I thought. The horse shifted slightly under our weight, keen to be off and away. 'I'll forgive you then.'

'But your people—your ancestors—they must have been here in Britannia long before the Celts ever set foot here,' he speculated thoughtfully. 'So, when the Celts finally did arrive, they would have pushed your people westwards I suppose.'

'If you say so,' I answered nonchalantly. 'After all, you're the historian.'

Legion XIIII Gemina

Gaius Julius Caecinianus

Chapter Four

AD 48 to AD 52

Glevum and Corinium, Gloucestershire and Manduessedum, Warwickshire

It felt strange riding off amongst an Army of some ten thousand soldiers—Roman soldiers—who up until yesterday were my people's mortal enemies and whom I would gladly have slain myself had I been able in order to avenge the deaths at Worlebury. Yet, here I was, and soon to be wed to one of the Roman Army's finest officers. There were a few other women around, I noticed, a few slaves and other wives of officers, both obviously native Britons from various tribes. A couple of the wives were Roman, having travelled with their husbands with the obvious intention of setting up home in Britannia. Yet I admit to feeling somewhat out of place during those first few days, knowing nothing of Roman custom nor how these people lived, although I knew that Gaius would teach me and would always take good care of me; still, these were early days for me and I had much to learn.

The Roman Army moved at a steady pace, finally halting for the night to set up camp on the banks of the Sabrina. Once the camp was set up proper, General Ostorius called his officers together for a tactical discussion. As I was feeling a little lonely and out of place, the General generously suggested that I could accompany Gaius to the meeting so long as I kept quiet this time and stayed out of the way, so there I sat, close by the entrance to the *principia* while the military elite discussed their next move.

It had begun to rain, and rain heavily. The wind blew hard against the tent and I shivered as a cold draught blew in. I listened to the rain as it pelted down upon the tented roof, for it was difficult to hear anything else, until finally the rain died down to a gentle pitter-patter before ceasing altogether.

Ostorius stroked his chin, deep in concentration. 'What I'd like to know now is, what's the best way of strengthening our defences against Caratacus and the Silures? We've lost too many men already.' He stared thoughtfully at the parchment laid out before him. 'Has anyone any suggestions?' he asked. 'Gaius Julius, your thoughts on this if you please?'

Gaius took a step closer to the table, his fellow officers gathered around him eagerly. Gaius looked at the map for a moment before reaching a conclusion.

'We need to establish more military forts,' he stated plainly after further deliberation. 'Here, and here,' pointing out the positions on the map.

The thought of yet more Roman forts popping up like toadstools and intruding upon British soil did nothing to ease my discomfort. Gaius glanced towards me, seeming to sense my disapproval of his plan. He excused himself for a moment, leaving his comrades and Ostorius to ponder his proposal.

'I'm sorry,' he apologised sincerely as he walked over to where I sat. 'It's my job.'

I gave him a quizzical look, not quite understanding the meaning of his words.

'It's what I do,' he explained patiently.

'I know,' I replied softly, my smile failing to hide the sadness in my eyes. This was something I would have to get used to if I was to become a Roman officer's wife.

'Do you want me to walk you back to our tent?' Gaius suggested with a smile as he held out his hand. 'I'm sure I won't be missed, just for a moment.'

'No, but thank you,' I declined gratefully. 'I'm all right.' I didn't want to be alone and I felt quite comfortable where I sat, despite the draught.

He nodded, and then fetched me a cupful of wine before returning to the General's side.

'Ah! Gaius Julius,' Ostorius remarked upon his return to the table. 'What would you say if we were to move the Legionary Base at Manduessedum and re-establish it here, on the very banks of the Sabrina itself?' His finger jabbed hard at an area on the map.

'Not bad,' Gaius agreed thoughtfully, studying the map again for a moment. 'It would certainly help defend the borders, and would be a good tactical move on our part, but I think that *here*, a little further north, would be a far better location.' Gaius indicated an area nearby. There were a few grunts and nods of approval from the other centurions.

'Place a Legionary Base here, and not only does it protect the borders, but it would give you optimum control of all traffic up and down the river,' he continued. 'Besides which, this position would place the fortress right next to the easiest crossing point, at this ford right... *here*.' Gaius pointed confidently to the location on the map.

By morning, the rain had returned and continued throughout the whole day, delaying the General's plans. He was impatient to get going, yet we could do little else but wait until the rain had eased off. It wasn't until noon of the following day that it finally ceased. We began to move out, the rain having caused the ground to become very treacherous and sodden, making for very slow going indeed. Occasionally, some of the soldiers would sing—Army songs mostly—to pass the time on these long and arduous journeys;

We are men of the Fourteenth, Legion of the Twin.
Away with you! Get out of our way!
The trumpet sounds advance,
Soldiers of Rome, forward!

Whether we follow the Eagles,
Or we go to the Ravens alone,
Our Pride is in the Legion,
And the fighting infantry are our family and home,
And the fighting infantry are our family and home.
We follow the Standards, wherever they lead us,
From the barbarous forests of Germany,
To the mist shrouded hills of Caledonia,
Tamers of Britain, March!'

Finally, we reached our destination just before sundown. It had been very tedious travelling at such a slow pace, but the Army needed to stay together and couldn't have had the cavalry charging on ahead and leaving the foot soldiers far behind, especially in such dangerous terrain so close to the Silures territory.

I was used to travelling much faster on horseback, and over a lot shorter distances, being only too glad to be able to eventually dismount and stretch my legs.

It didn't take too long for the legionaries to begin setting up camp once more, busily digging the defensive ditches before finally erecting the tents.

The surveyors immediately began working on the site of the new Legionary Base. An Auxiliary fort for the VIth Thracian was to be located also alongside the river, nearby, and a little to the south of the Base.

I sat beneath a small tree on an elevated position from the river and watched the activity with interest while Gaius unloaded the horses.

General Ostorius drew up alongside him and surveyed the scene with a keen eye. 'See that they place the fort in the correct location, Commander!' he ordered brusquely as the builders from the Twentieth Legion arrived and began to start work.

'Yes, sir.' Gaius saluted, promptly tethering the horses to the tree. 'You down there!' he called, giving me a wink as he marched off down the hill. 'Not that way. Parallel to the river!'

As lunch time approached a cry went out from one of the sentries. Soldiers everywhere ceased work, instantly on the alert for danger.

I gazed down the slope to see a small band of native Britons approaching from the southeast. General Ostorius was heading towards them accompanied by two centurions.

I gazed fixedly at them. Gaius returned and stood beside me bringing with him some morsels of food and fresh water. He placed the items down and seated himself beside me.

'Friends of yours?' he queried good naturedly, taking a bite of bread and handing me a piece.

'Ha!' I spat. 'These are no friends of mine!' I took a bite of bread angrily and swallowed it down whole. 'Northern Dobunni!' I added brusquely. 'Traitors and quislings the lot of them, especially that excuse for a chieftain down there!'

Gaius raised a quizzical eyebrow and took a swig of water. 'Who, Cattigarus?' he asked placidly. 'He's been nothing but polite and most helpful to us Romans.' He taunted me deliberately, and then he grinned.

'Coward!' I retorted. 'He isn't even of Dobunnic blood,' I added. 'He was put in charge of the Dobunni by one of our neighbouring tribes, the Catuvellauni, a very large and powerful tribe.'

'I know of them,' Gaius remarked, offering me some water.

'Well, that's why we split,' I continued on, taking a sip. 'We of the south refused to accept a foreign chieftain, and then his ideas sometime later of letting you Romans just walk in and take over, well…' I sighed deeply. And now where has it got us? Where had it got me? Would I ever fit into this Roman world that at the moment felt so alien?

Gaius placed an arm about my shoulders. 'He's probably come to ask more favours of his Roman allies,' he said speculatively. 'Or he's just being nosey.'

He paused thoughtfully, watching Cattigarus and Ostorius talking amiably. 'He wants to know what we're doing here,' he continued as Ostorius waved an arm about expansively towards the building work. 'What it is we are constructing. What's in it for him?'

'I wonder if he'll like having a full-sized fortress on his doorstep,' I pondered thoughtfully.

'Oh, I should think he'd love it,' Gaius replied. 'There for him to ask for anything he wants. Plus, he won't have to worry about any raids from the Silures anymore.'

'I'd still like to test the sharpness of my sword on him!' I said with a laugh. 'See how fast he runs!'

Gaius frowned at me. 'You promised me you wouldn't draw that sword on anyone again except in self-defence,' he reminded me sternly.

'I was only joking,' I replied abashed. 'And, I promised I wouldn't attack any more Romans, not natives!'

'Nevertheless,' he warned sternly, and then smiled.

'Nevertheless,' I repeated, and we both laughed.

While the forts at Glevum were being constructed, Ostorius had given Gaius orders to take his men across to the old Legionary Base at Manduessedum and see that it was taken down. As it would take a little while before the new Bases were to be fully complete, and with no sense of urgency required, our land finally at peace, I set off with Gaius and the VIth Thracian towards the midlands.

I was slowly getting to know the Thracians, and I liked them much better than most of the Romans I'd met so far, for they were much more well-mannered and respectful of others and possessed a peculiar sense of humour that never failed to make me laugh.

It took just under a week to reach Manduessedum, travelling at a leisurely pace. We stopped at Vertis in the Cornovii territory and then stayed a while at Salinae to enjoy the sacred spa waters briefly before heading further northward to Letocetum, calling at the small fortress there, and then headed eastward to our final destination of Manduessedum in the lands of the Corieltavi.

Both the Cornovii and the Corieltavi had agreed to the *Pax Romana* so, for the first time in my life, I had no concerns about being suddenly set upon by warring tribes. It felt strange, not to have to be on one's guard and I found it difficult at first to relax entirely.

I had never glimpsed a Roman fortress before now. Indeed, up until the last few days, I had not even so much as sighted a small mile castle. The fact that this was a Legionary Base of so much larger proportions made it all the more awesome.

The Base had been left only lightly manned, utilising a bare minimum of troops. There had been no need to continue to defend the fortress with a full garrison, the neighbouring tribes remaining peaceable for some time now.

With the number of soldiers at the Base, and with the small number of Thracians Gaius had brought with us, it was good to feel uncrowded once again. Even better was the fact that there were no superior officers, in particular one General Ostorius, to watch our every movement.

The time spent at Manduessedum however was short, but we enjoyed the peace and tranquillity and the feeling of freedom it brought. The Thracians and legionaries soon began to disinter the fort upon Gaius' command, smashing any items that were not to be brought along to the new Legionary Base, then digging a ditch in which to toss them before covering them up with soil.

Whole walls were pulled apart and any reusable timbers stored neatly on the awaiting carts. I stood back and watched in amazement as little by little the fortress disappeared before my eyes, like magic. Gaius was standing nearby, overseeing the whole operation. I looked across at him, somewhat perplexed.

'I don't understand,' I remarked at length. 'Why do you destroy your own fort?'

Gaius strolled over and stood beside me. He laughed in amusement. 'Well, the Legions are going to a new fortress. We shan't need this one anymore,' he replied patiently. 'And should any trouble break out in the future, an enemy won't be able to use our own forts, or technology, against us.' He smiled gently.

I gave this some thought for a moment, running the information over in my mind. 'But what if you should need the fort later?' I reasoned. 'If there was any sort of trouble in this area, surely you would have need of the fortress then?'

'We can easily build another,' he responded casually, folding his arms across his chest as he surveyed the destruction. 'Or we can resurrect this one if need be.' He turned towards me, smiling as he stroked my cheek affectionately before kissing me gently on the forehead. 'Time to leave.'

Upon returning to our new fortress home, we found that a house, the *praetorium*, had been constructed in our absence for our own personal use alongside the *principia* within the Auxiliary fort. It was of single storey design with a central courtyard, and while not overly spacious, the *triclinium*, or dining room, provided ample space in which to entertain any future guests.

After some weeks we managed to have a little leisure time to ourselves. While Ostorius could not spare Gaius for too long, the time he was granted was most welcome. We spent most of this familiarising ourselves with the surrounding area, which from a military point of view was required and sensible anyway, so we would go riding on many occasions, although we never ventured too far from the fortress for fear of attack from the Silures.

'I don't know why they insist on placing the stables so far from the barracks,' Gaius complained as we walked across the Legionary Base, the Auxiliary fort stables not quite completed, at least not to Gaius' satisfaction.

It had been a warm summer's day on the first occasion he had taken me riding. The sun felt quite hot upon our backs as we laughed and chatted merrily, meandering along without a care in the world.

Gaius possessed two horses, a white mare and a bay horse. Most centurions always had the use of two horses. We would ride one each, Gaius often preferring to ride the white in preference to the bay.

We took the horses out around the *Prata Legionis*, or Legion's Meadows, an area adjacent to the forts that was used for manoeuvres and training, and held fodder for the horses and livestock from which the native population were normally kept away.

July of AD 48 proved to be an exceptionally busy time. General Ostorius was yelling out orders as usual, the soldiers scurrying to obey his every command. Both the Legionary and Auxiliary forts had been fully completed by now.

Come the August, Gaius returned from a meeting with Ostorius, grinning broadly.

'Good news then?' I ventured hopefully.

'It seems I've been granted some leave,' Gaius replied happily. 'Not much, but a bit,' he added. 'In view of my "exemplary service" these past few months.'

'Some what?' I asked perplexed, hearing his words but not quite comprehending them. 'What's that?'

'That means,' Gaius answered, putting his arms around me, 'that I get some well-earned time off, and you and I, at last, have the chance to be wed!'

The town of Corinium was not all that far from Glevum and quite close to the Northern Dobunnic Centre of Bagendon, not that this particularly mattered to me. Corinium was a fairly new Roman town, and as with many towns of the same period construction work was continually taking place.

What was important, at least to us, was that there was a small Roman temple already completed. It incorporated four columns atop a number of steps leading up to the entrance. When we arrived, there were but a few people gathered around the temple making their daily offerings.

Marcus had accompanied us. Ostorius, being in an unusually generous mood had granted him time off too, so he had agreed to come along—our only guest. Marcus made sure that he enjoyed himself, happily downing any and all wine that he came across.

The ceremony was fairly short and quiet. Gaius had managed to find for me a brightly coloured veil from the *macellum*, where he also bought for me a bangle that was shaped like a snake, similar to a torque bangle, but with a snake's head at either end. It was truly the most beautiful piece of jewellery I had ever seen.

We stayed at a newly built inn for the night and strolled around the town the next day before heading back up. Marcus was very quiet. He said he had a headache.

I found adjusting to the Roman way of life a little difficult to begin with, although Gaius was very patient and willing to compromise wherever he could, but sometimes this was not always possible. The subject of slavery was one of them.

It was quite commonplace for Romans to own slaves, but having seen people from my own tribe taken to be sold into slavery in the early years of the invasion, my own baby brother one of them, this had left me with a bitter memory.

Gaius had but one slave, Goilladyn. Goilladyn was a native of Gaul, who was employed as a manservant and who had travelled with Gaius for many years. He was friendly and always willing to be of assistance. He didn't really give the impression that he was a slave at all, for which I was grateful. Goilladyn proved to be of an extremely reliable nature and Gaius always treated him as if he were a faithful and trusted friend, rather than a manservant or slave. Gaius was now looking to purchase a girl to help around the house and to assist with the preparation of food. After a few arguments over this, Gaius came across Caitilin. She was from the Catuvellauni tribe, and about the same age as me. Caitilin had been orphaned soon after the conquest had begun. Her hair was as fair as mine was dark, and we soon became good companions.

In the meantime, some of the veterans from Legion Twenty were being established alongside the Legionary Base. All soldiers in the Roman Army were given a grant of land upon retirement, and placing these veterans at Glevum would not only ensure that a back-up force of experienced soldiers was on hand if required, but also that these veterans would be able to show the native population how to live a decent, civilised, Roman way of life.

As for myself, residing within the Auxiliary fort was to prove both interesting and far less stressful than it would have been had we lived inside the larger, Legionary fortress. Apart from the fact that General Ostorius was rarely seen at the Auxiliary fort, being at the Thracian fortress meant that Gaius was the highest-ranking officer there.

The Thracian soldiers too were quite different to those of the Romans. They were far more courteous, and seemed especially loyal to their commanding officer, and therefore as their commanding officer's wife they would always treat me with the greatest respect.

Now that the major construction work had been completed, the Army invited traders in to set up shop outside the fortress walls. This not only helped with supplies for the Legionary Base but would provide a constant stream of custom for the merchants themselves. Thus, a small *macellum* was founded, only to grow in size over the ensuing years to come.

Gaius took great pleasure in escorting me by the hand for a tour of the new market place. He led me endlessly around the many stalls, stopping every now and then to sample some of the wares, and providing a running commentary on many of the objects that were new to me. Leading me over to one of the stalls, Gaius reached out and picked up a shiny, metallic object, with a short handle attached.

The table was laden with many such objects, some plain and others with a fancy, decorative motif across, such as the one Gaius now held out before me. He turned it over in his hand

and raised it up a little. The reverse side was flat and shiny enough for me to see my reflection in.

'You see,' he whispered in my ear as his left arm encircled my waist. He leant forward, resting his chin upon my shoulder so that I could see his reflection also in the mirror. 'You're beautiful.'

I laughed at his playfulness as his reflection smiled back at me.

'That's just a small hand mirror,' he added. 'They come much larger and more elaborate too.'

'And more expensive?' I quizzed.

'Of course!' he laughed.

Gaius asked the stall holder the price of the hand mirror, and after a bit of haranguing he handed the man some coins and then gave me the mirror.

A little further along, Gaius bought for me a pair of very fine hair combs. Caitilin and I spent ages later trying out various styles with them as we tried to work out the best way to wear the combs, and ensuring too that we made good use of the little hand mirror.

It was the first of many happy trips through the market place. Over the years, it was to become one of my favourite pastimes, ambling along and discovering new and exciting things to purchase for our home, or merely just to buy something tasty and fresh to eat for our meals that day.

Gradually, as things became more settled, we took time out to visit my people at Dolebury, stopping for a while to reminisce at the location where we first met, beneath the Mendip. The lake was usually present, changing its shape as the course of the River Chew which fed it continually altered. The level of the water fluctuated with the seasons. When the winter snows had melted, water was abundant, the lake growing to almost twice its normal size, with a small island or two at its centre. In the summertime, the lake had been known to dry up altogether.

In time Gaius was to teach me many things, not in the least my most fervent wish, how to use the sword, or at least, how to defend myself with it. We would head out, past the *Prata Legionis*, to find a quiet spot in which to practice where we wouldn't be disturbed, or else we would wait until Goilladyn and Caitilin were out and utilise the small courtyard to the rear of the house. It was on such a day that I had received my first lesson in the use of the sword. Caitilin had prepared lunch early that morning and left it covered and ready for eating when required, and Goilladyn had been given some free time to do as he wished so he had gone out for a stroll around the *macellum*.

Gaius pushed aside the remains of his breakfast and leaned back casually on the couch. 'So, what would you like to do today, my love?' he asked as I finished my last mouthful. 'You know I've nothing scheduled.'

I thought for a moment, then smiled mischievously. 'Mmm, I can think of one thing,' I replied, lying back and picking idly at a bunch of grapes.

'I could think of a few,' he replied, with a grin.

'Teach me now how to handle the sword?' I sat up enthusiastically, eyes pleading, 'Yes?'

'Dana!' he retorted reproachfully.

'You did promise!' I complained.

He shook his head, 'You're incorrigible!'

'Well?' I pursued.

'All right, all right,' he relented. 'I suppose I did promise, didn't I?'

While the courtyard housed a small rectangular garden within the centre, there was a good deal of paving remaining on which to practice, the only piece of furniture being a small bench opposite the entrance.

Gaius checked the swords over, giving them both a brief polish, and then tested my sword in his hand before passing it across to me.

'You know, you really would be much better off with a lighter weight sword,' he remarked at length. 'I know, I know,' he continued before I had a chance to protest. 'The sword is special to you.'

'It was my father's,' I stated simply.

'I know,' Gaius replied softly. He paused. 'It is a good sword. One of the best I've seen.'

'It was given him as a gift, from Antur's people, as part of the peace treaty,' I added. 'And something to do with trade. We got Antur, and the sword was a gift for the chief.'

'That's fine, as long as you're happy using it,' he smiled. 'All right,' Gaius began. 'The first thing you need to know is how to stand. Balance is important.' He made a few flourishes with his *gladius*.

I tried to follow his movements, waving the sword about a little awkwardly to begin with. Gaius was right. It was a little heavy for me.

He saw my difficulty. 'The sword needs to feel like an extension of your arm,' he continued.

Gaius sheathed his sword and came and stood behind me, placing one arm about my waist. 'Here, like this,' he said as he helped to steady my sword arm with his until I was properly balanced.

'Try holding the sword with both hands if you find it is too heavy for you,' he suggested. 'At least to begin with.'

I changed my posture a little so that I could balance while holding the sword out with both hands. When I was ready, he continued.

'Now, let's see how you get on. Try a few practice swings.'

'Like this?' I asked, slashing heavily at the air around me.

'Slowly, slowly to start with,' he said. 'Good, that's better.' Gaius moved around in front of me, placing himself directly in my path. 'Now, come at me.'

I began to take a tentative swing, and then I hesitated. 'I don't want to hurt you,' I said sheepishly.

'You won't, come on,' he laughed. 'That didn't seem to stop you before!'

By the end of the first lesson I felt as if I was beginning to get the hang of it and I was a little more used to balancing the weight of the sword than I had been before.

Gaius had insisted that I refrain from carrying the sword around with me as I had become used to, even though it was well concealed beneath the multitude of Roman robes, arguing that there was little need of it with two Roman Legions and a Cohort of Thracians to protect me. It took a long time however for me to feel comfortable about leaving the sword behind whenever I went out, but begrudgingly, I complied.

Gaius often spent his spare time teaching me new things, a task that he seemed to enjoy. With his help, I not only learnt to speak the Latin language a lot better, but to read and write as well. He taught me how to count and write in Roman numerals, and a little about Roman history and that of other lands besides, lands that I could only ever dream about as I listened to these epic tales.

By AD 51, the rebel Caratacus still remained free to cause mayhem and rebellion, and Ostorius Scapula was keen to the point of obsession to obtain his capture. Ostorius had decided to make a firm stance once and for all against him.

Caratacus had been chased further north by now, into central and north-western Cambria, and into an area occupied by a tribe known as the Ordovices. When he'd heard that Ostorius was coming in search of him, Caratacus had ensured that the battlefield was of his own choosing. Caratacus therefore chose a site to his maximum advantage.

General Ostorius had employed both of the Legions plus the Auxiliary units which included the VIth Thracian. On the eve before they were to move out the soldiers were in high spirits and eager for the fight, having every confidence in the officers that were to lead them. Ostorius however did not now seem to be so keen

Having learnt the location of Caratacus and his warriors, he was now beginning to have second thoughts about attempting to capture this British Chieftain who had evaded capture these past eight years, his battle tactics expert enough to rival that of any Roman.

Caratacus had chosen a craggy hill with rocky slopes between it and the river. Upon the summit lay a stone walled fort. While the Roman troops far outnumbered those of Caratacus, the rebel's position seemed practically impregnable—but then so had Worlebury, once.

Ostorius, urged on by the confidence of his own men, had apparently divided his troops into several columns, launching them simultaneously along different points of the river bank where it seemed most fordable.

The first onslaught had carried them across the river and far up the slope on the other side, but upon reaching the fortress walls the legionaries came under heavy attack. The constant fire of missiles from above forced them to lock shields, then, tearing down the stone wall, they broke into the fort on every side.

The Romans had chased the rebels to the very top of the hill, where, hopelessly outnumbered, they finally surrendered. The wife and daughter of Caratacus himself, plus his brothers, were all taken prisoner. Caratacus however had once more miraculously evaded capture, escaping to fight another day, but Cambria was lost to him.

His only choice now was Brigantia, to encourage a rebellion against Rome amongst Queen Cartimandua's already defiant subjects. Queen Cartimandua herself, however, had remained staunchly loyal to Rome, enjoying the absolute power that her position as Queen of the Brigantes had brought her. Nevertheless, she was not abject to trickery and deception in order to maintain that power. Whether she had managed to overcome Caratacus by force or guile will never be known, but Queen Cartimandua had proved her loyalty yet again by delivering Caratacus right into the astonished Romans' laps.

'I met him, you know,' I remarked idly as news came in of the rebel chieftain's capture.

'Met who?' Gaius enquired.

'Caratacus, of course!' I replied plainly.

He raised an eyebrow at me with interest as we entered the *triclinium* together.

'He came to our settlement at Worlebury promising great victories. You should have heard his speech! I can see him now, standing in the firelight, giving these great speeches on how we could drive your Romans from out of this land.' I smiled a nervous smile and we sat down together on one of the three couches. 'The whole tribe was transfixed,' I continued, blinking away a tear as the memories came flooding back. Now Worlebury, and most of those people, were gone. 'He made it all sound so easy.'

'It always does,' Gaius acknowledged, placing an arm about my shoulders.

'Caratacus stayed with us for a while, attempting to unite the tribes against your soldiers.' I lay back and stretched lazily, leaning my head against his shoulder. 'We began to fight alongside the Silures instead of against them, and the Durotriges, but the Dobunni of the north would have no part of the rebellion. Even the Belgae, Antur's people, the Atrebates tribe, were not too keen to fight,' I added. 'Caratacus had such enthusiasm, such charisma. He didn't tell us about the deaths that would follow.' I gazed up at Gaius and he smiled grimly. 'What will happen to him now?'

'I imagine they'll take him to Rome, show him off before the Emperor,' he replied practically. He got up and walked over to the window, gazing up at the clouded sky through which every now and then shafts of sunlight streaked through, and then deep in thought he turned to face me once more.

'Oh, he'll be paraded through the streets of Rome as a prize of war, I've no doubts about that,' he continued solemnly. 'They may let him live, but…' he let his words tail off. 'I don't really know.'

It was some weeks later before we were to hear any more of Caratacus. It was Marcus who came to the door bearing the latest news.

'Did you hear?' he began excitedly as he rushed into the *Atrium*.

'What?' we replied in unison.

'Caratacus made such an inspiring speech before old Claudius that he not only decided to spare his life but gave him a house in Rome and a pension besides!'

What was this? It was unbelievable! We all thought this to be highly amusing, shaking our heads in disbelief, and relief.

'It's true!' Marcus added. 'It seems we've been fighting on the wrong side!' He laughed aloud.

'No, no,' Gaius responded. 'It makes perfect sense. Think about it. Had they executed such a celebrated hero, Rome would merely have made a martyr of Caratacus,' he continued on, pressing his point home. 'Far better that he remains an example of the Emperor's mercy. Politically, it's a very wise move by the Emperor.'

So, all was well, at least for the time being. I was both pleased and relieved to hear that Caratacus and his family were safe. It would have been a shame to see such a proud and valiant warrior brought down. The world suddenly seemed a lot brighter place having learnt of his safety, his dignity intact.

The Macellum

Glevum

Chapter Five

AD 52 to AD 57

Glevum, Gloucestershire and Stanwick Hill-Fort, Yorkshire

In a way, the Legionary Bases turned out to be the best "friends" the local native population could have, for they protected against further incursions by warring tribes.

This had been the case when Legion XIIII Gemina was stationed in the midlands following the initial invasion of AD 43. The Cornovii tribe was quick to realise what devastating enemies the Roman forces made, and equally, what powerful allies they could become, offering protection against further invasions.

No longer would they be hounded by the over-powering Brigantes of the north, nor bullied by us, the Dobunni, who prior to the Romans' arrival had complete control of the shipping movements along the River Sabrina.

With the establishment of a Legionary Base at Glevum, and with the Fourteenth Gemina, detachments of the Twentieth Legion, plus Auxiliary cohorts to defend it, we Dobunni were now in the same position.

Nevertheless, this failed to deter the warlike Silures of Southern Cambria from continuing their rebellion. Roman forts and garrisons were totally destroyed as the whole tribe arose to avenge their conquered hero, Caratacus.

General Ostorius had tried many times to suppress the attacks with his "Camp of Legions", but to no avail. Although the Silures had been seen off yet again, Ostorius Scapula was continually frustrated by the recent raids and spate of attacks and had ordered the complete extermination of the entire Silures tribe, in much the same way he had earlier planned to eliminate my own people.

While this was, in many eyes, seen to be a little drastic, it was however an efficient way to quell the rebellion once and for all. General Ostorius was put under considerable pressure as his officers argued against the move.

Although the Silures had been enemies of my people for many a year, only once joining forces with us briefly in order to fight an even greater foe—that of the Romans themselves— I felt uneasy, and I could not warrant the complete annihilation of their own kind any more than I could condone the attack on mine.

'You can't just let them all be wiped out?' I protested wildly to Gaius when he informed me of the Governor's decision.

'What do you expect me to do?' he replied curtly. 'As a Roman officer, I'm duty bound to abide by my superior's decisions, whatever they may be. You know that, Dana. All I can do is advise against it, which I have done.'

'You convinced him not to attack my people,' I countered.

'That… was different,' Gaius remarked, softening a little. 'I had more incentive there.' He gave my cheek a playful tweak and smiled mischievously. 'If I argue the point too much, Ostorius will refuse to listen altogether,' he added practically. 'Natalis may already have pushed him too far on the subject. He was going to speak with him last night. If he has, it will only have made matters worse.'

'Worse? How could it possibly be any worse?' I responded in disbelief.

'Believe me,' Gaius answered. 'It can.'

The decision had been made. Ostorius sent some legionary detachments under the control of a Camp Prefect into the Silurian territory, where they began to construct Auxiliary forts in preparation for the attack.

General Ostorius had planned to trap them within their own mountains and extend the frontier line in one foul sweep. The Silures however, experts at guerrilla warfare, attacked first, swiftly and without warning, almost annihilating the few cohorts which had been sent.

Fortunately, a messenger managed to get through to the nearby forts now in use and the cavalry were sent in to disperse the Silures, but not before the *Praefectus Castrorum* and eight centurions had been killed. The entire detachment was all but wiped out, yet some of the legionaries managed to hang on until help arrived.

Meanwhile, the VIth Thracian Cohort was about to be deployed. Before leaving, Gaius assured me not to worry and that he would be returning soon.

Now, as I watched him bravely leading the VIth Thracian out across the mighty Sabrina, a knot of fear wound its way up inside me.

It was some days later when a messenger arrived, bringing dire news. The VIth Thracian had been attacked, suffering heavy losses. Further Auxiliary units which were stationed nearby had failed in their defence.

I felt numb, too afraid to ask the question that I knew I must.

'What word of… Gaius Julius?' I stammered tearfully.

Titus Flavius Natalis smiled gently. He had come across from the Legionary Base to give me the sad news personally. I had known something was wrong the moment his presence was announced. It was not customary for the *Legatus Legionis* to deliver messages.

I invited him into the *triclinium*. 'Won't you sit down?' I offered nervously, deliberately gripping the back of a couch hard for support.

'No, no, I won't stay,' he declined graciously, his voice strained and tired. 'But thank you anyway.' He heaved a heavy sigh running his fingers through his already greying hair.

'Listen,' he continued. 'Gaius is probably all right. It was he who sent the messenger. And, General Ostorius himself is leading both Legions off right now in order to assist them,' he added encouragingly. 'They'll be there by nightfall.'

I thanked Natalis for coming personally to inform me. All we could do now was to wait.

Days seemed to pass before the Legions returned, the auxiliaries following on behind, tired and bloodied. The two Legions had suffered only slight losses before the Silures had retreated at the sight of General Ostorius in the lead, but all the auxiliaries had suffered heavy losses, and two had been completely devastated, one of which was Gaius' VIth Thracian.

Natalis stood alongside the river, determined to see every unit and every man safely back. I stood there with him for a time, discussing the disastrous campaign while trying not to give vent to the thought that Gaius might be one of the casualties. Natalis was quieter than usual, understandably so, yet he still maintained his friendly and caring manner as he tried his best to keep my hopes up. He was of Greek origin and not unlike the Thracians, whose homeland I had learnt lay close by. Natalis was another officer who had wed a native Briton during the early days of the invasion, by the name of Veldicca.

Most of the auxiliaries were now returning, either already dead, or dying. The injured were hurried off into the Base hospital for emergency treatment.

It was a sorry sight to behold. Then, against all odds, there was Gaius. My heart skipped a beat when I spotted him, bringing up the rear with what was left of the VIth Thracian. He looked tired and defeated as he rode slowly up to where we stood.

Gaius gave a weary salute to Natalis before dismounting, almost falling out of the saddle from sheer exhaustion. I reached for his arm as he stumbled slightly but he suddenly and unexpectedly snatched his arm away.

'I must see to my men,' he murmured, his face pale and gaunt. 'My men,' he paused for breath, 'my men need me— what's left of them.'

'Your men will be fine; we have people here to help them,' Natalis told him reassuringly. 'Why don't you go with Julia Dana and freshen up?'

'No!' Gaius snapped. 'I must see to my men!'

'Later,' Natalis responded firmly.

Gaius hesitated, he seemed dazed and confused.

'That's an order, commander!' Natalis added, sterner this time.

Gaius gazed all around, and then taking a step backwards he placed a hand to his forehead as if trying to remember something, and he closed his eyes tightly.

'You're tired,' I whispered softly to him, reaching out towards him once again with concern, yet the moment I touched his arm he swiftly pulled it away. 'You need to rest, my love,' I persisted, trying to ignore the feelings of rejection. I had never seen a man so broken, so utterly defeated. 'Come home,' I urged. 'You'll feel better once you're rested.'

He took a deep breath to steady himself then looked at me as if seeing me for the first time. Slowly he nodded his agreement. I took his arm gently and we began to walk off.

'Wait!' he uttered suddenly, coming to a halt and pulling himself free of my grasp. 'My horses, I have to... have to see to my horses.'

'Someone will see to them for you,' Natalis reassured him. 'I'll see to it myself personally. You don't have to worry about anything.' He smiled warmly. 'Go on, soldier.'

Natalis took hold of the reins of Gaius' horse, the secondary one tethered alongside. Gaius then followed me back to the Thracian Base, and to our home, not speaking another word.

The Base seemed almost deserted, and deathly quiet, with only a handful of men left to defend it and a few of the other women. I had Caitilin fetch some wine for him as soon as we entered. Goilladyn immediately began to help Gaius out of his armour. Fortunately, he didn't seem to be wounded, just very, very tired. Between us, we led him into the *triclinium* where he swallowed his wine down in one single mouthful.

Caitilin returned moments later with some freshly baked bread, but Gaius was already asleep, stretched out across the couch, exhausted. I had her fetch a blanket, tenderly tucking it around him before curling up myself upon the opposite couch.

I watched him for a while before dozing off into a restless sleep myself. I awoke at some point in the middle of the night. Caitilin had thoughtfully tucked another blanket around me, so I snuggled down for the rest of the night.

I slept quite soundly until the dawn when I awoke to find Gaius seated there beside me. Although he'd slept quite heavily, he still appeared tired and drained. He leant forward and stroked my hair gently.

'You slept here all night, with me?' he asked suddenly.

I smiled up at him, taking his hand and trying to imagine what he must be feeling.

'I can't remember much of the last few days,' Gaius admitted, frowning as he tried hard to recall the events. 'Was I rude to you? I was, wasn't I?' he continued in afterthought. 'I'm sorry.'

'You were tired,' I replied softly, easing myself up to a sitting position. I tucked my knees under my chin. 'It's all right. You're home, safe. That's all that matters.'

Gaius brushed his golden hair back off his forehead, his wavy locks all matted and dirty and in desperate need of a wash.

'Our foraging party was attacked suddenly, completely out of the blue,' he began to recall. 'I remember, I remember I'd reasoned that it was fairly safe as we'd seen no sign of the Silures.' He closed his eyes in concentration. 'When we had news of the attack, I immediately sent forth our cavalry to assist,' he shook his head sadly, clenching his fist. 'All those men. None survived. Not one of them returned. I lost them all.'

He stood up and began to pace up and down. 'Worse was yet to come,' he continued on. 'Rebel groups were everywhere. We tried to track them down, but they knew the hills and valleys too well. I think other tribes must have joined with them, there was so many of them. They came at us all of a sudden, out of nowhere, chasing us up and around those damnable mountains! Did you know we'd lost two entire Auxiliary cohorts before the Legions arrived?' He clenched his fist repeatedly again as he continued to pace agitatedly up and down the room.

'Do you know how many men I have left?' he asked abruptly, his voice becoming louder as he turned on his heel and finally came to a halt. 'Do you?' He slammed his fist down so hard on the back of the couch that it made me jump. Gaius then slumped down heavily on the edge of the seat, placing his head in his hands. He closed his eyes briefly and I placed my hand gently upon his arm. When he eventually looked up at me his eyes were wet with tears.

'I could count their numbers, on my fingers,' he stammered.

My heart felt as if it would break at any moment. I had never seen him cry before.

'It's not your fault,' I replied, tenderly stroking his wavy hair. 'No one could have foreseen those events.'

'They were my men, my responsibility,' he retorted sharply. 'It *is* my fault they are all dead. I was their commander!' Tears rolled down his cheeks. 'A commanding officer is responsible for the safety of his men,' he tailed off, weeping bitterly.

Gently, I pulled him towards me, cradling him in my arms for a moment or two. 'It's all right, it's all right,' I whispered soothingly. 'There was nothing more you could have done. You did your best.'

'My best, ha!' Gaius snapped, pulling away suddenly. 'They should not be in *Elysium*—not yet.' He glanced across at me then ran a finger gently down my cheek. There was a flicker of a smile, just for a moment. 'My beautiful warrior,' he added softly. 'If anything was ever to happen to you, I… I…'

I pressed my finger to his lips. 'Nothing's going to happen to me,' I stated firmly. 'I'm here. I'm here with you, whether you like it or not!' I jested.

Gaius laughed and held me to him so tenderly, so delicately, it was as if I was made of the finest porcelain. 'I'm so glad you're back safely,' I whispered.

It took some time to build the VIth Thracian back up to a quingenary of five-hundred men, during which time Gaius had been granted some leave to recover from the traumatic loss of his unit.

Meanwhile, Ostorius Scapula's health had deteriorated very rapidly. It was as if the stress and strain of these past few weeks had caught up with him in a single moment. He looked as if he had aged twenty or thirty years overnight.

'The General is unwell and wishes to see Gaius Julius immediately.' Fulvius Biticus stood in the doorway. 'He bids him attend at once.'

'Gaius is not yet well enough himself,' I argued back at him.

Fulvius removed his helmet. He shuffled his feet about nervously, his eyes downcast, silent for a moment.

'He's dying lady Julia,' he stated simply, looking up at me with a saddened expression.

I was stunned. I had no idea Ostorius was that ill. What could I say? I had no choice now but to inform Gaius. I bid Fulvius he would attend shortly and went to find him. Having looked all around the house, I asked Goilladyn if he knew where Gaius was.

'He's outside, talking to some of the new recruits, mistress,' Goilladyn informed me.

'Fetch him, would you please, Goilladyn,' I requested.

Goilladyn bowed slightly, 'At once, mistress.'

Gaius strolled across towards me, smiling. The fresh air and free time had done him some good at least I thought.

'It's General Ostorius,' I began meekly as he approached. 'He wants to see you,' I said, stammering a little. He nodded and turned to go. 'And Gaius,' I added in a whisper, 'he's dying.'

Gaius halted in his tracks briefly, and then he turned and looked at me in surprise. 'I knew he wasn't well, but, I never expected...' failing to complete his thoughts.

'Nor I,' I replied softly.

'I'll go at once,' he said. 'Do you want to come along?'

I shook my head. 'I wouldn't wish to intrude,' I replied. 'But do give him my regards, won't you?' I smiled thinly. What does one say at a time like this? Gaius nodded and headed off quickly.

He was gone but a short while, returning later, ashen faced. 'He's gone, Dana,' he said. 'The strain of this last campaign I expect. He collapsed last night apparently.'

'Oh,' was all I could think of to say.

"Worn out with care" was what the Roman reports were saying. I cannot say I was unhappy to see him go, this arrogant Roman General with whom I would argue and debate endlessly on many occasions, although over these last few years, we did seem to have a gained a healthy respect for one another. I prayed that he reached his *Elysium* safely.

Ostorius' death brought even more troubles for us left in the land of the living. Once word had got out that Ostorius Scapula was dead, the Silures saw it as a perfect opportunity to renew their attacks full force, coming well into Dobunni territory and causing endless devastation. The Silures never gave up. They did not know the meaning of the word "defeat", and continued attack after attack after attack with relentless monotony.

It was not safe to travel anywhere. So, there we were, trapped within our own fortresses. The Silures were the perfect warriors. They came rampaging across the Sabrina at low tide, attempting to storm both the Auxiliary and Legionary fort walls at the same time. Some even made it to the top, only to be cut down by our soldiers lying in wait.

Gaius had assembled what remained of his Thracians into groups as best he could, the Silures almost upon us.

The majority of his troops consisted of the few he had left behind to garrison the fort, plus the handful of survivors, and a century of legionaries on loan from the Fourteenth. He had just over a hundred men at the most. The odds were against us.

All I could see from my position within the house where I stood attempting to peer out of a narrow, very high, window, Caitilin and a couple of other women behind me, was the top of their helmets and the tips of their spears as they stood to attention in neat, straight rows.

'This group, take the northern walls,' I heard Gaius command urgently. 'You lot, the southern perimeter. The rest of you, come with me!'

The soldiers moved like lightning as they scurried off to defend the fort.

'Get those *ballistae* over here, pronto!' Gaius called out. There was a rattle of wheels as the artillery was moved into position. Gaius climbed up one of the towers to get his bearings. 'Wait!' he shouted. 'Wait for my command.' He surveyed the machinery with a critical eye. 'You there, you're too close,' he called to one soldier. 'Move it back or you'll only succeed in knocking the top off our own walls!'

I could hear the sound of the Silures' battle cries, a sound I had heard many times before as they had attempted to scale the walls at Worlebury, and failed.

Gaius waited a moment while the *ballista* was moved to the correct position while a company of archers kept the enemy at bay. Every now and then, small rocks skittered across the ground as they were flung from beyond the fortress walls, or occasionally pelted upon the rooftop like large hailstones. I tensed, waiting to see what would happen.

'Get ready!' Gaius ordered, then moments later, 'Fire!'

Hundreds of huge rocks were suddenly launched skywards by these giant catapults, up and over the fortress walls, exploding when they hit the ground outside. Again they fired, and again. 'Bring those *catapultae* up, quickly!' Gaius commanded. There was a moment to bring the machines into position. 'Fire!' Multitudes of javelin were shot skywards, presumably finding their targets as they sped downwards outside the fortress walls.

Meanwhile, the Legionary fortress had begun to follow suit, launching everything and anything they had over the top of the walls until the Silures had at last retreated back across the river.

Natalis was well pleased with Gaius' grasp of battle tactics and initiative at seeing the Silures off, especially with the very few men that he had at his disposal.

'We shall need someone to train the replacements properly when they arrive from Rome,' he said later. 'I'd like you to take on that task, but I want you to train them in tactics as well as with the sword and spear,' he added with a smile.

'Thank you, sir,' Gaius replied. 'I'd be only too pleased.'

It would be some time before a new governor could be sent out from Rome to regain control, over which period of time the unthinkable happened. With renewed determination, the warring Silures managed to defeat the entire Second Legion in the field in one bloodied battle that was to cost many Roman lives.

Legion II Augusta had been called in to help protect the Dobunnic lands and Roman forts that were constantly being destroyed. The entire Base was in shock. Never before had a Legion been so utterly defeated in this land.

The Fates, paying them back perhaps for the destruction of Worlebury, I thought.

'I'll say one thing for them,' Marcus remarked as we sat reflecting in the *triclinium*. 'The Silures' grasp of battle tactics is almost as good as yours, Gaius.'

'Better, I'd have said,' Gaius stated, no doubt recalling the loss of his own cohort.

Marcus raised an eyebrow. 'Yes, worrying, isn't it?' he agreed.

'But there must be some way of stopping them?' I asked aghast.

'Name one?' Gaius replied sardonically.

It was a dire situation, and with the new governor not due to arrive for a further month or more, the Legionary Base would just have to hold out as best it could while the Silures did as they pleased.

We were fairly safe within the forts now we knew that the Silures would not be able to breach the walls, and there was enough food in store to see that we were all fed well enough, especially as there were now less mouths to feed. There were times when the Silures were not around, and hunting parties would be sent out, but the soldiers had to be ever wary of surprise attacks with extra guards being posted, leaving less men available to hunt and forage.

Once the new governor arrived one of his first tasks would be to oversee the rebuilding of the Legions and Auxiliary units back up to their original numbers. This would be done by taking soldiers from other units, perhaps from different parts of the Empire.

'It certainly won't ordain well for Manlius Valens,' Marcus commented. 'To have a whole Legion under one's own command defeated like that.' His expression completed any further thoughts on the subject.

'So, what's this new governor like?' I enquired, changing the subject slightly. 'Is he another military General?' By the gods, I hoped he wasn't. I couldn't stand another Ostorius!

'Didius Gallus? No, no, he's a politician or something,' Marcus replied. He thought about it for a moment. 'Hell, that could be worse!' he grinned and winked at me with a laugh.

'They say he's quite old,' Gaius added, helping himself to some fruit.

'So, why send us some old politician?' I asked, puzzled. 'Perhaps they just wanted to get rid him from Rome?' I was expecting them to send some young, warmongering General who could frighten the Silures all back into their own lands!

'I don't know,' Marcus said thoughtfully. 'What we really need is someone like the great Caesar himself to sort this mess out!'

Gaius laughed. 'There will only ever be one Caesar,' he said with a wry smile. 'There will never be another great General like him—or so my father would have had you believe! 'Tis true though what you say, Marcus my friend,' he continued. 'But who knows? We may be better off with some doddering old politician than another arrogant General!'

'True,' Marcus agreed with a laugh. 'That is if he actually ever gets here! We've been waiting months already.'

Didius Gallus did eventually arrive after a long wait of some six months. He may have been getting on in years, but surprisingly he seemed to be just the man to regain control of the situation. Although quite small of stature, he retained a razor-sharp mind when it came to the political tactics of keeping both sides happy. The powers that be in Rome did know what they were doing after all.

Instead of trying to defeat the Silures, an impossible task for anyone, Gallus decided it was wiser to leave them well alone, settling for strengthening the existing borders in order to "keep them at bay". He seemed to be content at this, although there were those who said that this was merely a temporary solution to the problem and that trouble was bound to erupt later if nothing more was done.

As a person, Didius Gallus was much more approachable than the usual Roman Generals whom the Senate saw fit to install. His diplomatic skills rivalled Gaius' own, and several times Gallus would complement Gaius, remarking that he ought to take up politics himself to which Gaius would always decline.

Indeed, his only failing seemed to be his memory for people's names. On many an occasion, he would refer to me as "Diana", a Roman name given to their goddess of the hunt, and a name which was to stay with me until the end. It wasn't the first time my name had been transposed from "Dana" to "Diana".

Marcus was the first to make this error upon our introduction, and had insisted on using it ever since, merely out of fun though, not from possessing a bad memory for names!

Having resolved the situation with the Silures, at least to his satisfaction, Didius Gallus then spent most of his time in Britannia governing from his residence at Camulodunum or Londinium, so we only ever saw him on occasion.

Although Governor Gallus had successfully prevented any future trouble from the Silures tribe by putting Scapula's frontier plan into action and stopping the exits from the hills, the tribes to the north of the Silures remained troublesome. The druids too had their main centre in Northern Cambria, with their seat of power lying just off-shore on the Isle of Mona. The druids wielded tremendous power over the Britons and had a communication network that spanned the length and breadth of the entire country.

They were the only thing that even Caesar had feared, and it was said that they could not only control the weather but were even capable of walking on water. The Roman Army had to stay on constant alert against any unexpected attacks.

The northern frontier also posed a similar threat. The Brigantes, one of the largest and most powerful tribes, so far had remained friendly to Rome, but there were other tribes further north still. The painted people of the far north, the barbaric Picts, had been known to travel as far south as the Brigantes' territory.

In AD 54, Cartimandua's position as Queen of the Brigantes came under threat from her own husband, Venutius. Queen Cartimandua had remained obstinately faithful to Rome, so it was in Rome's best interest that she remained as ruler of the Brigantes.

It was well known that she enjoyed the Roman luxuries and the power that her position brought. Venutius however now threatened that position as he moved to dethrone the queen and turn the whole of the Brigantes people against the Romans.

Didius Gallus had to move quickly to settle matters and had ordered that Gaius lead the VIth Thracian into the Brigantes territory to see that the queen maintained her rulership. Wisely, he saw that a Legion was sent along not too far behind, just in case reinforcements were needed.

Cartimandua meanwhile had captured her husband's relatives, and Venutius had retaliated by invading the kingdom with a group of hand-picked warriors.

'Why you?' I argued with Gaius when he told me of his mission. 'Why does it have to be you? It's always you!'

'It must be my diplomatic touch,' he replied with a wry smile. 'Actually,' he added in afterthought, 'it might be advantageous if you were to come along too.'

'Me?' I replied, stunned for a moment. 'What can I do?'

'Yes, you,' he continued. 'Well, you could help convince the queen that it is worth staying on our side.'

'How?'

'Well, you're a Celt... a Briton,' he corrected himself rapidly before I had a chance to complain, yet again, that I was not. 'You've lived amongst us now for some six years. There must be something about us you like? You can tell her about all the benefits, and how much you now like it—here with me!' Gaius teased, wrapping his arms about me playfully.

'Do I?' I teased in return.

'You know you do!'

And so, with the Fourteenth Legion tagging along not too far behind us, we headed off towards the Brigantes' Camp in the north. It was an extremely long haul, and it was to be some days later before we would arrive. Fortunately for Queen Cartimandua, the Ninth Legion was much closer at hand and by the time we arrived they had already seen off Venutius' warmongering rebels.

Cartimandua sat tall and erect, as Gaius was bid to enter. About to follow him in, and with a few of our soldiers behind me, we were suddenly halted by a spear that was thrust out before us, barring our entrance, so we just stood and watched from the doorway as best we could. Cartimandua held out a hand in greeting to Gaius so formally that it looked as if she expected him to bow and get down on his knees to her, but as it was, he merely took her hand for the briefest of moments and remained standing, at which the queen frowned.

'I am Gaius Julius Caecinianus, Commander of the VIth Thracian Cohort,' Gaius began, 'and I bring you greetings from Governor Gallus.'

Cartimandua gave the impression she wasn't very impressed, tapping her fingers impatiently upon her knee. 'So, Commander, have you come here to tell me that Rome will continue to support me, and save me from my overly aggressive husband, if I and my people in turn will continue to support Rome?' She gave an overly-exaggerated flourish with her arm as she spoke. 'Is that correct?' she added brusquely.

'It would go something along those lines, yes,' Gaius replied thoughtfully. 'We can offer you support, help you defeat Venutius…'

'Well, I'm sorry, but it's not enough!' she snapped, as if trying to make an impression upon those of her advisors who were watching and listening close by. She toyed with her long, braided hair for a moment, twirling it around her fingers, the strawberry blonde highlights occasionally catching the lamplight becoming as spun gold.

'Forgive me, lady, but you have already been well paid and rewarded by Rome upon your capture of Caratacus, for which may I add we are truly grateful,' Gaius replied promptly. 'Added to which, in case you hadn't noticed, our glorious Ninth have just saved your hill-fort, and your throne!'

Cartimandua's cheeks flushed with anger. She arose and strolled over to Gaius, seductively running her hands across his shoulders. 'Well I want more,' she purred in Gaius' ear.

Gaius took a step back. 'I'm sorry, lady, but I am not part of the bargain.'

'And why not?' she retorted haughtily. 'Do you want my allegiance or not?'

From my position within the doorway, I began to clench my fist in anger, all the while muttering under my breath. Queen or no queen, how dare she flirt with my husband!

Cartimandua hadn't seen me yet, but Gaius took a deep breath and turned towards me. 'Then let me introduce you to my wife,' he stated simply, holding out a hand. The spear barring my way was removed momentarily and I found myself ushered into the room, standing there alongside Gaius, hand in hand.

Cartimandua gazed down upon me with some puzzlement for a moment. She was an extremely beautiful woman, with her long-braided hair pinned back by what I was sure to be Roman hair combs, and expensive ones at that.

'Dana is Dobunni,' Gaius explained helpfully. 'We've been wed some six years now.'

'You took her for your wife?' She sounded surprised.

'I didn't "take her", it was Dana's choice,' Gaius replied. 'We may have been among the first of our peoples to wed, and we certainly won't be the last.'

'And your tribe, they agreed to this marriage?' Cartimandua asked me, her temper seeming to settle somewhat as her curiosity was aroused.

'After a while,' I answered softly, as I remembered Dolebury and Antur.

She smiled unexpectedly and bid us both sit.

'So, you see,' Gaius continued patiently. 'Our peoples can get along, we can learn from each other, help each other, and we are here to help you now—to defeat Venutius once and for all.'

It was some weeks later that we returned home triumphant, much to my relief. Having managed to settle the dispute to Rome's satisfaction, the balance of power had now been restored. Venutius and the rebel faction had been successfully driven out.

Didius Gallus was most pleased with the outcome and complimented Gaius once again on his efforts.

As word spread around the forts, Gaius earned the title of "peacemaker" amongst the soldiers, for not only had he prevented a massacre at Dolebury some six years hence, but now he had this to his credit.

Cartimandua was well settled once more upon her throne, and all was right in her kingdom of Brigantia. Eventually, she was to swap her husband Venutius for his armour-bearer Vellocatus. Not surprisingly, she became known as quite a strong and warlike queen, and with a reputation for adultery that was second to none. Somehow, she seemed to possess an uncanny knack of survival in troubled times.

Shortly after things had settled down in Brigantia, Gaius announced he was purchasing another slave to help out in the kitchen and with general chores about the house, therefore taking some of the pressure off Caitilin. Daireann was from the Cornovii tribe that lay a little further northward. She was a petite young girl only just into her teens and had long, brown hair that reached down to her waist.

Daireann was of a quiet disposition and would move around the house like a mouse. Sometimes I would not even know that she had entered the room until I'd turned around and nearly bumped into her. She was so different to Caitilin, who was always bright and cheerful.

Meanwhile, news came from Rome that Emperor Claudius had drawn his last breath and the Empire had passed over to his successor, Nero. Although Claudius was getting on in years, his exit from this world and entry into the next did however receive a little help by way of his loving wife, who was also Nero's mother. It was rumoured that she had fed Claudius some poisonous mushrooms. So it was that Claudius took his place on high with the gods, and the Empire continued on under the ruler ship of Emperor Nero.

The recent spate of trouble in Britannia had not gone unnoticed back in Rome. Nero's advisors had recommended that he should withdraw from the land altogether. It had become a burden on the Empire, and it was costing much in both financial and military losses, added to which the mineral wealth of Britannia was not as much as was originally thought.

Emperor Nero however staunchly refused to give up the land which was so valiantly won and conquered by the great Caesar, and over which he, Nero, now ruled.

Didius Gallus was spending his last few years in office strengthening the northern frontier with strategically placed forts right across Brigantia. It was about this time that Gaius was granted the post of *Armatura*, in charge of training the soldiers.

Natalis had earlier recognised his skills in training the new recruits they'd acquired in both tactics and weaponry after the disastrous confrontation with the Silures, and he had now decided to make the position a permanent one. Gaius didn't really mind that much, as most of the original Thracians were no longer with us, and the new auxiliaries sent to replace them were not even from Thrace. Besides which, Gaius had never really got over the loss of his men.

Sadly, the new post meant that we would have to move out of the Thracian fortress, and so we were moved into a regular house just outside the Legionary Base walls, where the retired soldiers resided. The new house was a single storey, Mediterranean design, having a courtyard at its centre.

In AD 57, the decision was made to expand the Empire westwards, heading back into Cambria once again. A new governor was chosen to oversee this task seeing that Didius Gallus had now served his term.

Quintus Veranius was an experienced military man who had fought in mountain terrain yet was also well known for his diplomatic skills. It was Veranius who had led the deputation to persuade Claudius to accept the role as emperor, and he had retained his position as the emperor's right-hand man even with the changeover to Nero.

He exhibited a youthful exuberance and was full of enthusiasm and zeal. He brought with him some fresh ideas and major changes of strategy, changes that would ultimately affect us all. Thus began the new campaign into the Cambrian heartland.

When Veranius first arrived, he conducted a complete overview of the military situation in regard to the placement of forts and military strongholds, and the ranks and positions of all the officers, including Gaius. While Gaius constantly remained the Army's chief tactician, he was taken out of the position of *Armatura* and promoted to the rank of Military Tribune.

This meant yet another change of residence, but before we had a chance to move into the Legionary Base, there came the biggest change of all that no one had expected.

General Quintus Veranius decided that the Fourteenth Legion should be now stationed in the recently constructed fortress at Viroconium, thereby creating a fully manned Legionary Base in preparation for the advance into Cambria while also helping to protect the northern frontier. The full detachment of Legion XX would then occupy the Base at Glevum. The only soldiers from the Twentieth Legion remaining at Viroconium were a small party of men who were there to continue constructing the town.

Gaius and I were not pleased about the move, for we'd lived at the same town for almost ten years now and we knew the surrounding countryside well. Besides which, it was not all that far away for visits to Dolebury. Being in the Army, Gaius was used to the endless travelling around, but I was not. I particularly did not want to move twice as far away again from my people as I was now.

Viroconium was in the Cornovii territory, near to the border of Cambria, where I knew no one at all. Daireann however, who by this time had been with us for three years, was only too pleased to be heading back to her home territory and eagerly helped to pack up all the household items. This was the first time either Caitilin or myself had seen her work so hard.

'Amazing!' Caitilin laughed, tossing her long blonde hair over her shoulder. 'How can we get her to stay like this?'

'I doubt it will last long,' I replied as I watched Daireann racing back and forth stacking all the kitchen things together. 'Pity about that!'

'Well, I'll tell you one thing for certain,' Caitilin added in a whisper. 'I'll not be doing her share of the work like I am now.'

'I know,' I agreed in sympathy with her. 'I'll get Gaius to have a word with her, again.' I placed my arm around her shoulder.

'I don't mind helping out too, you know,' I continued. 'I'm just as native to this land as you are. As far as I am concerned, you are a good friend and companion, not a slave.' I gave Caitilin a hug. 'So, you just let me know.'

Caitilin smiled. 'Thank you, mistress,' she said. 'I am glad I am here with you and the master,' she continued. 'I could have done a lot worse.'

Her words warmed my heart but made me think of my long-lost baby brother yet again, and what had become of him. Was he a slave somewhere too? Was he even still alive?

Goilladyn meanwhile had obtained a small wagon onto which some of the furniture was loaded along with our more personal items. Mounting our horses, we then began the journey northwards, following alongside the Sabrina, and at the back of the majority of soldiers of the Fourteenth Legion.

Legion XIIII Gemina

Marcus Petronius

Chapter Six
AD 57 to AD 58
Viroconium, Shropshire

It was a dark and dismal day when we arrived at Viroconium, the clouds hung like leaden weights in the sky threatening a summer downpour at any moment. It seemed to match the mood of us all, the weather only adding to the sense of upheaval we felt and made the town itself seem gloomy and uninviting.

'This looks a fun place,' remarked Gaius sarcastically as we rode towards the fort, which was positioned again upon the banks of the Sabrina only further north.

'Great,' I replied, tired from the long trek northwards. 'I hate it already.'

'Oh, cheer up you two!' It was Marcus, who reined his horse up beside ours. He seemed to be the only one in good humour this day. 'It might be fun here,' he grinned. 'New places to see, people to meet.'

'Women to be had,' added Gaius in jest.

'What?' Catching Marcus off guard. 'Oh yes, certainly!'

We hastened to locate the small townhouse that had been allocated to Gaius Julius Caecinianus, Military Tribune. It was one of a row of six, all being for the use of the Military Tribunes and their families. The house itself was again of Mediterranean design and had a small courtyard at its centre, as before, and with rooms all coming off it.

While the courtyards were a pleasant enough place to relax during the summertime, the winter snows made them quite impractical for the British climate.

This time, the townhouse was a sort of double storey construction, having a small wooden staircase from opposite the front entrance leading up to a small, singular room above and to one side that was used as the main bedroom. Beyond the staircase, an archway led out onto the courtyard while off to each side were the main living areas. The servants' quarters, kitchen and a small storeroom lay towards the rear.

The house did not seem to let in as much light as the ones at Glevum, perhaps because of the double storey design, making the overall impression of Viroconium seem more dismal still as they shadowed the streets below. This time of course we were housed within the Legionary Base walls, surrounded by rows upon rows of barrack blocks and an Army of some five-thousand soldiers, which was quite a contrast to the small Auxiliary fort or the open countryside alongside Glevum Legionary Base. It made me feel a little claustrophobic to begin with, but our soldiers of the Fourteenth were always respectful and honourable, and at least we were safe from attack within the walls of the Base. Gaius too felt a little uncomfortable, for Viroconium was within sight of "The Wrekin"—the hill-fort that he and the VIth Thracian had been commanded to attack in the early days of the invasion.

We had not been at Viroconium long before Daireann took to her heels and fled, apparently to re-join her tribe.

She didn't seem to understand the punishment that Roman Law decreed for runaway slaves should they be caught, but Gaius decided to let her go.

A couple of weeks passed by before Gaius obtained another slave girl to replace Daireann. Aine was also a local girl, who had been left an orphan when she was quite young. She had medium length brown hair and green eyes, and was not abject to hard work, unlike Daireann.

Having been at Viroconium now for some weeks, I quickly got into the routine of perusing the *macellum* each day for some fresh fruit and bread for lunch. This I liked to do myself rather than send Caitilin or Aine, although sometimes one of them would accompany me helping to carry the baskets.

While the territory itself was unfamiliar to me, at least the Roman forts were always built to the same standard pattern, the streets and buildings in exactly the same position, so that there was a kind of familiarity about the Legionary Base itself. The *macellum* had sprung up alongside the fortress, as it had at Glevum, with similar rows of stalls and shops. The *vicus* adjoined the market place and contained several shops alongside the houses of the local population.

Running along the northern perimeter of the Legionary Base and above the southern edge of Bell Brook Valley, was the *canabae* area, a place which catered to the "recreational needs" of soldiers and where good, hot food could be found. This area was under the control of the military to a certain degree but was run by the locals.

As winter drew in, the streets became less crowded. I would take my time ambling around the shops and market place. It was on such an occasion as I strolled around the stalls on my own that I took a walk past the row of silversmiths' shops that Gaius was always keen to show me. All the silversmiths here seemed to produce some excellent pieces, but one in particular caught my eye. The silversmith himself was standing behind the stall, a strong, red-haired man with a long moustache. He smiled amiably as I inspected his work.

'All half-price today,' he said with a wink of his eye. 'Not much custom at this time of year!'

I smiled back, but I was really more interested in looking than buying.

'You from around here then?' he asked.

'Yes... and no,' I answered, much to his confusion. 'I reside within the fort, but I'm from the south.' I clarified.

'Hmm, married to soldier, eh?' he remarked gruffly. 'Where about in the south?' he queried. 'I didn't think your colouring belonged around here.'

'I'm Dobunni.'

'Ah, yes of course!' he remarked with a grin. 'I should have realised. Northern or southern?'

'Southern, if you please!' I exclaimed, feigning insult.

'Ah!'

'What's that supposed to mean?' I snapped sharply.

'Nothing, nothing at all,' he replied, taking a step backwards. He held his hands up feigning surrender. 'Calm down,' he added. 'Don't be so tetchy.'

'Sorry,' I apologised, slightly embarrassed by my outburst.

'So, do you know many people around here then, apart from the five-thousand in the Legion that is?'

'No one,' I answered gloomily. How I wished we could have stayed at Glevum.

'Hmm, my wife would most probably like to meet you then. She doesn't have any friends here either,' he continued. 'Wait here and I'll fetch her.'

That was how I met Sabina. She and her husband, Creag, had been at Viroconium but a short while themselves. While Sabina was from the local Cornovii tribe, her family lived some distance away and there was only her old grandmother left now.

Creag, as it turned out, was one of Antur's people, a Belgae of the Atrebates Tribe. I had thought his craftwork looked familiar and toyed with the idea of showing him my sword one day, perhaps.

Sabina was quite slender and dainty alongside Creag who was of a large and muscular build with broad shoulders. She had long, light brown hair that she wore tied back in a braid that reached almost to her waist.

'So, how did you two meet?' I enquired politely.

'Creag was on his way up here looking to sell his silverware. I guess we kind of got talking over lunch, and I suggested he should open a shop in the *macellum*,' she shrugged her shoulders. 'And well, here we are!'

'And doing quite well it seems,' I remarked, gazing around the shop display which was laid out with precision.

'I have Sabina to thank for that,' Creag remarked. 'She sees that every piece is polished up and placed in precisely the right location to catch the buyer's attention!' He grinned broadly. 'Don't you my love?'

When the spring of AD 58 arrived, General Quintus Veranius decided to put into motion the plans he'd been formulating throughout the winter.

He would set forth into the very heart of Cambria, taking the majority of the Fourteenth Legion with him, including Gaius and Marcus. After the devastation brought by the Silures in previous years, Gaius was hesitant at first and warned Veranius to avoid rushing in. He had instead suggested a slow and steady advance, starting in the north. As far as I was concerned, setting foot in any part of Cambria was a bad move and I objected to this most strongly, especially after the loss of the VIth Thracian some years ago. I tried to argue my point on this with Gaius but to no avail.

'Dana, I can't not go,' he argued back at me. 'It was my suggestion.'

'Then "un-suggest" it!'

In retrospect, I suppose there was nothing he could have done about it, as Veranius was determined to see this through, but my mood became sullen and depressed. The night before he was due to leave I had argued with Gaius quite fervently about him going until I had ceased talking to him altogether.

'I'm off now,' Gaius proclaimed the following morning as he stood in the doorway of the *triclinium*. How handsome he looked with his armour gleaming and his lovely golden hair. He looked towards me but I was unresponsive.

'Back in about three months,' he added hopefully. Saying nothing, I turned away in a sulk.

'Fine!' he snapped impatiently, stepping through the doorway.

A sudden panic came over me. I couldn't let him go in the midst of an argument. What if I was to never see him again? 'Gaius!' I called out urgently. He stopped and turned about to face me.

'Well?'

I beckoned him inside.

Gaius re-entered the *triclinium* and walked over to where I sat. I didn't want him to go, but I couldn't make him stay either. I arose swiftly and hugged him so tightly, wishing that time would stand still.

'I love you, Gaius Julius,' I whispered. 'I always will.' I wanted to hold onto him forever. I looked up at him tearfully. The thought of losing him I tried to banish from my mind, but there was always the possibility that one day he may not return, at least not alive.

'I know you do,' he replied softly, and smiling, he kissed me gently on the lips.

'Don't go!' I pleaded one last time.

'You know I have to,' he replied solemnly. 'Orders.'

'Then take me with you?'

He shook his head. 'Not this time—it's too dangerous.' Gaius stroked my hair tenderly and turned to leave once more. 'Don't worry, I will be returning. I'm not going anywhere near *Elysium*, without you.' He strolled over to the door. 'I'll be back by August the third,' he added, with a mischievous smile and a wink, and then he walked out.

That was our special date, the date of the anniversary of our wedding, and ten years this year. I prayed hard each and every day for his safe return.

The remainder of the month of May passed swiftly, yet June seemed endless. When finally, the month of July arrived, my prayers were answered. Praise be to the gods as Gaius and the Legion returned safely. I had not slept well at all since the day he'd ridden off with the Fourteenth, the memories of how vicious the Silures could be haunted my dreams each night.

My worries were proven unfounded however; for Veranius had led them valiantly across and into the unconquered territory, only to return safe and sound.

'You should have been there!' Marcus remarked with a laugh.

We sat in the *triclinium* eating a hearty meal that Caitilin and Aine had prepared especially for their return.

'There was Veranius, up there in front, chin held high, as we approached the Dematae tribe,' Marcus continued.

'We were advancing quite steadily, when suddenly,' Gaius added, taking a piece of bread and popping it into his mouth, pausing to chew the mouthful.

'What?' I could not stand the suspense.

'They gave up!' Marcus finished. 'Just like that!'

'Without even a fight?' I asked, astonished. What sort of a tribe was this? We Dobunni would certainly not have done so.

'Yes, just like that,' Gaius answered, taking a swill of wine to wash down the bread. 'Amazing!'

'And, what of the Silures?' I queried, worriedly.

'Oh, we went into their territory all right, but we didn't see them,' Gaius replied. 'They were probably there somewhere, watching us, but thankfully, this time, we had no trouble from them.'

'So, I could have come along then after all?' I pointed out brusquely, feeling somewhat cheated and annoyed that I'd been left behind to worry and pray for Gaius' safe return each day, although thankful of course that he was now home safe. Yes, I should have been there!

'We had no way of knowing that,' added Marcus helpfully, seeming to sense my anger. 'Of what it would be like.'

Gaius reached across and lovingly took my hand in his, holding on to it tightly.

'I think it's time I was off,' said Marcus politely. He arose from his seat, smiling broadly. 'I'll see myself out.'

'I will make it up to you,' said Gaius apologetically, pulling me closer to him. 'I'll not leave you again; I promise—orders or no orders.'

The Silures had in fact remained quiet for some time now, but Veranius was taking no chances. He had established forts right across the Silurian lands and had begun to establish a Legionary fort boldly within the Silurian territory itself, a major stroke for the Romans. The fort was established at Usk, known to the Romans as *Burrium*. It was the Fourteenth Legion and my Gaius that had begun to build it, after which detachments of the Twentieth Legion were then sent across to man it, and they would continue to complete the construction while Veranius and Legion XIIII Gemina had returned home victorious.

General Veranius' somewhat over-zealous approach to the conquest of Cambria quickly earned him the reputation of being an "insane military commander" as he became quite hell-bent on subduing all the Cambrian tribes. His energy and enthusiasm could be matched by none, his courage unwavering, but he expected his men to be filled with the same amount of energy and zeal as he himself had, which was of course impossible, although every man was trained to fight, and fight well.

By the summer, much of Cambria had been taken with many forts established across the width and breadth of the country. There were a few minor raids against the Silures. Only in the far north did Cambria remain unconquered.

However, at the height of the summer tragedy struck, not once, but twice. Firstly, General Quintus Veranius, this extremely fit and energetic commander, was struck down by a sudden fever and died but a short time later. He had claimed on his deathbed that he could have conquered the Province had he but two more years. Everyone was in shock for it had happened so fast. Yet again began the process to find a new Governor of Britannia.

Shortly afterwards, a second tragedy hit. Creag passed away from an infected wound, a minor injury that he'd received at his forge during the previous month and with the summer heat the injury had refused to heal, despite the constant ministrations of physicians and Sabina's never-ending attention.

I was so sad to hear this news when I arrived at their shop, only to find it dark and un-illuminated. I knew he was quite feverish from his wound, but to die from such a small injury I could not comprehend. It seemed odd how a man so fit and strong could be taken by a mere scratch of a wound. Sabina, of course, was distraught with grief.

With Creag gone Sabina was now faced with making repayments to the moneylenders for the shop on her own. While she was not a silversmith, she came up with the idea of turning the shop into a bakery.

Once the last of Creag's silverware was sold, she set about baking a variety of cakes and breads which were second to none, managing to scrape together a meagre living that was just enough to pay the debts. Sometimes, I would help her sell her wares, minding the stall while she baked extra cakes, or when she had a break, and of course we could chat and keep each other company.

It was toward the end of the summer, the days still long and hot. I had been helping Sabina all morning and took a stroll through the *macellum* on my way home, making the occasional purchase. It was almost lunchtime and I had worked up quite an appetite. I decided to purchase something to eat and drink from the *canabae* and so made my way out of the crowded market, passing some new construction work and northwards to the *canabae* area.

A couple of soldiers from the Fourteenth Legion whom Gaius had trained two years ago were seated at one of the tables about to enjoy their lunch, and they beckoned me over to join them.

Quintus and Gnaeus were two of the most polite and respectful soldiers that the Roman Army had enlisted. They were still quite young and had a lot yet to learn, not having encountered any serious fighting to date.

I placed my basket on the table and seated myself down beside them.

'Here, try a little of this wine. It's absolutely delicious,' Gnaeus offered, passing me a cup. 'Help yourself, there's plenty.'

'Thanks,' I replied gratefully, pouring a little into the cup and taking a sip. 'How's the Army treating you these days?' I enquired.

'Good, but it's hard work,' Gnaeus replied. 'At least we had good training!'

'Yes, the best,' Quintus agreed, taking a piece of freshly cooked bread. 'We have your husband to thank for that.'

'I'm sure he'd be very pleased to hear you say that!' I replied with a laugh.

'Well, well, look who we have here!' A voice suddenly whispered close to my ear and instantly I froze, for it was a voice I had not thought to encounter again.

The summer heat seemed to become quite chill and my appetite had vanished altogether.

A clammy hand touched my shoulder, sending shivers down my spine, and I turned my head slightly to see Vecilius leering down at me. The touch of his hand made my flesh crawl and I abruptly shook him free.

I was gripped by fear that tied my stomach up in lots of little tiny knots. I hadn't come across Vecilius since our first encounter ten years ago.

'You two may leave,' he addressed Gnaeus and Quintus, with a wave of his hand. 'Old friends, catching up; you understand?' Vecilius glared at them meaningfully.

Apologetically, Gnaeus and Quintus moved to another table. I could see them looking across every now and then, curious and perplexed.

Vecilius walked casually around to the other side of the table and leant his back against the wall. He hadn't changed all that much over the years, his face retaining a youthful expression, his wavy brown hair was now cut quite short and had become sun-bleached in places, his eyes burned with the same hatred I had glimpsed years ago. Or had his hatred grown, I wondered, festering like some infected wound such as Creag had suffered from?

'Thought you'd seen the last of me, eh?' he jeered, stepping forward and reaching across the table to cheekily help himself to an apple from my basket. He tossed it about for a moment before sitting down opposite me and taking a large bite.

'I've advanced quite a bit since we last met you know,' Vecilius boasted grandly, chewing on the apple. 'Chief Architect in fact, in charge of all the construction work in the area.' A trickle of apple juice ran down his chin and he caught it on his finger, licking it off with obvious delight.

'You may have noticed the recent building work around here?' he added proudly, with a flourish of his hand. 'I'd only just finished working on the new forts in Cambria when my cohort was recalled by Suetonius himself.'

Namedropper, I thought! General Suetonius Paullinus was the newly installed governor who had arrived to take charge the previous month and had wasted no time in settling himself in at Viroconium in preparation for his advance into Northern Cambria. Indeed, I'd seen very little of Gaius since his arrival, the two of them constantly engaged in discussing tactical warfare.

Vecilius took another bite of the apple, all the while his gaze fixed upon me as if daring me to speak or move. Quintus and Gnaeus were of little help. Perhaps they did really believe that he was an "old friend" after all? I pursed my lips in annoyance.

'Well now, imagine my surprise when I saw you strolling about the *macellum*,' he continued on, unabated. He folded his arms across his chest. 'Have you nothing to say to an old "friend"?' he snapped impatiently.

'I have nothing to say to you,' I replied blandly. 'Go away.'

Vecilius' manner changed suddenly. He leant across the table and grabbed hold of my wrist hard. 'Now listen here you little bitch,' he snapped menacingly. 'I haven't forgotten the insult you did me and I will make you pay for it, sooner or later, do you hear me?'

Just then, Marcus arrived. He walked up to the end of the table, ensuring that Vecilius had seen him, and placed his hand upon the hilt of his *gladius*.

Vecilius took the hint. Letting go of my wrist, he stood up. 'I haven't forgotten,' he repeated.

'Would you see me home please Marcus?' I asked, trying hard to ignore Vecilius' taunt. I stood up abruptly, taking hold of my basket as I did so.

Vecilius instantly broke into fits of raucous laughter, pointing towards me as everyone around turned to see what was going on. The laughter spread like the plague. Vecilius was laughing so hard that he was doubled over.

I gazed around to see what he was laughing at, looking over my shoulder.

'She still doesn't know!' he cackled like an old harpy, pointing a finger directly at me.

I looked down and to my horror I saw that my fibula brooch had become unfastened, my sleeveless summer gown now partly down around my waist. Hastily I covered myself back up, nervously fumbling with the catch of the brooch in an attempt to re-fasten it.

'Be quiet! You'll laugh on the other side of your face when my fist hits it!' Marcus scolded Vecilius.

I glared angrily at Vecilius, my embarrassment turning to rage as I realised it was he who had unfastened my brooch pin when he'd come up behind me.

'You! You did this!' I accused wildly, my basket flying out of my hands as I swiftly grabbed a sharp bread knife from off the table. He was still laughing at me as I rushed towards him without even thinking. 'I'll kill you!' I screamed. 'I'll kill you for this!'

Marcus acted quickly, grabbing at my arms and holding them fast. I struggled to get free. 'Easy, easy,' he whispered. 'Let's get you home. Come on.'

Quintus retrieved my fallen basket, rapidly collecting up its contents that were spewed across the ground, and he handed the basket to Marcus. With a glare towards Vecilius, Marcus gently guided me out of the *canabae*.

The remainder of the walk home was all a blur. I was in a daze. In the back of my mind I could still hear Vecilius laughing, and I wanted revenge.

Aine came to the door and Marcus handed her the basket then whispered something to her. He then led me into the *triclinium*, and once comfortably seated Aine entered with some wine. She handed me a cupful and then offered some to Marcus, but for once he declined.

'It'll be all right,' he said to me. 'I'll keep an eye on him whenever I can.'

I nodded and gave him a weak smile. 'Thanks,' I replied.

'I should tell Gaius,' he added after a moment's thought.

'No!'

'At least to let him know that Vecilius is around, eh?' Marcus pursued. He smiled warmly.

I suppose it made sense.

'All right,' I agreed at length, pushing my hair out of my eyes and flicking it over my right shoulder, as I always did, 'and thank you, Marcus.'

Marcus grinned, that cheeky irresistible grin of his. 'My lady,' bowing and kissing my hand. 'May the goddess, Diana, smile upon her namesake, the lady Julia *Diana*!' And I laughed.

When Gaius returned later I was in a quiet, introspective mood. He could tell straight away that something had happened, but when he asked me what was wrong I could not bring myself to tell him.

'Is it Vecilius?' he asked gently. 'Marcus told me he was here in Viroconium. Did he hurt you at all?'

'No,' I sniffed. 'Not really.'

'It's my fault,' Gaius added softly, a genuine tone of guilt to his voice. 'I should have dealt with him more severely ten years ago.' He stepped forward, wrapping his arms around me and running his fingers through my long hair, playing with the Roman braids. 'It's all right,' he whispered. 'I'm here.'

For weeks afterwards I refused to go anywhere, staying inside the house and becoming more and more depressed.

I wanted to see Sabina but I was too afraid of bumping into Vecilius again. Finally, Gaius coaxed me into accompanying him around the *macellum*, the sun shining brightly on this crisp, autumn day. I held tightly to his arm, looking all about me warily for any sign of Vecilius.

Gaius had assured me that Vecilius and his cohort from the Twentieth Legion would most likely be moving off elsewhere come the winter, their work here almost done.

'They may even be joining Suetonius on his campaign into Northern Cambria,' he had remarked earlier that day.

Then, I spotted him, just up ahead. He was chatting up one of the stall holders, a pretty, fair-haired girl who must have been half his age. A couple of his legionaries were there with him, obviously making crude remarks.

'Don't look at him,' Gaius advised as he too had noticed him. 'Turn your head aside. Just ignore him.'

I wanted to turn around and go back, but Gaius urged me on.

'Come on,' he whispered, 'don't let him see he's upset you.'

'Take me home,' I begged, hiding my face in his shoulder. 'I want to go home.'

'On such a fine day?' Gaius remarked.

He wouldn't take me straight home, but led me down to the river's edge where we could sit peacefully by ourselves and relax for a while.

'I shouldn't worry about Vecilius,' Gaius said. 'He's just a prankster, that's all. He likes to tease,' he continued. 'Oh, I know he's bigoted. Most of the Twentieth Legion are; "A Legion is the sum of their training", you know,' he added, as if quoting some long ago learnt lesson. 'Plus, they tend to follow their commanding officer's example.'

I looked at him with interest. 'What do you mean?' I asked, my curiosity aroused.

'It's true,' he replied earnestly. 'I can't say it's true for all the soldiers of the Twentieth, but many of the veterans at Camulodunum have been treating the native Britons there like slaves for quite a while.'

'And they are not slaves?'

'No,' he affirmed.

'So, what about the Fourteenth Legion?' I asked, leaning back and resting my head upon his shoulder.

'The Fourteenth? Oh, we're the worst of the lot!' Gaius jested, and I giggled in amusement.

'No, seriously,' he continued. 'We were favoured by Augustus, and we've always been quite fortunate to have good commanders, at least while I have been with them. You know; leaders with a diplomatic touch who are more interested in finding a peaceful solution.'

Like you?' I remarked with a smile.

Gaius laughed. 'I was thinking more of Natalis actually.'

'What about the other two Legions in Britannia?' I pursued.

'Hmm, let's see,' he replied, obviously giving the question some thought. 'The Ninth Legion, they're a pleasant enough bunch, not much different to the Fourteenth. Very courageous in battle, the Ninth,' he paused a moment. 'They say that their new commander, Cerialis, has something going with Cartimandua. I don't know if it's true.'

'Well, that wouldn't surprise me,' I remarked brusquely. 'What do you think?' I remembered how attractive Cartimandua looked, and her quite forceful personality. She was the sort of woman who could always get her own way and seemed to love the little Roman luxuries that she'd managed to acquire.

'Oh, she's certainly capable of anything,' Gaius remarked, smiling.

I'd only seen Petulius Cerialis once, just after he'd arrived in Britannia. He was sent for by Suetonius to meet with him and the other Generals. Cerialis was a muscular man with a very round, full face and short cut black hair. I would certainly not have called him "handsome" or attractive, although he did seem to have a lot of energy and enthusiasm. I shook my head, recalling our visit to Cartimandua's hill-fort not so long ago.

Gaius sighed deeply, thoughtful for a moment. 'And then there's the Second, you know all about them,' he added, stroking my hair with his fingertips. 'They're the ones that destroyed Worlebury.'

'I know,' I said sadly, snuggling down into his arms.

'It was at the hands of the Second Legion that other native settlements besides Worlebury, have also suffered,' Gaius continued. 'They're the only Legion responsible for massacring entire settlements. Ostorius had told Vespasian to use "whatever means necessary" to quell the rebellion, you see,' he added, pausing for a moment. 'That virtually gave him the authority to do as he pleased. They attacked your friends, the Durotriges, too you know.'

'I know that also,' I said, my mind losing itself in the past. Maiden Castle was one of the Durotriges' best defended hill-forts, as Worlebury was ours. Its inhabitants too had been massacred.

'You see, the Second Legion have always had quite ruthless commanders, at least within living memory,' he added. 'They were trained to fight, and fight hard, showing no mercy. They wouldn't have thought twice about killing an innocent woman, or child, if that's what they're ordered to do.'

I shivered at the thought, remembering those slain at Worlebury.

It was as we had returned that fateful night that the true desolation had hit us. We had entered cautiously back the way we'd come, through the western gateway, once Antur had signalled that it was safe to do so. The sight that met our eyes was horrific. Our once mighty hill-fort now blackened, the thatched roofs of our huts still smouldering. The sickening smell of charred timbers mingled with the stench of blood.

'Stay here,' Antur had said to me and the woman, her two children clinging desperately to her side. 'We'll check for survivors.'

Antur and the two warriors had then moved forward, and I had begun to follow. The woman quickly grabbed my arm. 'Antur said to stay here,' she'd said sharply.

'So, stay here then,' I'd replied with a shrug. I'd shook her off and sprinted across to catch up with the menfolk.

They had started going through the debris of the largest hut, the chief's hut, my home. Antur was beginning to move a large piece of timber when my father's body suddenly came into view. I gave a stifled cry. He had been hacked and mutilated almost beyond recognition.

Antur looked up sharply. 'Get her out of here!' he'd snapped in irritation.

The copper-haired warrior had taken me by the arm and dragged me some distance away. He too was of the Belgae people.

'Stay here, this is not work for women,' he'd said gently but firmly, his eyes moist and wet with tears. 'And to think, they call us savages.'

I'd stayed put this time, numbed with shock, and watched as they went through the debris, burying what dead they found. In the distance, a wolf howled.

Antur stopped, listening hard for any sign of movement. He peered around into the darkness. 'We'll have to hurry,' he'd called out. 'The wolves will be here soon.'

After they'd moved onto the other huts, I had begun to go through the ruins, absently looking for anything recognisable, but nothing in particular. It was difficult to see amongst the shadows, but then I caught a glimpse of something glinting in the moonlight—it was the sword. My father had always kept it by his bedside each night in case of trouble. As it was, the sword was still in its leather and bronze scabbard. He hadn't even had a chance to use it.

Frantically, I'd started to dig it out from underneath the fallen timbers. Something moved a short distance away.

'Dana, let's go,' Antur had called out. 'We have to go now, the wolves are closing in, come on.'

Frantically, I'd pulled at the sword until finally it came free. Antur came running over, scrambling through the ruins.

'Come on, what are you doing?' He saw the sword. 'Give that to me.' He'd reached his hand out towards the sword and I had rapidly snatched it aside, fixing the sword-belt around my own waist.

'Oh, all right, keep it for now,' he'd snapped, impatiently, 'but we have to move.' Urgently, Antur grabbed at my wrist. 'Here, take this,' he'd added, thrusting an urn filled with grain into my arms.

Antur dragged me through the rubble, passing the bodies that they hadn't the time to bury, and towards the main gate

'Don't look,' the copper-haired warrior had called out. The woman and children had turned their heads aside, but I had already caught sight of what he didn't want for us to see. Bodies—skulls crushed in, limbs hacked on many; some of our best warriors, and even babies and children. Why they did not take the young to sell, as they did my own baby brother, I could not understand. To destroy our homes, and kill our people was bad enough, but to continue to butcher them so?

One warrior had been pinned to a piece of timber wall, impaled with his own spear. I had given a yelp and Antur had swiftly removed it, the man's body slumping heavily to the ground.

I shivered at these memories once more. 'Can we go home now?' I asked Gaius, pulling my shawl closer around me as the wind began to get stronger.

'Yes, of course,' he replied with a smile as he helped me up. 'It is getting a little chill.' He pulled his cloak to and we headed back home.

Gradually, I returned to helping Sabina at her bakery. It was hard work and very little profit. On one particular day we had just set up the stall with the cakes and bread that Sabina had baked earlier that morning, arranging them neatly, and then sat back to enjoy the fine autumn sunshine. I closed my eyes for a moment. Upon looking up I was startled as a shadow was cast across me. Vecilius was standing arrogantly before us.

Vecilius grinned mischievously as he pretended to inspect the cakes, breaking some open and then dropping them back down again, occasionally sampling one or two.

'Hmm, not bad,' he remarked casually, licking his fingers. 'A little dry though, I think.'

'I trust you intend to pay for those!' Sabina snapped angrily, flicking her long braided brown hair off her shoulders with a brush of her hand as she stood up to face him.

Vecilius raised an eyebrow in surprise, staring at Sabina. 'Pay?' he remarked, as if this was something new to him. 'I don't think I've got any coins on me,' pretending to look for any money. Reaching for his money pouch, Vecilius suddenly produced his dagger instead and before we even had time to react he had plunged it swiftly downwards and right through the centre of the largest cake, making both of us jump.

He picked up a piece of the cake with the tip of his dagger, grinning at our discomfort before taking a small bite.

'It's very good, my pretty,' he remarked casually to Sabina who was looking decidedly angry. 'Not bad, not bad at all.' He then turned on his heel and impudently marched off, tossing a coin over his shoulder toward Sabina as he left.

Sabina gazed at the coin in astonishment. 'It's a silver denarius!' she exclaimed with delight. 'But who is he?' she pondered.

'Believe me, you do not want to know that person,' I replied with a scowl.

I hadn't told Sabina about Vecilius and of my previous encounters with him, and I didn't wish to think about them either, so I said no more to Sabina and left it at that. It was the worse decision I had ever made.

A week or so later, I was making my way as usual to help Sabina with the shop, just as I'd done every day for the past few weeks. Strangely, I arrived to find it all locked up and with no sign of Sabina. Puzzled by this, and a little worried to say the least, I began to wend my way back through the *macellum*. I was so concerned as to her whereabouts that as I passed by the construction work that was still going on I failed to see Vecilius until I was right upon him. He grinned with delight as I rounded the corner, quickly reaching an arm across and pinning me against the wall to prevent my escape.

'You know, I must say, I'm enjoying myself immensely here!' he said. He leant in closer to whisper in my ear. 'I've just raped your friend—no witnesses,' he boasted arrogantly, his hot breath breathing down my neck. 'Cause me any trouble, and I'll do the same to you!'

I stared at him, wide-eyed with terror. Vecilius smiled meaningfully, then withdrew his arm from the wall and released his grip on me. I could hear him laughing loudly as I ran from him in fear. I had to get away before my anger at his insolence got the better of me, but more than that, Sabina was my closest friend, the only friend I'd made since arriving at this miserable place!

After what seemed like miles I returned home, slamming the door firmly shut behind me then sent Goilladyn to locate Gaius. In a short time, he arrived home and I related what had happened. He took it all in silently while I ranted away, my sense of panic rising all the time.

'I'll kill him!' I swore angrily, 'I'll kill him for what he's done!' Before I could think what I was doing I had picked up Gaius' *pugio* from off a small table near the entrance and reached for the door, swiftly pulling it open.

Gaius immediately ran at the door and quickly slammed it shut again. 'Put the knife down,' he said calmly but firmly. 'You have to let the law take care of this.'

I glared at him, my anger unabated, as I spun around to face him.

'Dana.' He held out a hand patiently and after a few moments, I reluctantly handed him the knife, but my anger still raged inside of me. Gaius placed the dagger back down on the table. 'Look, you kill Vecilius and you'll be the one on trial, not him,' he pointed out sensibly, gently stroking my cheek.

Once I'd had a chance to calm down a bit, Gaius and I managed to locate Sabina. She was sitting in the cemetery at Creag's graveside, weeping bitterly. Between us, we helped her home. I stayed with her while Gaius went to report the incident.

Sabina had lost all confidence in herself, her peaches and cream complexion now sporting two massive bruises, her upper arms revealing where Vecilius' fingertips had grasped her a little too firmly.

After what seemed forever, Sabina ceased her sobbing and dried her eyes. 'I'll never trust another man again as long as I live!' she stated bitterly. 'What do we need them for anyway? They're only good for making babies!' she added, picking up an empty wine cup and throwing it full force across the room. It shattered into pieces as it hit the opposing wall. 'If this land was ruled by women, we'd all be safe to walk the streets at night. Men! They're always starting wars and fighting. I hate them! I hate them all!'

'Take it easy, Sabina,' I said soothingly, attempting to placate her.

'Easy?' she retorted sharply. 'I've just been beaten and raped by that, that… creep, and you tell me to take it easy?'

'Look, I don't like Vecilius either, he's had it in for me for a long while,' I stated as calmly as I could manage, although I was still seething underneath. 'I'm sorry. I should have warned you what he was like. I never expected even him to do what he has done, but Gaius will ensure he pays for his crime.' I couldn't help feeling that he'd done this to Sabina merely to get back at me.

Unfortunately, as it turned out I was wrong. There was little Gaius could do to bring Vecilius to justice. It was some weeks later when Gaius returned home after a closed trial that I learned why.

'He's been let off, scot free!' Gaius informed me. He placed an arm about my shoulders. 'It was her word against his,' he added, 'and, as it turned out, fresh evidence came to light of which neither of us was aware.'

'Evidence?' I queried. 'What evidence?'

Gaius heaved a heavy sigh, throwing his cloak down over the back of a chair. 'Did you know that Sabina had been working nights at the brothel in order to supplement her income?'

I was stunned. I could not believe what I was hearing. 'Of course not,' I replied aghast. 'Are you sure? That can't be right. Your information must be flawed, surely?'

'Vecilius had apparently become a "regular customer" of hers over the previous couple of weeks, so since that was her "profession" bruises don't count it seems. Part of the job you might say, and no one saw anything of course.'

As Vecilius had remarked—no witnesses.

I angered. I wanted recompense for Sabina, for what he had done to her, and to me; and for my injured pride. 'So much for your Roman justice!' I snapped, running swiftly out of the house and slamming the door behind me. In my confusion, I had no idea where I was going but eventually I found myself at Sabina's door. The whole investigation had been a farce.

168

Vecilius knew full well that we'd get nothing on him else he would never have boasted about his crime to me in the first place.

Sabina was in the middle of packing when I arrived. We both stared at each other in silence for a moment before she bid me enter.

'You're leaving?' I asked, although it was perfectly obvious that she was.

'I'm going home to my people, my tribe,' she replied coldly. 'I shall stay with my Grandmother and take care of her. We can look after each other, there's nothing left for me here now. I should have done so straight after Creag died, then I wouldn't have been in this mess!' She threw a handful of shawls into her bag. 'I'm beginning to think that this Roman world is not for us,' she added, shaking her head. 'We are the foreigners here; they have different ways, different laws.' She looked around in frustration for a moment. 'I cannot possibly carry all the things I wish to take, and I've no money left for a cart!' She sat down heavily on the edge of the couch and sighed deeply.

'Don't worry, I'm sure Gaius will help you with that,' I said soothingly. 'You can borrow Goilladyn for the day.'

I sat down next to her on the couch for a moment, neither one of us speaking another word, lost in our own thoughts.

I recalled all the trouble I'd had with Vecilius, of how I'd met Gaius, of my family that had perished at Worlebury, and my baby brother, stolen not long after he was born by the Romans, and I wondered where he was and if he was even still alive. Then I thought of Sabina, and of Creag, until I could contain myself no longer.

'Sabina,' I said suddenly, breaking the long silence. 'Why didn't you tell me about the brothel?'

Sabina looked down with embarrassment, her face turning bright pink. 'I don't know,' she muttered eventually. 'I mean, well, it's not something one talks about, is it? After all, it wasn't exactly out of choice you know,' she added hastily. She paused for a moment, wiping away a tear with the sleeve of her gown.

'When Creag went, when he died, the money-lenders came around. They demanded so much money be repaid—I just couldn't cope with the cost. What I was making at the shop wouldn't even have covered half the amount.' She looked up at me, tears welling in her eyes once more. 'There was nothing else I could do,' she explained. 'I didn't want to admit defeat and run away, but now it seems I must, and I am.' Sabina sniffed. 'Why did Creag have to die?' she cried mournfully. 'It's not fair!'

Sabina turned to me for an answer, but I had none to give. 'Only the gods know these things,' was the best I could manage in reply. 'The Fates have not been kind.'

It was not long after I had arrived home and related what Sabina had said that Marcus turned up at Sabina's door, having borrowed a donkey and cart from the Base in which to take Sabina and her belongings back home to her people. That was the last I saw of her.

Shortly afterwards Vecilius returned to working on the building site, the construction work all but complete and requiring only the finishing touches.

'He'll be gone soon,' Gaius assured me. 'Suetonius is planning to take his unit along into Cambria. Perhaps one of your druids will take care of him? They could use him as a sacrifice!'

'Nice thought!' I replied with a laugh. This was something to look forward to perhaps. Wishful thinking, I knew, but his presence still worried me.

'Meanwhile, just try and stay out of his way,' Gaius advised solemnly. 'If he so much as touches a hair of your head I swear I'll kill him myself!'

Despite Gaius' previous warning, I could not rest while Vecilius remained at Viroconium. At first, I thought it coincidence that each time I went out either alone or with Caitilin, I would see him somewhere along the way, and then it dawned on me—Vecilius was stalking me—deliberately

170

following me around or waiting somewhere that he knew I'd be. I began to feel frightened and intimidated, and I thought about mentioning this to Gaius but then Vecilius hadn't really *done* anything. He was just *"there"*.

Nevertheless, he was either intentionally trying to frighten me, or else he was planning something worse. I tried varying my route, but he would soon work this out and be waiting at either end.

I made a decision to begin wearing my sword once more. Whether through anger or fear, slowly but surely, I plotted my revenge. On this day, I had strapped my sword about my waist, concealing it beneath the many folds of my gown and overdress, and it hung heavily, but I felt all the better for feeling it there even if I never had call to use it. Nevertheless, a plan was beginning to formulate in my mind. Although the wearing of my sword made me feel a little more secure, I confessed to a certain trepidation. Would I even have the opportunity to carry out my plan, or would Vecilius be the one to strike first?

I happened upon Vecilius almost immediately as I headed into the *macellum*. He was busily chatting with some ladies, two of them hugging up to him on either arm, so I ducked quickly out of sight and watched him unnoticed for a moment.

Perhaps this was not such a good idea after all? Nevertheless, I was here now. I thought about visiting the temple and cursing Vecilius, wondering absently if the Roman curse tablets would truly work? I turned around and began to walk in the opposite direction, passing a stall selling ladies clothing. With one eye on the look-out for Vecilius, I began sorting through the woollen shawls. I needed a new one as winter was fast approaching and my old one was getting quite threadbare.

Finding a colour that I liked, I handed the stall keeper some money and placed the shawl about my shoulders. It was a lovely blue one and quite heavy. I was adjusting the fit when I saw Vecilius pass by, having shaken off his admirers. For once, he hadn't noticed me. The gods had presented me with the opportunity I was seeking, so I made a rash decision and decided to follow him for a change. Now that I had my sword upon me, I somehow felt braver. Perhaps I would get the chance to strike him from behind?

Quickly, I skirted around the stalls, walking as fast as I could in order to keep up. I had lost him for a moment in the crowd, and then I spied him just up ahead, heading towards the river. He turned a corner and I followed. Vecilius was waiting for me. Abruptly, he pushed me up against the wall, his arm across my neck.

'Are you following me?' he snapped.

'No,' I lied, startled. 'What makes you think I'd want to follow you?' My voice was trembling. I tried to sound more convincing. 'Don't flatter yourself! I cannot help it if you happen to be going the same way as me.' I wasn't sure whether he believed me or not. He looked me squarely in the eye for a moment, and then relaxed his grip a little.

'Oh yes,' he added menacingly, as if he'd almost forgotten something. 'You remember what I said I'd do to you should you cause me any trouble?'

I swallowed hard, too afraid to answer. My bravado had vanished. My hand rested upon my sword, but I had no room in which to unsheathe it.

'I tell you what, I'm going to be fair about this,' he continued almost amiably. 'I am going to let you go. I'm going to give you a sporting chance, and let you have a head start.' Vecilius stood back, releasing his hold on me. His eyes narrowed and his lips curled into a sneer. 'Go on. Run!'

The pure hatred in his eyes spoke volumes. After a moment's hesitation I needed no further incentive. I did just as he suggested, I took flight. I thought I heard him laughing as I rounded the corner, but I couldn't be sure, that evil cackle of his, echoing in my head as I ran. After a while, I slowed down and sneaked a look over my shoulder, breathless and certain that I'd given him the slip. I couldn't see him anywhere and I breathed a heavy sigh of relief.

Terrified and shaken, I decided I'd best head for home. I walked quickly past the row of stalls. The crowds were thinning out a bit towards the remaining rows and I risked another glimpse behind me. To my horror, Vecilius was right on my heels! Panic set in and I began to walk faster, but the faster I walked the faster he walked, until gripped with fear I started to run again. There were no more stalls to lose him amongst so I turned and ran along an alleyway.

I was somewhere between the *macellum* and the river. I could hear his footsteps running behind me, getting closer and closer all the time, then suddenly they ceased, but I wasn't going to stop until I reached home. I came to a corner and sped around so fast that my shoes skidded and I nearly fell. The alleyway ahead was even longer and I was running as fast as I could. I had almost reached the end when Vecilius suddenly leapt out in front of me.

'I warned you not to cause me any trouble, didn't I,' he remarked coldly. 'I told you what would happen.'

He lunged towards me, grabbing my arm fast as I tried to escape. His grasp was so strong that I cried out in pain. In vain, I attempted to pull free but his grip got even tighter. He wrapped an arm about my neck, half choking me as he dragged me backwards and through a side entrance and then into one of the buildings.

In the struggle that ensued, we both all but fell down the few steps which lay beyond, but the unexpected stumble had fortunately managed to free me from his hold. Vecilius marched angrily down the steps towards me and I backed away in fear as far as I could, noticing that we seemed to be in some sort of a cellar. Many large storage vessels were neatly placed around the walls. The only exit was the one by which we had entered and I'd have to get past Vecilius to reach it. I decided to risk it and made a dash for the door. Vecilius lunged at me, clutching my sleeve and I spun around and skidded to the floor. He grabbed hold of my long-braided hair and yanked me to my feet throwing me up against some amphorae and urns, many of which shattered, spilling their contents across the floor, and then slowly, he withdrew his *pugio* from its sheath.

'Now I'll make you sorry you ever insulted me!' he threatened. 'First, I'm going to rape you, just like I did to your friend. Then I'm going to kill you,' he waved the dagger around menacingly close to my face, 'slowly! I think I'll leave your body lying around here in little pieces for Gaius to find,' he added, a look of pure hatred on his face. 'Oh, he'll probably know it was me who killed you, but he'll never be able to prove it. Hey, guess what?' he looked around dramatically, 'No witnesses!'

In my panic to get free I somehow managed to wriggle out of his grasp, pulling my arm away sharply and tearing the sleeve.

'Gaius will kill you if you so much as touch me!' I yelled at him fiercely, my heart beating like a drum as I ducked down and dodged round behind him.

'Oh, I don't think so,' he replied casually, turning about to face me once more. He shrugged his shoulders almost apologetically. 'Friends in high places, I'm afraid. Too bad.'

He lunged towards me rapidly, and I dodged to one side, knocking over more amphorae. Red wine oozed out across the floor. Vecilius pursued me around the urns, dodging and weaving in and out, obviously enjoying the chase. I had but one hope, one chance.

Reaching beneath my long woollen overdress and newly bought shawl, I placed my hand upon my sword. I had obediently done without it all these years. It felt strange to be wearing the sword again, feeling the weight of the weapon as it hung about my hips, but it was also most comforting.

It was difficult to say what happened next in the scuffle that followed. There was a moment when I thought I wouldn't be able to withdraw my sword in time, wedged between the urns as I was for protection. Vecilius clambered between them, pushing some of them over in his effort to reach me. I struggled against Vecilius for what seemed an eternity, feet skidding, Vecilius lashing out with his dagger.

Finally, I got my sword free and held it out before me, remembering what Gaius had taught me and holding it firmly

174

with both hands. Vecilius halted in his tracks, watching me warily with a keen eye.

How I hated this Roman! I hated him almost as much as I hated those who had destroyed Worlebury. My temper mingled with my fear.

'If Gaius won't kill you, then I will!'

I brought the sword down hard upon him before he had a chance to draw his own. I sliced at the arm that held the *pugio*. It flew from his hand and skittered across the floor. Vecilius clutched at his wrist, blood dribbling out between his fingers from the cut my sword had given. He staggered, holding his injured arm out before him, the hand dangling by a thread, his face pale and gaunt. Shocked, yet with anger spurring me on, I then brought the sword down on him again in a death-wielding blow. There was a momentary look of surprise upon his face as he fell to his knees and collapsed, his blood spilling out across the floor to mingle with that of the spilt wine. Stunned, I gazed down at my sword, now smeared with Vecilius' blood.

I felt a small sense of triumph for a moment, but only for a moment, as the horror of what I'd done slowly dawned on me and I did what any Dobunni does best: I panicked. Fleeing the scene as fast as I could, I abruptly pushed my way past a couple of legionaries who had unfortunately now appeared at the top of the steps.

'She's killed Vecilius,' I heard one of them cry out as I ran back into the alley. 'Get her!'

From then on, soldiers seemed to appear around every corner joining in the chase. With no time to sheath my sword, all I could do was run up and down the alleyways once more in an attempt to lose them, until I had no idea where I was, and then finally I sighted a gateway into the Legionary Base.

I ran directly past the soldiers that were on guard duty at the gate before they knew what was happening. I sped around a corner, my sandaled feet slipping upon the stony ground as I ran along the rear of the barracks. I could hear the soldiers not far behind me, shouting and yelling for retribution. There seemed to be more of them now. I rounded yet another corner and found myself at the stables. I breathed a sigh of relief as I spied Marcus out the front preparing his horse for his daily inspection of the nearby forts.

'Marcus! Marcus!' I called out, careering into him as full speed. 'Help me, help me Marcus,' I pleaded desperately, grabbing him by the arm.

'Why? What's happened?'

'Hide me, quickly!'

The sound of the soldiers' hob-nailed boots was coming ever closer. They would be here at any moment, and they were out for blood—my blood!

Marcus was quick to react. He looked around. 'It's no good hiding,' he remarked, sizing up the situation in an instant. 'We've got to get you away from here.'

'I must get to Gaius!' I cried in a panic.

'There's no time!' he snapped, abruptly pulling me aside and into the shadows as the troop of soldiers ran past the courtyard. 'I'll tell him,' Marcus whispered confidentially, noting my blood-stained sword and garments for the first time. 'What on earth did you do?'

'It, it was self-defence,' I stammered, swallowing hard, my mouth dry with fear. 'Vecilius…'

'All right, all right,' Marcus soothed, placing a hand upon my shoulder, his bright blue eyes full of sympathy. 'I get the idea. Come on, you can take my horse.'

'Where?' I asked panic stricken, gazing around anxiously lest the soldiers should return at any moment. 'Where shall I go?'

Marcus thought for a moment. 'What about one of the local settlements?'

I gave him a blank look in reply. I didn't even know where the local Cornovii settlements were, let alone the people who lived there. I wished I knew how to locate Sabina, but I didn't. She would help me. Meanwhile, the soldiers had begun a thorough search of all the nearby buildings. They had turned into a lynch mob and it would not take them long before they headed back towards the stable block.

'Well, what about the Northern Dobunni?' Marcus suggested.

I shook my head vigorously. Even if I could reach Bagendon by nightfall, there was no way I was going to beg for help from our traitorous cousins. They would more than likely hand me over to the Romans themselves.

'No,' I stated firmly, as I reached a decision. 'I shall go home.'

Marcus looked perplexed. 'Home? You mean all the way to the Mendip?' he said aghast. 'You'll never make it!'

'Yes I will,' I replied boldly, my mind made up and filled with fierce determination. 'Now, give me your horse.'

Having sheathed my sword, we walked across to where the mare was obediently waiting.

'What should I tell Gaius?' Marcus asked as he helped me up into the saddle.

I thought hard for a moment. 'Tell him... tell him to seek out Antur,' I replied quickly. 'He'll know where to find me.'

Marcus nodded. 'Just remember,' he added as I prepared to ride off. 'You may not want to rest, but the horse will.' He stroked her muzzle affectionately.

I smiled down at him, knowing how much he cared about his horses. 'Don't worry, I'll look after her,' I promised.

Southern Dobunni

Antur of the Attrebates

Chapter Seven

Autumn, AD 58
Cadbury Tickenham,
North Somerset

I was alone and desperate. The only thing on my mind was that I had to get away, to leave the Legionary Base, as quickly as I could. I had ridden Marcus' horse as fast as I dare towards the main gate, and now paused for a moment trying to gauge my chances of getting through. I was in luck. The gate remained open and there were just the two guards. I could hear the soldiers that were pursuing me coming up fast. The soldiers on the gate looked the other way briefly and I made a quick dash, urging the horse forward at full gallop. Before the guards had time to realise what was going on, I had ridden directly out of the fortress, the horse knocking one of the guards aside as we sped through the gateway. The mare continued to go at full speed as we reached the open road.

The soldiers were continuing in their pursuit, some taking to horseback themselves, but they were failing to keep up and I managed to lose them after a few miles. Where the road crossed the river Sabrina, I decided to head across country, slowing down to a more moderate pace and following the course of the water as best I could.

I re-joined the road at *Vertis* and by nightfall I gauged I was about halfway to my destination, wondering whether Gaius was following behind somewhere. I had been taking it in easy stages, letting the mare canter for a while, then walk, before galloping briefly and then resting for a time, occasionally stopping for water for both myself and the horse. Marcus had left a small pouch of food in one of the saddle bags but it would not last long, and there was a flask full of water that I could easily replenish from the river.

Throughout the entire journey, Gaius' words kept haunting me, his warning of years ago—"Roman Law can be very severe"—and I was terrified. The sound of wolves howling in the distance brought yet another terror and I halted abruptly. I decided I ought to find somewhere safe to spend the night, safe as I could anyway. I located a large tree and tethered the mare to it, hoping she would be all right, and then climbed up onto a low bough above. Needless to say, I got very little if no sleep that night, the sound of the wolves keeping me constantly vigilant and on the alert for danger, added to which the memory of this dreadful day's event was still fresh in my mind.

At the first sign of daylight I set off again, moving closer to the roadside and following the Glevum to Abonae Road, then picking up the Fosse Way for a while which ran south towards the Mendip. Several times I spotted a Roman patrol and had to duck and hide behind bushes and trees until they had passed. This made my journey painfully slow and with winter drawing near, the daylight would soon turn to dusk.

I had decided not to head right into Dolebury itself, although I desperately wanted to ask my people for help, I did not wish to place them in any danger by leading the Romans there and implicating them in this whole mess. I had therefore made up my mind before I left that I would head for a rock shelter that lay a little north of Dolebury and Worlebury, at the location known as Cadbury Tickenham. The rock shelter was in fact a small cave which didn't lead very far into the rock face. There was an old hill-fort nearby that had been the place of my birth and where I had resided for many years, so I knew the area well. It had been abandoned shortly after the invasion began.

I was not far now from the rock shelter which lay within the woodland. With the daylight failing, I had reduced the horse's pace to that of a slow trot. Suddenly, out of nowhere, a pack of hungry wolves appeared, surrounding us on all sides. The horse reared up in fright and I clung onto her as tightly as I could for fear of my life, wrapping my arms about her neck. The wolves were moving in closer, snarling and drooling. The mare spun around in a circle looking for an escape route. She kicked her hooves about wildly as two wolves tried to grab hold of her legs, and then abruptly, she bolted.

I didn't mind her bolting just as long as I remained in the saddle and hopefully she'd be able to lose the wolves. Keeping my head down, I held on for what seemed an eternity, crossing streams and puddles, twigs and branches occasionally brushing the top of my hair.

Eventually, the mare came to a halt, tired and sore. I looked all around. There didn't seem to be any sign of the wolf pack and I realised that it was now just a short walk up the hill to reach the rock shelter.

The mare had suffered an injury to her hind fetlock and I could see where the wolf had tried to sink its teeth. The wound did not seem to be too deep, but nevertheless I was concerned.

'Poor girl,' I said, stroking her mane. 'There, there.'

She seemed to have calmed and rested a bit now, so I walked her the rest of the way up the hill, bathing the wound upon reaching the cave. There was plenty of fresh water around for it looked as if it had been raining, and quite heavily at that, the rainwater having gathered into a multitude of puddles and in the indentations atop some of the loose boulders.

I tethered the mare to one side of the cave where there was a bit of grass for her to eat and then retired inside. The night air began to draw in and it became freezing cold. I pulled my bloodied shawl about myself in an effort to keep warm and settled down behind some fallen rocks near to the cave entrance.

My stomach pained me. I began to feel hungry, but the food had run out some way back. There was little else I could do now but sit tight and hope that Gaius would soon find me.

Despite my tiredness I was afraid to sleep, trying to remain ever vigilant in case the wolves had managed to track us. No doubt eventually, they would. I could hear them now, howling in the distance, Marcus' mare having put many miles between us.

I remembered the wolves stalking the woods around Worlebury. During the winter months they would become braver, the scent of food drawing them ever closer to our settlement. I recalled an expedition with my aging grandfather when I was about thirteen years of age. We had ridden across to Dolebury and had left a little later than we'd intended. The sun was already setting and my grandfather wanted to rest. He halted his horse up ahead and turned to face me.

'Can't we rest now?' he'd asked wearily.

I shook my head. 'We have to keep moving or the wolves will track us,' I'd replied with determination.

Then, right on cue, there came the sound of wolves howling somewhere behind us. They were already on our scent. We had immediately begun to move off again when suddenly there came a ferocious, growling snarl from a thicket directly in front of me.

My horse reared up in fright and the wolf had jumped up at me, knocking me to the ground. I didn't recall any more, but I learnt later that my grandfather had saved me and slain the wolf. From then on, I'd had an innate fear of wolves, and I didn't even like dogs much.

Fitfully, I began to doze, but each time I slept I saw visions of Vecilius and the wolf pack. I dreamt of Gaius' voice calling me, and those fateful words warning me not to break any Roman laws.

The night seemed to stretch forever but eventually daybreak came. It was a miserable day which just about summed up my mood. Rain poured from the heavens and I'd nothing to eat. At least the horse had enjoyed a bit of grass, I thought. Pity we couldn't eat the grass also. I'd brought the mare into the cave entrance now to keep her dry. With the days shortening, I began to worry about the darkness and the wolves returning. Would Gaius ever find me here? Would Antur remember this place, the place we played in as children?

Daybreak came and went. I'd lost track of how many nights had passed since arriving at Tickenham. I was so tired, so very, very tired. I felt weak from hunger and lack of sleep, so I decided to snuggle down as best I could and grab some sleep while it remained daylight, at least for a little while yet.

The horse was quite comfy, sheltering at the entrance of the Rock Shelter but still within reach of some grass should she feel hungry, yet she could still do with more than mere grass to feed upon and I worried about her leg.

I was so cold and tired that as I began to doze once more, I began to dream of Gaius calling me again, then slowly, dazedly, I realised that I was hearing him!

'Dana! Dana?' he called.

Cautiously I peered out of the entrance, dazed and unsteady on my feet. I leant against the cave wall for support. I thought at first it was all an illusion, for there he was, he and Antur together, slowly walking their horses up the path. I couldn't believe it! Tears of joy and relief filled my eyes.

Gaius halted when he saw me and handed the reins of his horse over to Antur. He then ran as best he could, slipping and sliding in the mud, toward the cave entrance. Shaking and cold, I ran to greet him, flinging myself into his outstretched arms, sobbing uncontrollably.

'It's all right, it's all right,' he whispered soothingly.

'I thought you'd never find me,' I wept.

'Well, you didn't have to run quite so far!' Gaius replied as he held me close. 'Let's get out of this wretched rain!'

We walked into the rock shelter and sat down on some boulders.

'Are you hungry?' he asked.

'Starving!' I brushed my tears aside with the back of my hand. It was difficult to tell which were tears and which was rain.

Antur tethered their horses next to Marcus's, then opening a saddle bag he brought some food across. He handed me a large chunk of bread and I looked up at him for the first time, noting the few age lines he'd gained since we'd last met, but basically, he was the same old Antur that I'd known and loved. I smiled gratefully up at my childhood friend.

'You look dreadful!' he remarked brusquely.

'Thanks!' I replied smartly. 'I feel it!'

'Let's get some warmth in here. It's feeling like the entrance to the Underworld,' he said. 'I'll see if there's anything we can use to make a fire.'

Antur walked down to the back of the cave seeking some dry timber. After a few moments he seemed to have found a little and began working on starting a fire.

'Marcus told me what had happened, well, at least all he knew from your brief conversation I gather,' Gaius said, handing me a little wine. 'I can help you, you know that, but you have to tell me everything that occurred, every last detail. It's important first of all that we get the story straight.' He took my hand gently in his. 'Did Vecilius touch you at all?' he asked, a worried frown crossing his face. 'Did he?'

I shook my head. 'No,' I replied plainly. 'Not in that way. He never got the chance.'

Antur went to fetch some more wood for the fire and spied my sword that I'd left leaning against a rock. He halted and unsheathed it, noting the blood that still stained the blade.

'I never thought I'd see you put this sword to good use,' he remarked nonchalantly. 'It's about time it drew some Roman blood!' He glanced across at Gaius. 'No offence,' he added.

'None taken,' Gaius responded curtly. 'If I'd had the chance, I'd have gladly run him through myself!'

'Thought I'd always told you to keep the blade clean!' Antur scolded me, but gave me a wink and a wry smile with it.

I managed a weak smile in return but the memory of it all still haunted me; the look on Vecilius' face as he'd fallen, the blood, the soldiers who pursued me. It was like a nightmare, only in a nightmare one could always awaken.

'Just how long have you been carrying that sword around for anyway?' Gaius asked suddenly. 'I thought I'd told you to leave it at home.'

'Only on that day,' I replied sheepishly.

'Just as well she did,' put in Antur.

Gaius looked at me sternly. 'Dana, were you hunting him?' He knew me too well. 'Were you? You need to tell me the truth.'

'Not at first,' I stammered, shaking my head fervently. 'And then I decided to follow him, I have no idea why,' I lied, 'but by that time he was pursuing me.'

'Roman pig!' Anturiaethus remarked sharply, spitting on the ground to show his distaste. 'He deserved to die then!'

'If I hadn't had my sword with me, it would be me lying there dead now instead of Vecilius,' I argued, trying to vindicate myself. It didn't help how I felt. 'The gods move in mysterious ways.'

'True, and sometimes they have a little help!' Gaius remarked, and then he smiled warmly. 'But I'm very glad that you disobeyed me, on this occasion at least!' He hugged me close then continued more seriously. 'Having said that, however, if you hadn't been hunting him he may not have attacked. Now, you'd better tell me all that happened, and I want the truth.'

Slowly and painfully, step by step, I began to recount my movements leading up to Vecilius' death, and then recalled my journey here to the rock shelter at Tickenham.

'Marcus' horse, the mare, her leg was injured by the wolves,' I added in concern. 'I promised I'd look after her for him.' I was beginning to get agitated, being forced to remember the terrible events that had occurred.

Antur walked over to the mare, checking her over.

'It's the rear right fetlock,' I called over to him, and he bent down to take a closer look. 'What am I going to tell Marcus?' I wept. 'I promised she'd be all right!'

'I'm sure she will be,' Gaius assured me. 'She's a strong mare, and a healthy one, and she's brought you safely all this way.'

'She'll be fine,' Antur remarked, running an experienced hand along the length of the mare's leg. 'Don't fret so! It's not as bad as it looks.'

'There, see,' Gaius added. 'We'll fix a bandage around the wound. That will help.' Gaius arose and tore off some of his clothing to provide a makeshift bandage.

'Now then,' he said, returning to the fireside that was now beginning to throw off some much-needed warmth. 'We need to get ourselves sorted out so that we can get you back home and straighten this mess out.'

'Oh, no no no no!' I responded abruptly, scrambling to my feet. 'I'm not going back there!'

'Dana's right,' Antur agreed. 'You can't seriously expect her to go back after what has happened!'

'Well now, what do you suggest?' Gaius snapped sharply. 'We can't all stay here forever! We need to get this sorted out, the Roman way. The authorities have already begun looking for her. It's only a matter of time.'

'The Roman way? Ha!' Antur scoffed, pacing up and down. 'I've heard about your Roman justice,' he added sarcastically. 'Justice, now there's a word! We'd all have been a lot better off if you Romans had never set foot on these shores!'

'Don't I get a say in all this?' I spoke up. 'I don't want to go back. I don't want to face your "Roman justice". I can't! Do you hear me? I can't!' I backed away tearfully until I could back away no further, hunched up against the cave wall.

'You can't take Dana back there,' Antur pointed out. 'Look at her! She's terrified.'

'All right, all right,' Gaius relented. 'We'll stay here for the time being, how long that will be I don't know, but I can get you out of this, and the only way is through the Roman Law Courts.'

'Like you helped Sabina when Vecilius got off?' I remarked coldly.

'It will be different this time,' Gaius replied. 'I promise.'

He stepped forward and placed his arms around me. I couldn't seem to stop shaking.

'I need you to trust me,' he added. 'We'll get through this.'

I nodded vaguely.

'I should probably head back up to Viroconium,' Gaius continued on in afterthought, 'and find out exactly what the situation is.'

'You can't!' I objected strongly. 'You only just got here!'

'Look, I can be back within five days, a week at the most,' he reasoned. 'It may not be as bad as we all think. Antur will stay with you, won't you Antur?' Gaius said, looking him straight in the eye.

'You sure you can trust me?' Antur replied caustically, folding his arms across his chest.

'Oh, I know I can,' Gaius answered confidently, steadfastly holding Antur's gaze.

Antur turned aside with an abrupt laugh. For once, they were on the same side.

'I'd best unload the rest of the supplies then,' Antur said practically, 'seeing as we seem to be staying.'

'I'll depart first thing in the morning,' Gaius said. 'And I'll take Dana's sword back with me.'

'What?' Catching this last remark, my head in a spin.

'It's for the best,' Gaius explained. 'The last thing you want is to be found with the sword.'

'The last thing I want is to be found at all!' I complained.

'I can take the sword back to Dolebury if you prefer?' Antur interrupted. 'That might be better.'

'Ha, better for you, you mean!' I retaliated swiftly. 'You've always wanted that sword. You can't let him take my sword, Gaius, please?'

'That sword should have come to me in the first place,' Antur pointed out. 'It was made by my people.'

'Your people?' I laughed, marching over and gazing up at him in defiance. 'I thought we Dobunni were your people. You've been with us long enough!'

'By the gods, Dana, try and see some sense!' Antur retorted hotly. 'I will give it back to you once this is all over with.'

'Liar!'

'Enough! Both of you!' Gaius strode across to us, pushing us apart. 'You behave like children,' he chastised, glaring at us each in turn.

I looked away, pursing my lips in anger.

'Antur, you'll need to fetch extra supplies from Dolebury,' Gaius added. 'You've not quite enough to last for a week.' He breathed a weary sigh. 'I'll take the sword. Let that be an end of it.'

Antur nodded. He glared at me and I turned aside in a huff.

'Can you be back at first light?' Gaius asked.

'Of course,' he stated curtly, as he prepared to ride off. 'Back at first light it is then!' Antur mounted his horse. 'Sleep well,' he added, as he reined the horse sharply about, and then rode off steadily down the track without so much as a backwards glance.

The rain had ceased now, but nightfall was almost upon us. The day was already becoming a blur as tiredness overtook me once again. I sat down on the ground and rested my back against a nearby boulder.

'So, what is the penalty for killing a Roman officer?' I enquired none too hopefully, and too tired even to care.

Gaius strolled over and stood beside me, obviously giving the question some thought before replying. 'We just need to prove it was self-defence,' he answered at length.

'And if we can't?' I asked, my voice beginning to tremble. 'What then Gaius? You haven't told me what happens then?'

Only last year, Pomponia Graecina, the wife of General Aulus Plautius, commander in charge of the invasion of AD 43, had been accused in Rome of the acceptance of a "*foreign superstition*", Christianity, they called it. Although he was now a Senator, Plautius' wife was still forced to stand trial. Fortunately for her, she had been acquitted. Had she not, however, the punishment would most likely have been banishment to some remote island, or in the extreme could even have been death. A lot lesser crime one would have thought than that of killing a Roman officer.

'If we fail,' he replied at last, 'then the charge will be that of murder,' he stated matter-of-factly. 'There is only one penalty.' He sat down and took my hand in his. There was no need to say further. The penalty was obvious, a life for a life. If I was found guilty of murder, the penalty would be death.

The following morning Antur returned right on time, just after sunrise.

'There's no sign of any Roman patrols around yet,' he remarked as he began to unload his horse. 'Are you sure they'll be heading this way?'

'Oh yes,' Gaius replied as he readied his mount. 'Dolebury will be the first place they look, and Vecilius had a lot of powerful friends back in Rome. They won't let it rest.'

That was comforting, I thought.

'I sneaked the extra supplies in when no one was looking,' Antur said, bringing them across in sacks. 'They think I'm on a hunting trip for a few days.' He heaved the sacks down in the corner and sat down by the fire. There was a frost this morning but at least there was no more rain for the present.

A short time later, Gaius was ready to leave.

He took the sword back with him with the intention of concealing it at the house, saying that the less evidence there was against me, the better. I supposed it was a fact that I really could not dispute.

'Do you have to go?' I complained fretfully. I could feel the panic returning, making me edgy and restless.

'We have to know what is going on,' he replied, smiling down at me, ready to ride off. 'I'll be back within the week, I promise,' he added. 'Meanwhile, should any patrols show up—no heroics, either of you. Do you understand?'

'I understand,' Antur acknowledged. He sounded disappointed. 'Good luck.'

Gaius gave him a nod, and with a glance towards me, he rode off.

During the days that Gaius was away, Antur and I spent many hours recalling childhood memories and visiting some of our old haunts nearby. This very rock shelter was one of them, which was why I'd chosen to take refuge here, hoping that Antur would recall playing here as children. I knew that Antur was just trying to cheer me up by keeping my mind off my current predicament. There were times when he really could become quite likeable.

We took a walk up to our old hill-fort home one day, just for somewhere to go and to see if anything useful remained there. A few broken pieces of pottery were all there was to be found. When the tribe had relocated, we had taken everything with us. Moving the people from the smaller hill-forts into our two largest and strongest ones at Dolebury and Worlebury had seemed the sensible thing to do at the time. Little did we know that doing so would see a third of our population wiped out.

As the darkness would draw in each night, Antur ensured that the fire was kept going. The wolves had managed to find us by now, probably smelling the food cooking, but Antur only had to fend them off the once with his spear, the fire helping to keep them at bay. We brought the horses just inside the cave entrance at night to keep them safe too. The fire was extinguished during the daytime in case it should alert any Roman soldiers of our location, but it was getting bitterly cold. Winter was just a month away now.

We sat down together amongst all the blankets, pulling them around us as best we could, the fire keeping out the cold at night. Antur tossed a handful of twigs upon it and it roared and sputtered. This was the third night since Gaius had been gone.

'What happens when Gaius returns?' I pondered aloud. 'Do you think I'll have to go back?' I asked. 'I don't want to go back, Antur. I'm so afraid.'

Antur turned his head and looked at me, his piercing blue eyes intense.

'You should have stayed here and married me,' he scolded brusquely, 'and then you wouldn't be in this mess.'

I sniffed and looked aside for a moment. 'You don't need a wife,' I retorted sharply. 'You just want someone to cook and keep house for you.'

'I wanted you!' Antur snapped back. 'I would have looked after you.'

Suddenly, I felt a pang of guilt. 'I know you would,' I whispered apologetically. I flicked my long hair over my shoulder and gazed into those piercing blue eyes of his. 'Oh Antur, I am sorry.'

Antur smiled a little and then he placed an arm about my shoulders. 'You know,' he said softly, 'I never even got to kiss you.' Gently he tilted my chin up towards him, and then leant forward to kiss me tenderly on the lips, just for a moment.

I was close to tears when he pulled away. 'Antur, it's all such a mess!' I cried forlorn. 'What am I going to do?' I rested my head upon his shoulder. 'I can't do this anymore. I can't face their Roman justice and their Roman Courts. I can't! I can't!'

'Are you sure you're a Dobunni? You do not speak as one!' Antur berated me sharply, instantly snapping some sense back into me. 'And yet here I am, an Atrebas brought up with Dobunnic beliefs and convictions. We are both fighters, not cowards!'

I swallowed hard, wiping my tears aside quickly. He was right, of course.

'We could run away to Hibernia together,' he continued, gentler now, 'you and I; stay with some of our distant cousins there?' He wiped a tear from off my cheek that I had missed.

'But what about Gaius?' I asked. 'I couldn't leave Gaius!'

Antur looked at me. He pursed his lips together for a moment, deep in thought. 'No,' he replied at length. 'I suppose not. He's all right, your Gaius—for a Roman,' he added. 'But you know, you didn't have to go off and wed a Roman just because you didn't want to marry me. I'd sooner have agreed to you marrying Dafydd, if that was what you really wanted.'

'Oh, Antur, is that what you thought?' I asked, somewhat shocked and distressed that this should even have crossed his mind.

Antur smiled thinly, repeatedly clenching his fists.

'That was not the way of it, no,' I continued. 'That was not why I married Gaius,' I added gently. 'Marrying you would have been like, like marrying my own brother.'

I snuggled up close to him and he placed an arm back about my shoulders. 'Oh, Antur,' I sighed.

Finally, on the sixth day Gaius returned. It was dusk and he was carrying a couple of rabbits he'd caught along the way.

'No one in sight,' he reported. 'Here!' Tossing the rabbits to Antur. 'I caught these for our supper.'

Antur caught them deftly and took out his dagger, beginning at once to prepare the rabbits.

'Antur thinks we should all flee to Hibernia together,' I announced abruptly and without hesitation making Antur drop his knife in surprise.

Gaius raised an eyebrow. 'All three of us?' he remarked. 'That'll be cosy.' He looked across at Antur. 'Is that really what you said?'

'Not exactly,' Antur replied honestly, retrieving his knife from the cave floor. He wiped it clean upon his cloak.

Gaius smiled. 'Well, it's one place my fellow Romans won't be looking for us, that's for sure!' he laughed. Then his manner changed abruptly. 'I'm not sure,' he added seriously.

'But I think I may have been followed.' My heart skipped a beat. 'Oh, not to here,' Gaius continued on. 'But at least as far as The Mendip.'

'I should check around then,' Antur remarked helpfully.

'It's all right,' Gaius asserted. 'No one followed me up here, I assure you.'

'Nevertheless,' Anturiaethus replied, scanning the bushes nearby for any sign of movement, his hunter's instincts kicking in. 'A quick reconnaissance down the track won't hurt.' He handed Gaius the rabbits. 'Here!' he said, wiping his hands on one of the empty sacks. 'You finish them, I'll check down the hill.' He picked up his spear and began to walk cautiously along the pathway.

'So, what did you find out,' I asked Gaius as he continued preparing the rabbits for supper.

'Well, it could be better,' he answered, finishing the rabbits off. He came over and sat down, rinsing his hands in some water and wiping them on his cloak, and then he brushed his fair hair back off his forehead with a sweep of his hand. He looked as if he hadn't had a lot of sleep.

'The incident in the *canabae* last summer,' he continued.

'What about it?' I queried, not wishing to recall the event.

'There are many witnesses who remember your threat to kill Vecilius, and your flying at him in anger there and then, knife in hand,' he stated. 'Plus, Vecilius' *gladius* was still within its scabbard. It would help if we could locate his *pugio* but it hasn't been recovered. An empty sheath proves nothing.'

'What! But it must be there!' I protested in defence. 'It has to be!'

'Look, I only had a quick look around myself,' Gaius added, 'but I could find nothing. Perhaps if we conducted a thorough search it might turn up, then at least that would prove that he had it in his hand.' He tried to sound hopeful but I wasn't convinced.

'It must be there!' I repeated frantically. 'It must be!'

'Don't worry,' Gaius stated calmly. 'If it is still there, we will find it. There are an awful lot of barrels and urns to search behind.

'I suppose so,' I said, still not convinced. 'But what if one of his men has found it already, and taken it?'

At that moment, Antur arrived back at the rock shelter. 'Everything's all quiet,' he reported happily. 'I can't see any sign of the soldiers having followed you this far.'

'Good,' Gaius replied. 'At least that gives us more time to think.'

'Look, if we can't find the dagger it makes it a little harder to prove your claim of self-defence, that's all,' Gaius replied, trying not to sound too concerned. 'Everyone knows what Vecilius was like, and the accusation of rape will still stick even though it was never proven.'

'I'll head back to Dolebury then,' Antur remarked. 'You'll be needing some more supplies.'

'Thank you,' Gaius replied thoughtfully. 'You'd best bring enough for two day's ride,' he added, placing an arm about my shoulders. 'We really should return and sort this mess out.'

'No! No, please Gaius,' I implored him, clutching at his wrist as I gazed pleadingly, desperately, into his eyes. I would far sooner stay here forever than return.

Gaius sighed deeply and raised his arms in surrender. 'All right, but just one more day and that's all,' he stated firmly but patiently, his tone indicating that he was not willing to compromise any further. 'Anyway,' Gaius continued, taking my hand and giving it an encouraging squeeze, 'it will give us an extra day to think and plan our best approach. Antur, can you return the day after tomorrow with those supplies for the journey?'

'No problem,' Antur responded confidently. 'If you're sure that's what you want to do?'

'I'm sure,' Gaius Julius responded promptly. 'It's the best way. We have to get this business resolved, one way or another.'

'See you both in two days' time then. Hope you know what you're doing!' Antur walked over to his horse and leapt up onto the stallion's back. He turned and called across to me, grinning mischievously as he reined the horse about. 'I still think my plan to go to Hibernia is better!'

'Antur!' Gaius added quickly. 'Be careful. The soldiers may not have followed me here, but they could certainly be headed for Dolebury.'

Anturiaethus nodded his head in acknowledgement, and with that, he rode off.

The next day came and went, a little too fast for my taste. It was good to be with Gaius and I feared being parted from him should things go badly back at Viroconium.

Come the second day, there was no sign of Antur. The morning became the afternoon, and the afternoon quickly turned into night. We were both getting very worried.

'There may be soldiers at Dolebury and perhaps he can't risk leaving without being followed,' Gaius suggested hopefully. 'Antur would not be one to risk leading them here.'

'True,' I agreed, it was a possibility but I wasn't at all sure that this was the reason. 'But if you are taking me back to Viroconium, why worry if your Roman soldiers find me first?'

Gaius looked at me for a moment. 'Far better for you to return willingly and give yourself up than to have the legionaries capture you, believe me,' he responded quite seriously.

As the third day began and with still no sign of Antur, Gaius decided to go and look for him, even if it meant going right into the hill-fort to find him. Antur would not have let us down deliberately.

'Then, I shall come with you,' I stated boldly.

'You'd be far safer here,' Gaius assured me. 'I'll be back as soon as I can, and anyway,' he added, scrutinising the heavy clouds that were rolling in steadily over the tops of the trees, 'it looks as if there's a storm approaching.'

Gaius was right about that. Just after he ambled off on foot, leading his horse down the track, the heavens opened. The rain came down in bucket loads, reducing visibility to almost nil. Gaius would be getting soaked! A chill wind began to blow and I moved further back into the cave, wrapping a blanket around me.

I prayed to the gods for Gaius and Antur and their safe return. Perhaps Gaius would decide to turn around and head back, resuming his search once the storm had passed? With this thought in mind, I strolled back up to the cave mouth and sat down to watch for him.

The trees lashed about in anger as the wind became stronger and stronger, the heavy rain making it difficult for me to see. I gave the blanket a tug, pulling it around my shoulders as I peered anxiously into the distance.

I had been sitting there for just a little while I suppose, although it could have been longer, when Gaius finally appeared from out of the mist. The wind was not so strong now, but it was still raining quite heavily, the ground sodden under foot. He took a couple of steps forward and then halted at the end of the track.

Why had he stopped, and where was his horse? Had it thrown him I wondered? What was he doing just standing out there in the rain? And then, suddenly, and to my horror, I realised that he was not alone. A large band of legionaries slowly came into view, marching up behind him, and from out of their midst came Governor Suetonius himself!

Cautiously, Gaius took a few steps towards me. I stared at him, wide-eyed, shaking my head in disbelief. How could he do this to me? He seemed to read the look of betrayal upon my face.

'I didn't bring them here,' he stated plainly, arms outstretched. 'I didn't have any choice.'

I began to panic, a foolhardy idea suddenly entering my head.

Glancing quickly over my shoulder, I somehow believed that I could make a break for it and outrun the Roman legionaries. Gaius was quick to realise my intentions.

'Dana, don't run!' he warned promptly, taking a few steps nearer.

I felt like a wild deer, poised to bolt away from the hunter's arrow. Gaius took one more step closer and I suddenly made a dash across the open ground. My feet skidded upon the sodden earth and I slipped in the mud, falling onto my knees just as a javelin whizzed past my head.

'No!' Gaius cried out in alarm, the javelin thudding into a tree just ahead.

'Hold!' Suetonius commanded immediately.

Terrified, I gazed up at the javelin hovering above me, yet I still wanted to run.

Gaius slowly walked forward, halting only when I turned my head to look at him. After ten years of living together he could read my thoughts and mannerisms well.

'Don't run,' he repeated, gently but firmly. 'They'll kill you.' Gaius held his hand out towards me through the pouring rain. 'Come on, we haven't any choice now,' he added. 'I didn't bring them here; you know I didn't—not out of choice.'

Shivering, I reached my hand out to clasp his and he swept me up into his arms, kneeling down beside me, the two of us on our knees in the mud, and the rain.

'I can't do this, Gaius,' I cried out pathetically against the howling wind. 'I can't, I can't!' I closed my eyes tightly and clung to him as if I would never release him, for my very life was dependent upon him and him alone.

'Yes, you can,' Gaius replied in a reassuring tone. 'I'll be right there with you. I'm not leaving your side again.'

Standing up carefully in the slippery mud, Gaius reached down a hand to pull me up and then swiftly swept me into his arms, carrying me back into the rock shelter. He found a dry blanket and placed it around me, cradling me gently in the warmth of his arms.

After a moment, Suetonius Paullinus walked over. He stood gazing down at us impassively as we sat huddled together on the ground, his dark eyes unreadable.

He was not a young man by any means, being perhaps in his early fifties, his dark hair thinning and with a balding patch to the centre, and while not particularly tall, from where we sat he seemed as a giant.

'Come on, we have to start heading back,' he commanded at once.

'Oh no, you're not dragging Dana all that distance in this rain!' Gaius retaliated firmly. 'You can't go ordering me about anymore! I'm not in your Army now; I resigned remember?'

This was news to me! I looked up at Gaius in surprise. I never imagined he would feel so strongly about all this so as to resign his rank and position. He had served his time it was true, but it was something that was never even talked about, despite his passion for Law.

'Come now, Gaius Julius,' Suetonius replied patiently. 'There's no need to be like that. You know how highly I have valued and revered your advice of late, but surely you can appreciate that I have my men to consider?'

Gaius was not to be appeased. 'Then I guess you had better kill us both, right here and now!' he exploded angrily, holding onto me tighter than ever before. 'And another thing,' he added. 'I don't see why you had to bring an entire Army with you just to capture one girl!'

Gaius glared stubbornly up at Governor Suetonius. I had never seen him in such a temper. Quite startled by his outburst, I glanced from one to the other, the two men seemingly having reached an impasse.

Suetonius was wise enough and old enough to know when to back off. He turned his gaze towards me, a hint of sympathy in his eyes. The look of determination relaxed into a smile as he came to a decision.

'We leave as soon as it stops raining,' he stated firmly, adding sincerely, 'I'm not your enemy, you know.' He stared thoughtfully at Gaius. 'I will do all I can to help.'

Suetonius turned swiftly about and walked over to where his men were hopelessly trying to take shelter from the driving rain. They stood in close formation beneath the trees, their commanding officer vainly attempting to establish some sort of order by ensuring they at least stood smartly to attention.

General Suetonius Paullinus ordered the centurion and most of the unit away with a wave of his hand. The centurion saluted promptly and began to lead the legionaries off down the muddy track. Suetonius then began to usher the remaining soldiers towards the cave to take shelter until the storm had passed.

After all the fear and torment I'd been through, I suddenly felt the need to speak.

'Stop!' I yelled angrily and all eyes turned towards me. The legionaries came to an abrupt halt, almost crashing into one another in the slippery mud.

'This site is sacred to the Dobunni. No foreign enemy may enter this cave!' I glared defiantly at Suetonius, daring him to cross me.

To my surprise, Suetonius merely bowed gallantly. He kept his eyes fixed upon me however as he waved his men back under the trees where he too joined them in a feeble attempt to keep dry. Even attempting to set up one of their tents would have been impossible in this blustering wind.

Gaius led me toward the back of the cave where it was a little warmer, and I could change out of my wet clothes in some privacy at least.

'Is that true, what you said?' he asked, removing his cloak which was absolutely drenched and hanging it over a nearby rock.

'Is what true?' I replied, pulling a blanket snugly about me.

Gaius laughed. 'About this cave being sacred,' he said.

'I don't know,' I answered truthfully, seating myself down and leaning back against the cave wall. 'We always used to imagine it so, Antur and I, when we were children. We found some bones here once, skulls and the like. They may or may not have even been Dobunni. We came here a lot when we were children,' I added nostalgically. 'This was our special place.'

Dobunni or not, my bluff had obviously fooled Suetonius. I felt as if I'd achieved some small yet meaningless victory at least; a small triumph.

Gaius sat down beside me, pulling up an extra blanket. 'So, it's more a case of likely to be sacred to Dana and Antur, eh?' he said with a laugh as he placed his arms around me.

I smiled contentedly, snuggling up against his warm body. Gaius reached across and pulled the blanket up around my shoulders. He looked thoughtful for a moment.

Talking of Antur had started me wondering. 'Gaius,' I said worriedly. 'What happened to Antur? Did you find him? Is he all right?'

Gaius was silent for a moment. A dark expression crossed his face and he frowned slightly. 'I'm afraid Suetonius found him first,' he replied gravely.

'Antur!' I gasped, immediately sitting up.

'He's okay,' Gaius assured me hurriedly, 'but he'd been beaten before I got to him.'

I let out a cry of despair.

'He'll be fine,' Gaius assured me, giving me a hug. 'He's a tough one, your Antur. Don't worry. He'll be safely back at Dolebury by now.'

I gazed towards the cave mouth, the driving rain still coming down in torrents. I could just about see Suetonius and the legionaries looking decidedly miserable and shivering beneath a large oak tree.

Serves them right for hurting Antur, I thought.

Gaius saw me staring at them. I could feel my hatred of the Roman enemy returning for the first time in the ten years I had been with Gaius.

'I hope they all die of the cold!' I snapped vehemently.

'You know,' he began, 'there are some good men out there, many I trained myself. The legionaries,' he shrugged, 'they just follow orders.'

'Suetonius then,' I corrected, 'if he's responsible for giving that order to hurt Antur!'

'He's not normally that bad—it's the Roman way—and before you say any more, I know it's not always the best way.' Gaius heaved a heavy sigh. 'We could do with him on our side at the trial, Dana.'

I was still not convinced, but after a moment's thought reluctantly I relented. 'Tell Suetonius they can come into the cave then,' I said.

'Are you sure?' Gaius enquired.

'No,' I answered honestly. 'But do it anyway.'

Gaius stood up.

'Tell them to leave their weapons outside though, eh?' I added hastily. 'Sacred ground and all that!' I decided to stick with my theory that the skeletons and skulls were ancestral. Best to show some respect, just in case. The Romans wouldn't know any more than we would whether they were Dobunni or not. Gaius nodded and walked outside into the rain to deliver the message.

Suetonius, like many of his predecessors, had come into office with "trumpets blaring and banners raised", instantly instigating many changes in order to align things to his way of thinking and fully expecting such changes to be carried out practically overnight. He treated his appointment as Governor of Britannia as if it was one long continuing battle. His rather heavy-handed attitude finally mellowed after about six weeks as Suetonius became more settled in his new position, however he still retained the tendency to use a "sledgehammer to crack a nut". This was perfectly apparent at this precise moment in time. As Gaius had previously observed, he had brought an entire Army, consisting of a complete century of soldiers, in order to capture but one girl—me.

Governor Suetonius Paullinus strolled slowly over towards us, attempting to wring the rainwater out of his wet robes.

'I'm not your enemy,' he reiterated solemnly as he approached, gazing down upon us both. 'Look Gaius Julius,' he continued sincerely. 'I will help Julia Dana in whatever way I can, but you have to understand that I must remain impartial during the proceedings. I cannot be seen to take sides.'

'I just wonder why you're taking a personal interest in this at all?' Gaius questioned a little sarcastically. 'After all, it's hardly a matter for the Governor of Britannia to concern himself with now, is it?'

If he wanted Suetonius on our side, impartial or not, he was hardly going the right way about it I thought.

Gaius glared resentfully up at Suetonius and Suetonius took a deep breath, clearly exasperated by Gaius' continuing manner, his patience beginning to wear thin.

'Ever since the murder… the death,' he corrected himself, 'of Vecilius Lascivus, the men have become unsettled, notably the Twentieth Legion mostly, and what concerns the men concerns me. I cannot lead them into battle, especially through the mountainous terrain of the Ordovices, with doubts and uncertainties. I must have total dedication.'

Suetonius paused for a moment, wiping the droplets of water from off his face with his already dampened sleeve. 'All they ask is for justice to be done.'

'You mean Dana's life?' Gaius snapped brusquely.

'No, no, not at all,' Suetonius objected promptly. 'Vecilius' own century of men perhaps, but no more than that. Most would be happy to see a fair trial take place,' he continued. 'Whatever the result, guilty or innocent, justice will have been served.' Suetonius glanced at me and smiled compassionately. 'You, of all people, should know that, Gaius,' he added patiently.

Gaius averted his eyes, somewhat disconcerted. He pursed his lips together out of sheer frustration. It was unlike him to be so bitter. He was clearly feeling uncomfortable in Suetonius' presence, which was unusual in itself. Indeed, from the first day they had met, the two of them had got along famously, Gaius coming up with ideas and strategies which would parallel the governor's own.

I had to wonder what exactly had gone on between them during Gaius' brief visit back to Viroconium which had made him so bitter, and had given him cause to resign.

'Well, if you'll excuse me,' Suetonius said politely. 'I think I'll get some rest.'

Gaius watched him intently as he walked over to a quiet corner of the cave where Suetonius then sat down and closed his eyes, seemingly oblivious to all else.

It wasn't as if there was an awful lot of space to find a quiet corner in, what with the Marcus' horse just inside the cave entrance and half a dozen legionaries all spread about. The entire situation could almost have been comical if it wasn't so distressing.

'I still have to wonder why Suetonius bothered to lead the search for you personally,' Gaius pondered, gazing thoughtfully across at the sleeping Suetonius. 'He must have followed me all the way from Viroconium.'

I allowed myself a smile of amusement and looked up at Gaius fondly as I snuggled down for some much-needed sleep myself. 'Isn't it obvious?' I replied. Gaius just gazed at me in puzzlement. 'You're his favourite.'

Morning arrived all too quickly for my liking. I awoke to see Gaius, smiling down at me as I lay, my head upon his lap.

Gazing bleary-eyed across at the cave entrance, I noted that the rain had finally ceased, the morning sun shining brightly down and onto the clearing beyond the cave mouth.

'The rain stopped some time ago,' Gaius remarked softly, gently caressing my hair.

I could see Suetonius and the legionaries outside, waiting anxiously to be moving off. Gaius' horse had been brought up along with another for Suetonius.

'Suetonius let you sleep on,' Gaius continued. 'I don't think he had the heart to wake you.'

The journey began with Suetonius collecting his cavalry escort that he'd left at the start of the track through the woods where he'd captured Antur, having followed him out of Dolebury.

While Antur had staunchly refused to reveal my whereabouts, Suetonius had then decided to use him as bait. It seemed ironic that the Romans should go to so much trouble when all they needed to do was to follow the track. They may have found the rock shelter, but then again it was extremely well hidden, and as Gaius had commented earlier, they just had to do things "the Roman way".

When Gaius had come upon Anturiaethus, he had found him tethered to a tree and looking as if he'd been beaten at least a few times for his refusal to comply. Gaius had agreed to lead Suetonius to me, provided that they release Antur immediately and let him return safely to Dolebury. This he had done, despite Antur's protestations to the contrary.

Although Gaius had mentioned to Suetonius that he was about to take me back to Viroconium himself anyway, and that the food supplies which Antur had brought with him were in fact for the journey back, Suetonius had still insisted on a military escort.

'I want to see Antur,' I stated as we neared the trackway that led to Dolebury. I sat behind Gaius, Marcus' mare in tow, not wishing to burden her with any weight given the injury she had sustained from the wolves.

Gaius reined his horse to a stop and Suetonius pulled up alongside.

'What's the hold up?' he asked at once.

'Dana wishes to see Antur,' Gaius replied. 'The one you beat and tortured,' he added bluntly.

'Legionaries, halt!' Suetonius called to the escort in front. He heaved an impatient sigh. 'We haven't time for pleasantries and visits to kith and kin,' he retorted sharply. 'And I think 'tortured' is a little exaggerated.'

'I don't,' Gaius snapped.

'I want to see him!' I insisted. 'I'm not going any further till I do.' I released my hold around Gaius' waist and slid off the horse. 'I want to see what you did!'

'There, see?' Gaius said to Suetonius. 'She'll cause you no end of trouble until she gets what she wants.' He grinned down at me mischievously. 'I ought to know!'

Suetonius folded his arms across his chest, impatient to continue the journey.

'Look,' Gaius added diplomatically, ''tis but a few miles from here. It will only be a short diversion and will take just a little extra time, but it will be worth it, besides which I think you owe it to Antur.'

Suetonius sighed wearily. 'Very well, so long as we can then get a move on.'

Gaius offered a hand and I climbed back up onto the horse.

We rode in silence and eventually arrived at the massive entrance gates to be greeted by the sentry on watch. We had to wait outside while he went and conferred with chief Eber. Suetonius was getting impatient. The sentry returned sometime later with strict instructions not to let any Romans, except for Gaius of course, through the gates. Everyone now knew what had happened, and they had seen the injuries done to Antur by the Romans and their governor. My people sounded as if they were on the verge of starting another war, which was the last thing anyone wanted.

While the sentry and Suetonius were arguing, Antur suddenly appeared at the entrance. Suetonius instantly became silent and he and the legionaries backed away, content to wait a little way further down the sloping pathway.

Gaius too backed off somewhat, giving us some space.

I ran up to Antur. He was leaning heavily upon a thick wooden staff, his left leg having a large splint strapped around it, and it was completely bandaged from thigh to ankle, his face cut and bruised. He was almost unrecognisable. I halted in shock, staring at him wide-eyed.

'Now you can complement me on how dreadful I look,' he said wryly, attempting a smile but finding it too painful.

'Oh, Antur,' I wept, gently stroking his cheek with an outstretched hand.

'It's not as bad as it looks,' he stated plainly. 'Anyway,' he continued, 'a good warrior has to have a few scars.'

'A few!' I ran my fingers lightly over a deep cut upon his cheekbone.

Tenderly, he took my hand in his. 'I'll be all right,' he said softly. 'This is what your Roman friends have done,' releasing my hand and caressing the back of my neck. 'Their ways are not our ways, Dana,' he added bitterly. 'They never will be.'

I was beginning to think that Antur may be right about this. 'Antur, I'm so frightened!' I stammered, on the point of tears.

'Your Gaius won't let them hurt you,' he remarked, 'but if he fails, they'll have me to deal with and I swear I'll take on every damn Roman myself if I have to, one at a time or all together!' he glared across at where Suetonius was waiting.

'So, you're going to take on the entire Roman Army, on your own?' I teased in reply, sniffing a little and managing a brief smile.

'Of course!' he replied boldly, feigning insult. 'Why? Don't you think I could?'

I smiled up at him warmly, 'Oh, I know you could. You're my hero!' I teased in return but meaning every word. 'Always my hero.' A tear ran down my cheek and he wiped it away gently with the palm of his hand.

We gazed across at Suetonius who was shuffling his feet impatiently. He then signalled to Gaius who started to walk back up the track towards us.

'Looks like time is up,' Antur stated plainly. He pulled me in closer and we stood, foreheads touching. 'You should have gone with my idea for Hibernia,' he added softly. Slowly, he moved in closer still, until our lips brushed lightly before kissing me firmly on the cheek as he saw Gaius approach. 'At least I got to kiss you properly at last!' he whispered in my ear.

I stood back and laughed quietly, a little embarrassed.

'Thought that would make you smile!' he retorted with a half grin.

'We have to go,' Gaius reported quietly, seeming as if he didn't wish to intrude. 'I'm sorry, Antur, for what they did to you,' he added, sounding quite ashamed of his compatriots. 'I don't agree with all the things we have to do.'

Antur turned to face him. 'It's not for you to apologise,' he retorted brusquely, glaring across at Suetonius.

'How is the leg?' Gaius enquired softly.

'Painful!' Antur replied plainly. He frowned, thoughtful for a moment. 'It will heal,' he added with confidence and determination. 'As soon as I'm able, I'll follow you up to Viroconium.'

'Are you sure?' Gaius asked in concern. 'It's a long journey.'

'Of course I'm sure!' Antur responded at once, sounding almost insulted. 'You don't think I'm going to sit here and do nothing do you? And you,' Antur continued, turning to me. 'You just give them hell! You're good at that!' He clasped hands with Gaius and we began to walk away.

'Hey, Gaius!' Antur called after him loudly, obviously intending for the Romans to overhear. We both halted and turned around. 'If you fail to get Dana free, we'll go with my original plan, eh?'

Gaius smiled, and then he waved and saluted in response.

Suetonius was instantly alongside, curious. 'Oh, and what plan would that be?' he enquired sharply.

Neither of us said a word.

Legion VIIII

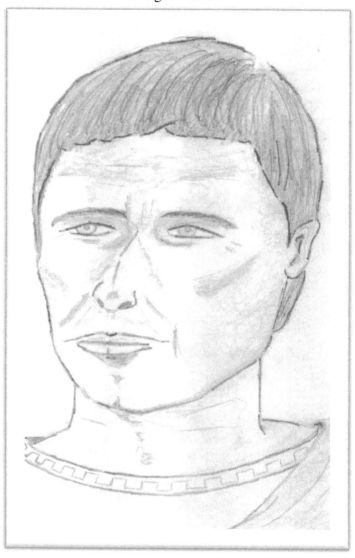

Petulius Cerialis

Chapter Eight
AD 58 to AD 59
Viroconium,
Shropshire

The long haul back to Viroconium proved to be very tedious, but it was far less hurried than the journey southward. At least we got to stay in proper accommodation once we reached Glevum Legionary Base. I only wish we could have halted there. It felt strange, like going home, but we weren't home and we couldn't remain at Glevum. We had to move on, and yet there was our old house just outside the walls, and there was the Thracian Base to the south nearby, yet without any actual Thracians, and they weren't ours to command anymore.

Suetonius left the legionaries at Glevum having collected them from here on the way down. This made our return journey faster although it was hampered further still by Marcus' mare. While her injury, Gaius had assured me, was superficial, I did not wish to push her any harder than necessary. I took great pleasure in frustrating Suetonius by insisting on a slower pace. Clearly, he was irritated by the continual delays and I had to wonder just how long his patience would last.

Finally, after a quite a few days had passed, we arrived at Viroconium. The soldiers now gathered around us in tight formation as we began to dismount. Small groups of legionaries were beginning to stare, halting in their duties and muttering amongst themselves. They were soon to be reprimanded and ordered back to work by their commanding officers.

Marcus came running over. He approached Governor Suetonius and saluted, requesting permission to speak with us. Suetonius signalled to the cavalry and they let him pass. The Decurion in charge however was keeping a sharp eye on Marcus as he walked over towards us.

'Gaius, thank the gods!' he exclaimed, clasping arms with his life-long friend before glancing across at me and smiling broadly.

'Are you all right?' he enquired.

I nodded and smiled nervously. 'Just about, thank you Marcus. It is good to see you again.' I felt conspicuous with everyone looking on.

'And you, my lady,' he replied gallantly.

'I'm sorry I stole your horse,' I added loudly, hoping that those nearby would overhear. I did not wish Marcus to be implicated in any way, so I tried to make it appear as if I'd merely taken his horse rather than that he had loaned her to me.

'That's enough talk!' The Decurion snapped as an armed escort of legionaries was brought across to lead us away.

'No, please?' I begged. 'I must show Marcus… his horse's leg, it was injured.'

'Quickly then!' the Decurion snapped sharply.

'Down here,' I said, leading Marcus to the mare's rear fetlock and showing him the injury. 'I'm sorry. It was the wolves.'

As Marcus knelt down to examine the fetlock, I whispered urgently in his ear. 'Will you let my people know all that happens here and keep them informed, please?'

The Decurion moved closer, suspicious, and Marcus stood up promptly.

'Don't worry,' Marcus said with a sly wink of his eye. 'She'll be fine.'

The Decurion then ushered Gaius and me towards the waiting escort.

'Hey! No need to push!' Gaius reprimanded him angrily as the Decurion shoved me hard between the shoulders. Suddenly, the legionaries began to close in and drag me away from Gaius. I struggled against them, helplessly, as Gaius tried to reach me.

'Gaius! Gaius!' I cried out desperately.

Gaius marched straight up to Suetonius. I could see him debating angrily with the governor for a few moments, and then Suetonius called the legionaries off. They released their hold upon me and I ran over to Gaius, terrified. We clung on to each other tightly, the tears rolling down my cheeks.

'Escort them to their house,' Suetonius ordered the legionaries sharply. 'Gently,' he added in afterthought. 'And I want armed guards posted at all the exits. No one's to be allowed in or out save at my command, do you understand?'

'Yes, sir!' they saluted in unison.

Upon reaching the house, we stepped gratefully over the threshold and closed the door firmly behind us. I wished that we could just shut the whole world out like that, forever, and that none of this nightmare would ever have taken place.

Goilladyn, Caitilin and Aine couldn't do enough, running around and fetching food, wine and a change of clothing for us both. While Gaius filled Goilladyn in on recent events, I curled up on the bed and drifted off into a restless sleep.

I awoke the following morning to the sound of Gaius' voice. He sounded angry and annoyed.

'This is ridiculous!' he shouted as I wandered down the stairs. 'How can I conduct any sort of investigation if I can't even get out of my own house?' A startled young legionary was standing on the doorstep before him. 'You tell Suetonius, for me to be able to legally defend my wife, I have to be able to come and go as I please!'

The legionary looked undecided for a moment, and then signalling for another legionary to take his place, he ran off to find Suetonius and Gaius slammed the door hard behind him.

Gaius breathed a sigh of relief as he walked up to me. 'Don't worry,' he said, taking my hand. 'Everything will be all right. We'll soon have this all sorted out.'

I smiled gratefully and he kissed my hand. 'I know,' I replied, although I had many misgivings.

The legionary returned shortly after breakfast and Gaius left the house to see what he could find out, having been granted his liberty to come and go as he pleased, and intending to take a look around the wine cellar where Vecilius had died. He returned about midday, somewhat disappointed, as he was unable to search the cellar at all. Suetonius had it cordoned off.

Yet, despite being unable to search for the missing dagger, Gaius still seemed very confident about the eventual outcome of the trial. Meanwhile, the delays and waiting for the trial to commence were beginning to take a toll on my health, although I tried to hide it. I had very little, if any, appetite, and as a consequence I was beginning to lose weight dramatically. Sleep came in snatches and I was continually on edge. I worried too about Antur, who had not arrived here yet, and wondered if Marcus had heard any news from Dolebury.

As the day of the trial drew near, the might and power that was Rome saw fit to take matters into its own hands. The Senate, in its infinite wisdom, was not only impatient for the advance into Cambria to begin, but they saw the trial of a native woman as a possible rallying point for further rebel attacks. Added to which, matters with Rome had been further influenced by the fact that Vecilius apparently had an uncle on the Senate, no doubt the main reason for their involvement in the trial at all.

It was early morning and I had been aroused from a restless sleep by the sound of raised voices. Quickly I secured my robe about me before carefully and quietly slipping out of the bedroom and onto the landing.

Governor Suetonius Paullinus stood below, his expression grave.

'I don't understand,' Gaius remarked brusquely. 'You assured us that everything was fine!' He was pacing up and down angrily, clenching and unclenching his fists.

'I know, I know I did, but the rebel resistance is escalating,' Suetonius explained, attempting to justify himself. 'The Senate has demanded a speedy end to all this. They insist that we concentrate on the campaign into Cambria.'

'You can't let Rome use Dana as some sort of scapegoat!' Gaius debated hotly. 'There must be something you can do? You can't just let her die!'

I froze in stunned silence. Was I to be condemned to death before the trial had even begun? For the first time since I'd known him, Suetonius Paullinus seemed lost for words.

'I'm sorry,' he said at last. 'There's nothing I can do.' Suetonius stepped out of the door. 'It's out of my hands now,' he added apologetically with a shrug of his shoulders.

'Then help us find the knife,' Gaius called after him. Suetonius halted and looked back over his shoulder expectantly. 'At least help us do that. If we could find the dagger, if we had some proof that Vecilius had threatened Dana,' Gaius continued. 'Would that make a difference?'

Suetonius nodded, scratching his chin thoughtfully. 'Perhaps,' he replied.

Once he had departed I crept slowly down the stairs as Gaius slammed the front door furiously behind him. He turned about sharply and I stared at him transfixed for a moment. I was not used to seeing Gaius this angry. In fact, it was rare to see him lose his temper at all.

'What's wrong?' I asked innocently as he came over towards me. He had no idea how long I had been standing there and I didn't wish to worry him. 'I've never seen you so angry before.'

'It's all right,' Gaius assured me, taking a deep breath to steady him. He stroked my cheek gently. 'Everything's fine.'

That afternoon, as a last resort, Suetonius allowed a thorough search of the cellar to take place. Although the cellar was the last place right now that I wanted to be, Gaius had insisted that I accompany them seeing as I was the only person who would have any idea where the *pugio* could have flown to.

So, with four armed guards, two in front and two behind, and with Suetonius himself in charge, we headed down the cellar steps. Suetonius had brought the legionaries along not only as guards but also as useful witnesses should the dagger be found.

It was a nerve-wracking experience just returning to that cellar. I had to keep reminding myself that Vecilius was no longer there, and while the blood stain on the floor helped to reinforce this fact, it only added to my discomfort. I was feeling faint just looking at it.

Gaius took me by the hand, seeing me falter for a moment, and led me close to where Vecilius had fallen.

'Before we start,' he began gently, 'where exactly were you standing in relation to Vecilius?'

I gazed around, trying to get my bearings for a moment. 'Over there, I think,' I responded shakily, pointing to the location. 'Up against some urns.' Everything had been cleaned up, the broken amphorae and urns removed—perhaps the dagger was too?

Gaius nodded thoughtfully. 'And he was facing you when he fell?' he continued logically.

'Yes,' I replied, closing my eyes briefly in concentration. 'I slashed his arm and the knife just flew from his hand.' I gazed about trying to recall the details. Damn it, it could have gone anywhere if it was still there at all! 'Over there somewhere,' I added, pointing vaguely. 'And then I heard it skitter across the floor.'

All right, then let's make a start by moving some of these storage urns,' Suetonius suggested, calling two of the guards over to assist.

'We should take a section each,' Gaius said, beginning a methodical search of the middle section close to the wall.

I joined Gaius in searching that section while the legionaries were paired together to take a section each, and Suetonius a further area.

Having searched endlessly for quite some time, I was beginning to become despondent when suddenly I spied something glinting behind some of the amphorae that were housed in a corner toward the rear. Bending down to take a closer look, my heart skipped a beat and I called out excitedly.

'Gaius! Over here, quickly!'

Both Gaius and Suetonius came rushing over. Suetonius motioned for all four guards to approach and had one of them move the amphorae aside. There at the back, almost completely hidden, lay the *pugio.*

Governor Suetonius bent down to retrieve the weapon. He turned the dagger over in his hands as he arose smiling.

Gaius breathed a sigh of relief. 'That … makes a difference,' he remarked drily. 'Doesn't it, sir?'

Now that we had some tangible proof that Vecilius had in fact withdrawn his *pugio,* the trial became more or less straightforward, as far as a Roman Law Court could be.

I was made to "dress down" for the trial, and so I wore a simple shift dress that was due for a wash, my hair left loose and uncombed. Gaius had said this would gain some sympathy perhaps from the judges who were called *indices.* Gaius, on the other hand, was dressed impressively with his full regalia and his very best toga.

I ran my fingers through my long hair, attempting to free it of knots. 'Can't I at least comb my hair?' I asked Gaius.

He walked over to me, gently helping to brush some of the stray locks back off my face with his fingertips. 'I like how you look with your hair down,' he said, smiling.

I looked up at him in astonishment. 'Now you tell me!' I replied with a laugh. 'You give me combs to pin my hair up with, have it braided like your Roman ladies, and now you tell me you prefer it down!'

'Well, I didn't like to say.'

It was a very public trial, and as it turned out, it was Vecilius' uncle who had filed a suit against me thus summoning me to the court.

Suetonius was seated high above the courtroom and the judges seated on benches below him. Some spectators stood around the edge of the room, many local people who were just inquisitive and there for the "show", and some of Vecilius' own men, who were obviously not on duty and intent on revenge. I spied Marcus amongst them, and he smiled and waved cordially. Although Marcus' presence was reassuring, I felt absolutely terrified, despite the finding of the *pugio,* seated as I was in the centre of the room for all to see.

Suddenly, there came a loud commotion outside the doorway to the court, with a lot of shouting and yelling. The doors burst open, and to my surprise and delight, there stood Antur, together with a group of armed warriors, some Roman guards forcing their way in behind them.

'What is this?' Suetonius raised his voice above the cacophony. As governor, he was the presiding chairman of the court.

'We have come to see our tribeswoman set free!' It was Antur's voice. A guard seized his arm and he struggled against him. 'We do not ascribe to Roman "justice"!' He almost spat the word back at Suetonius.

It was fortunate that Suetonius recognised Antur, who was leaning heavily upon his wooden staff, but at least he was here.

Suetonius bid him enter and find space for him and his comrades to stand. He then called for calm. 'Very well, but sheath your weapons if you are to enter here,' he said, waving the armed guards aside, and they returned to their posts outside the door.

The warriors did as they were bid. Antur smiled across at me and waved a little too enthusiastically, but I began to feel a bit better now that he was here.

After Gaius had given his introduction, he then began to relate to the court what had happened before the crime was committed. 'Only recently, Vecilius Lascivus was accused of raping one of the local native women.'

'Objection,' the prosecution interrupted, 'the woman was a whore! He was cleared of this accusation.'

'Silence!' Suetonius called out. 'Over-ruled! Please continue Caecinianus.'

Gaius bowed formerly and went on to explain how and more importantly, why the crime was committed. 'Nevertheless,' he said, 'the accusation had been made, and his name tainted. I believe that Vecilius Lascivus wanted revenge. He wanted revenge for the slur against him, against his character. I believe, in fact I know,' Gaius added dramatically, waving an arm in an exaggerated manner, 'that he has been looking for a reason, an excuse, to attack my client, my wife, since the very day they first met.'

Gaius then presented his "proofs", including the *pugio* itself. A picture had been drawn, painted upon a piece of cloth, showing the layout of the cellar and giving mine and Vecilius' positions, plus that of the newly discovered dagger. This was passed along for all the judges to see.

'After my wife had narrowly escaped death at the hands of Vecilius Lascivus, she was then hounded by this lynch mob to such an extent that she felt it necessary to flee hundreds of miles away,' Gaius accused, pointing an angry finger at the soldiers concerned. 'Cold, hungry, and hounded by wolves, it was a journey that could very well have proved fatal!'

Antur and his friends began to jeer, with many of the locals joining in. After a moment, Gaius held up his hands for silence as he began to sum up.

'Vecilius Lascivus was a soldier, but more than that, he was a ruthless soldier,' he stated plainly. 'He was a soldier who liked to fight—lived to fight—and we prevented that,' he added with a shrug, spinning round and holding out one hand to indicate him and me. 'You see, Dana and I have something unique,' Gaius added as he walked across to me and took my hand in his, entwining my fingers tightly with his own. 'Our love has prevented battles, stopped wars. Something Vecilius could never hope to achieve. We ensured peace between us Romans and the local native population, the "Celts".'

It was eerily silent for a moment and I wondered whether Gaius' last words had been completely understood. Had he exaggerated a little too much? And then, surprisingly, applause began to reverberate around the room. Suetonius eventually held up his hands for silence, and then Gaius' time was up.

Suetonius called for any witnesses to come forth. Marcus was called to give his account of events, during which it was inferred that he had, in fact, assisted in my escape. Even though Marcus and I had both vigorously disputed this claim, although we knew it to be true, this slight against Marcus' character had been made.

The remainder of the trial went completely over my head as the intricacies of Roman Law took control. In my extremely nervous state, I found it difficult to concentrate on what was being said, the entire proceedings taking on a kind of surreal atmosphere as I tearfully recounted the death of Vecilius.

The speaker for the prosecution was quick to react. He began by bringing up my previous attempt to kill Vecilius with the knife at the *canabae*, and produced witnesses to this effect.

'And why, I ask, was the defendant armed and carrying about upon her person, a sword? Every citizen knows this to be illegal in itself, and yet, there she was, brandishing this sword,' he made an overly dramatic gesture, sweeping his arm around with a flourish, 'obviously intent upon slaying Centurion Vecilius Lascivus with this same weapon!'

'Rubbish! Lies! All lies!' Cried out Antur and his assembled cheer squad. 'Dana is a Dobunni woman. Dobunni women are not trained in the sword!'

It was fortunate that Gaius had taken my sword back to our home at Viroconium when he'd returned to check on the situation, so it had not been presented amongst the "proofs".

'This is true,' Gaius interceded. 'And "if" there was ever a sword, may I ask where this weapon is now?'

'Well, she was carrying one when Vecilius was cut through,' the prosecution accused. 'She must have got it from somewhere, and someone must have been teaching her!' He glared across at Gaius who was forced to back down.

'If she was carrying a sword, then it was in fear of her life,' Antur yelled back. 'She knew that this soldier of yours would attack her. You have seen the dagger, which is proof enough!'

'Vecilius Lascivus may very well have withdrawn his dagger in order to defend himself!' The prosecution retaliated.

'Against a mere girl? More lies! What sort of soldiers do you have here; men or mice?' Antur was gaining ground. 'Perhaps the wound was self-inflicted!' The court erupted in raucous laughter and the prosecution was then forced to withdraw.

'Silence!' Suetonius called out. 'I will have silence! Enough banter.' He turned to address the judges below him.

'You have heard the evidence; you have seen the evidence,' he breathed a heavy sigh. 'It is time now for you to consider your verdict, and in so doing may I remind you of the situation in Cambria at present. We don't wish to fuel any discord there,' he added with some emphasis.

A subtle hint I thought.

The judges began to whisper and debate amongst themselves. It seemed to take forever, and then finally they seemed to reach a decision and they placed their voting tablets into a jar. This was then handed up to the clerk of the court who had the job of counting the votes. After but a short time, which seemed as an eternity to me, this was finally done and the result was handed up to Suetonius.

Suetonius looked at the result, and then he smiled.

'The court finds the defendant absolved of the accusations made against her, but she shall be fined the princely sum of two denarius for the carrying a sword illegally. Other than that,' he added, 'she is free to go.'

Such a commotion then erupted all around, both cheering and arguing, the noise was quite deafening. Suetonius waved his arms for silence.

'And,' he yelled out, waiting a moment for the cacophony to die down. 'I should like to add that in the case of the deceased; Vecilius Lascivus, is seen to have brought about his own demise by his continuing bravado and disrespect. This court is closed.'

Suetonius stepped down looking as if he was pleased it was all over with. He wasn't the only one.

Gaius gave me the biggest hug, and Marcus came running over. Antur was trying to make his way through the throngs with some difficulty, the guards continually pushing him back.

'I knew we'd do it!' Marcus exclaimed, grinning broadly.

'Oh, did you?' Gaius replied. 'I am honoured by your faith in my talents.'

'No, no, it's not that,' he said, winking slyly. 'Not that I don't have faith in your expert skills,' he added hastily with a mock bow. 'I bribed the judges, well, some of them anyway.'

'What?' Gaius responded in astonishment. He raised a questioning eyebrow and Marcus gave an embarrassed shrug of his shoulders before explaining further.

'Oh, only the ones with the most influence!'

Tears of joy and relief were cascading endlessly down my cheeks. I felt weak at the knees and needed Gaius for support. Antur caught up with us outside, and it was only when the fresh air hit me that I blacked out completely.

I awoke in a daze a short while later back at our house to find an anxious Gaius gazing down at me as I lay upon the bed. The physician had been brought across and was sitting perched on the edge of the bedside.

Aine immediately came bustling into the room carrying a jug full of water, a cup and a towel. She hastily poured out some of the water into the cup, spilling a little on the floor as she did so, and then she handed the cup to Gaius.

'Here, drink this,' he said, gently helping me to sit up and pressing the cup to my lips. I took a few sips and then slumped back onto the cushions, smiling gratefully.

'I'm all right,' I said weakly. 'I just suddenly feel so tired.'

'Hmm, well that's only to be expected,' the physician remarked as he arose. 'Well, there's not much I can do here.'

He scribbled something upon a wax tablet and handed it to Gaius, then gave his robe a sharp tug to straighten it out. 'Get this made up,' he said, gruffly. 'And you, young lady, you get some sleep,' he added, turning toward Gaius as he took his leave. 'If I might have a private word with you?'

'Of course,' Gaius responded, and he followed the physician out. Aine damped the towel with the remaining water from the jug and placed it gently across my forehead. She stayed with me until Gaius had returned and then she left us alone.

'What did the doctor say?' I enquired sleepily, and not really all that interested. 'Did he say anything else?'

Gaius smiled warmly but failed to hide the concern upon his face. 'He said, you need to eat more,' he berated me, removing the towel and tenderly smoothing back the wisps of wet hair. 'He also said to rest,' he added. 'You've nothing to worry about now. It's all over.'

Despite the trial now being over and done with, I still had very little appetite, for food or for life, and now the pain in my stomach had returned.

Perhaps it was hunger? Who knows, but I didn't much care.

Antur had stayed with us for a short time after the trial. I could tell he was concerned, as was Gaius. They didn't know that I'd overheard them talking one morning when they thought me still to be sleeping.

'I've only seen her like this once before,' Antur was saying to Gaius. 'That was when we lost Worlebury. Dana wouldn't eat. She wouldn't even talk to anyone for days.' He paused slightly, and I heard his footsteps move towards the doorway. 'I should have put my arms around her then,' he berated himself, 'but I didn't, so Dafydd did, and he took her from me—and then you came.'

At this point, I thought I'd better let them know I had awakened; Antur could be so temperamental, and so I stretched noisily. Gaius instantly poured some mulled wine into a cup and brought it over to the bedside. I struggled to sit up but managed somehow, refusing assistance.

'Here, drink this.'

I took a sip, but would take no more, my hands trembling slightly.

It was to take some time before I would manage to regain my full strength. Food was brought up to me on a tray, but often it would be returned to the kitchen untouched.

Gaius would look on in concern as he sat beside me, a worried expression on his face as he tried to encourage me to eat a morsel or two.

While Antur was still with us, the winter snows began to arrive somewhat earlier than expected, and were quite heavy in parts, making it difficult for him to depart. Meanwhile Suetonius had spent the remainder of the winter preparing his Army to move out at the first hint of spring.

'He means to cut off the rebels at their source,' Gaius announced one day. 'The druids at Mona.'

'What!' I exclaimed in alarm, sitting bolt upright upon my sickbed. 'But, Dafydd is there!'

'Not anymore!' A familiar voice rang out suddenly.

'Dafydd!' I was so overjoyed, and relieved, to see him.

He stood in the doorway, leaning casually against the frame, arms folded. He looked so different now to how he used to when we were younger, his short neat hair was long and slightly silvered, and with weathered lines upon his face.

'Dafydd,' Gaius greeted him cordially. 'Come in, please. Perhaps you can shed some light on the goings on within the druid circle?'

'Not much, I'm afraid,' he replied.

'But the druids are healers and lawmakers,' Antur stated plainly, strolling into the bedroom and pushing his way rudely past Dafydd as if he wasn't even there. 'They are the one source that can bring all the tribes together.'

'Glad you appreciate my value at last,' Dafydd responded coyly.

Antur ignored him.

'But don't you see, that is just it,' Gaius continued. 'That is what we fear—we Romans—that they will unite the tribes, against us!'

'Precisely why I'm here,' Dafydd replied. 'Oh, I heard about the trial by the way, but I couldn't get here in time anyway. There was just too much going on at Mona.' His brow furrowed as he scratched at his chin, deep in thought. 'Nevertheless, I did make sure I had news of the proceedings and I'm pleased it all turned out well,' he added with a wry smile.

'So are we,' Gaius said, gesturing for Dafydd be seated.

Dafydd walked over to the side of the bed and sat down on the chair that was placed alongside. 'There's something going on that I just can't quite fathom,' he continued, pushing his long hair back from off his face. He looked thoughtful for a moment and then he added, 'Call it intuition if you like. Only the fully-fledged druids, the elders, are privileged to such information. I don't know what it is,' he shrugged, 'but something big is brewing.' And then he smiled slowly as he took my hand in greeting. 'So, what's all this about then?' he asked, noticing yet another untouched lunch tray.

'The result of the trial,' Gaius replied, folding his arms across his chest. 'She needs to eat,' he added sternly.

'Ah,' Dafydd remarked. 'Then, we'll have to do something about that!'

'Well, if you're going to play doctor, I think that I should leave for Dolebury now,' Antur announced. 'I might just be able to make it there before the next snowfall.'

'Oh Antur, must you?' I implored.

'I know when I am outnumbered,' he added wryly, gazing from Dafydd to Gaius. 'Don't worry, I'll see you before I go,' his eyes resting on me for a moment before he strolled out of the room. Gaius followed him out.

'So, what about some of this food,' Dafydd said.

'I'm fine,' I argued back. 'I just need to rest.'

'You also need to eat,' Dafydd berated me, reaching across and placing the tray upon my lap. 'Now, don't argue with your doctor. Who's the healer here, me or you?'

'But I'm not hungry... really,' I lied.

'No?'

'Some of it, some of it was making me nauseous,' I added.

'Was it?' his tone softening somewhat.

'And I had this pain. It's gone now.'

After a little while, and some general conversation, Dafydd leant across and kissed me gently on the forehead, and then suddenly upon the lips.

Surprised, I tried to sit back further.

'I seem to have done this before,' he whispered softly. 'At Dolebury, eleven years ago. I stole a kiss from you then too,' he recalled, smiling, 'and more,' he added with a mischievous twinkle in his eye.

'Then why did you not stand up to Antur?' I retorted, feeling a little angry and embarrassed at the same time. 'Why did you not fight for me then?'

'Oh, I'm not a fighter,' he replied, gently taking my hand. 'You know that. Perhaps I am better suited to serving the gods.'

'You are the only Dobunni I know who is not a fighter!'

'And that's what you should be doing now,' Dafydd retaliated sharply. 'Fighting! Not lolling around here feeling sorry for yourself.'

Touché! 'If you'd have fought for me all those years ago, we could have been together now, raising chickens or something,' I argued back. And I wouldn't be in this mess, I thought glumly.

'Chickens?' he laughed. 'That would never have satisfied you! You'd have been bored within a week. You're far too adventurous by half.'

I had to agree, he was probably right. And then, there was Gaius, of course. Meeting my Gaius had been the best thing to happen in my entire life, despite our somewhat unusual first encounter.

He asked me a few more questions regarding my health, to which I replied that I'd suffered some pain to my abdomen and that my monthly bleeding had been a little late—no more than that. After a brief examination, Dafydd then deliberated for a moment or two, scratching his chin in deep thought.

Gaius re-entered the room, knocking lightly on the door frame as he did so. 'Everything all right?' he asked.

'Of course,' Dafydd replied, giving my hand a little squeeze before arising from the chair. 'Dana will be fine,' he added, 'but I think you should both know. I believe Dana was with child.'

I was stunned, and the look of surprise on Gaius' face spoke volumes, and then Dafydd's words slowly sunk in. 'Was?' Gaius asked.

'She must have lost the child, what with everything going on, the stress, the horse ride,' Dafydd smiled weakly. 'I'm sorry Gaius; Dana.'

Gaius sat down on the chair. 'Are you sure?'

'Fairly sure, yes,' Dafydd replied. 'Have your physician confirm it if you like.'

'He was here earlier,' Gaius remarked. 'He didn't seem to pick up on anything then.'

'Well,' Dafydd said. 'It just goes to show that he's not as good a healer as I am!' He grinned broadly and headed towards the door. 'I'll make up a potion for Dana,' he continued. 'It will have her back on her feet in no time. Mind if I wait in the *triclinium*?'

'No, no, go right ahead,' Gaius said, and Dafydd strolled out.

'Why didn't you say something?' Gaius asked me as soon as he'd left.

'I didn't know,' I replied. 'Truly I didn't.' I still felt stunned by this revelation, but it did make some kind of sense and Dafydd was probably right I reasoned—he usually was. He had an instinct for these things. Plus, this was not the first time I had miscarried, and now that I thought about it I recognised a few of the symptoms.

'I thought it was just all the worry, and the running; the long horse ride. I'm just as stunned as you are.'

Gaius took my hand tenderly. 'It's okay,' he whispered. 'The important thing is that you are here now, and safe, and we shall have you well again in no time.'

The next day, having taken some of Dafydd's "magic potion" as he called it, I began to pick at a few morsels of food, much to Gaius' relief.

'I'm sorry if I worried you,' I remarked huskily as he took my hand in his. 'I didn't mean to.'

'It's all right,' he said, smiling.

Now that I was on the road to recovery, Dafydd announced that he was heading back down to Dolebury. He didn't feel safe in Mona anymore he'd said.

Although Gaius had officially resigned now from the Roman Army, Suetonius had stated that there was no need for us to vacate the tribune's house for some time yet, seeing as both Legions would soon be heading off for Cambria.

Time would soon pass however, and we knew we'd have to find somewhere else to live by the time that the Legions returned if not before. The Army would grant him some land now that he'd served his twenty-five years' service, but where? And with Dafydd now safely back at Dolebury, my thoughts turned towards home. I pondered on whether we should just go there too, return to hill-fort life, even though years ago I couldn't get away fast enough? One thing was for sure in that neither of us wished to remain at Viroconium, the memories of our life here now well and truly tainted.

Spring finally arrived and before the Army headed off, Governor Suetonius sent for Gaius one last time. He returned a while later from his meeting at the *praetorium,* a dazed look upon his face yet with the hint of a smile. He walked into the

226

triclinium where I was seated, idly picking at a bunch of grapes as I awaited his return.

He sat down heavily on the couch opposite. Gaius looked across at me as I waited expectantly for him to speak, my legs curled up comfortably beneath me.

'Well?' I prompted impatiently. 'What happened?'

'He offered me his house,' Gaius said in astonishment, shaking his head in disbelief and with a look of bewilderment upon his face.

'What?' I enquired, somewhat perplexed and stunned at the same time. 'What do you mean? Where?'

Gaius drew in a deep breath. 'Suetonius, he's given me his house—if I want it,' he continued. 'As Governor of Britannia, he has several villas dotted all around the country for his own personal use,' Gaius explained further. 'He's offered me one of them.'

'A villa, well where? Where is it?' I asked, excitedly, uncurling my legs and sitting bolt upright. I could hardly contain myself.

'It's a fair way from here, at Verulamium.'

'Verulamium?' I repeated slowly as I pondered the thought. 'Do you mean Verlamion?' That was what the native population had called it. 'That's close to Londinium, isn't it?'

'Yes, Verlamion. It's not that far from Londinium,' Gaius confirmed, 'and the villa itself is not overly large. In fact, it is quite new. Suetonius hasn't even had the chance to use it yet.' He leant forward and plucked a grape, popping it into his mouth before continuing. 'It lies atop the original Catuvellauni settlement which was given over to Rome by the Catuvellauni kings.'

Catuvellauni, I thought—that was where Caitilin was from. 'So, have you accepted his offer?'

'I have until he leaves for Cambria in a few days' time to make a decision,' Gaius informed me, 'but I don't want his charity.'

'It's not charity, Gaius,' I remarked, arising from my seat and sitting down next to him. I took his hand warmly in mine.

'I told you—you're his favourite. He's probably trying to make amends for all that has happened.'

Gaius smiled. I don't think either of us realised just how much he did think of Gaius, of both of us really, until this moment. I suppose we were both somewhat overwhelmed by his generous offer. That such a stern, military leader, a man who didn't often show his feelings, should hold Gaius in only the highest esteem, was just so flattering. Surely, it should be the other way around?

'At least there should be plenty of legal work required down there,' Gaius remarked idly, his dream of having his own legal practice now seemingly within his reach. 'The local Britons at Verulamium and Londinium are having trouble with the money-lenders, and the Britons are deep in debt.'

'But that's no good,' I said. 'How are they ever going to be able to pay you if they've no money?'

'Guess I'll have to help them as a kindness and hope they can pay me later,' he replied with a laugh. 'Donations only! But there's also land with the villa; it's a proper working farm too, some several hundred acres, so we could always sell some produce at the *macellum,* and people could repay us with their labour perhaps. Goodness knows we'll need some help with that much land to farm!'

The next few days were spent weighing up the pros and cons of moving to Verulamium. The town itself was in a territory that neither of us was familiar with, yet it seemed to be in an ideal location in which Gaius could set up his law practice, and with the major port of Londinium not far away.

As for myself, I would have been quite content to return to the Mendip, to live out our days farming and hunting the land as my ancestors had done. To run across those hills with the breeze upon my face brought a true sense of freedom and belonging. That much I had missed, it was true. I'd had enough of Roman ways and excitement to last a lifetime, and now all I wanted was some peace and tranquillity.

Had I mentioned this to Gaius, I know he would have forsaken his dream in favour of mine and tried his hand at living the Dobunni way, but I knew how strong his interest in Roman Law was. It was his passion and his dream, and what's more he was good at it. Now that he was free of the restrictions of Roman Army life, he at last had a chance to achieve his life-long ambition. I did not wish to ruin that chance, and no doubt I would enjoy working on the farm and having land of our own.

The day before the Legions were due to depart Gaius informed Suetonius that we would be grateful to accept his offer of the villa—for the time being at least. If it didn't work out, then we could easily retreat to Dolebury, but all things considered the villa sounded perfect.

On the evening, Marcus came to dine with us for the last time at Viroconium. Aine had prepared a banquet fit for a king, with far too much food for just three diners. She must have drained the storeroom dry or spent the entire week's housekeeping in just one day!

The clever girl had even managed to find some imported fruit. There were breads and cakes of every description, and a fine hot stew to warm us as the chill of the night air drew in.

'You're not heading a cavalry unit?' I remarked in surprise as Marcus informed us of his latest piece of news. 'But that's what you're best at.'

Horses were his life and meant just as much to Marcus as law did to Gaius. He would be incomplete without his horses.

Marcus merely shrugged his shoulders in resignation, and then he grinned broadly. 'Suetonius requires more foot soldiers on this mission,' Marcus replied, 'or so he says. All those mountains I expect.' He reached over and picked up a chunk of bread, tearing it in half before taking a large bite. 'So, I've been transferred.'

'And what of your rank?' Gaius asked curiously. 'A centurion rank, surely?'

Marcus appeared a little ill at ease. 'No, not exactly,' he answered slowly. 'I'm to carry the standard of the First Cohort.'

'A *signifier*?' Gaius responded in surprise. 'No longer in command?' He leaned back on the couch and scratched his head in thought while taking a sip of wine. 'Surely, you should have been advanced to *Decurio Princeps* by now?'

Marcus shuffled in his seat uneasily, his eyes downcast.

'Why no longer with the horses?' Gaius pondered.

A sudden thought came into my mind. 'Is it because of the trial, because you helped me to escape?'

'No!' he said a little too sharply. 'No, not at all,' he added. 'It's a great honour, to carry the standard, especially that of the First Cohort. And, I'm only one rank below the *Optio*.'

Both Gaius and I knew that he was bluffing although he had tried to sound as convincing as he could.

'It would have been more of an honour to let you carry the eagle standard,' Gaius observed matter-of-factly. 'If Governor Suetonius had wished to honour you, he should have made you *aquilifer*.' He placed his wine cup down on the table, resting his hands upon his knees as he sized up the situation. 'The First Cohort,' Gaius mused. 'That puts you in the front line. You'll be right in the middle of any fighting.'

'Ha! No worries!' Marcus scoffed. 'In any case, I had my fortune told only yesterday, and she said the portents were good.' He tried to sound convincing, but his expression said otherwise.

'You don't sound too sure about that,' I said worriedly.

'Nonsense! Of course I'm sure,' Marcus retorted smartly. 'See, I have a new charm for luck,' he added, producing a tiny idol from out of his pouch and waving it about before us. 'In any case, those Britons have never managed to so much as scratch me yet!'

Despite his false courage and bravado, I was deeply concerned for his safety, as was Gaius. A sad tone had fallen upon this last evening together at Viroconium, and we all prayed that it would not be the last ever.

'Don't look so melancholy you two!' Marcus berated us both as we said goodnight. 'You just get yourselves down to that upper-class villa of yours and I'll be knocking on your door in no time.'

As Marcus departed with Suetonius and the Legions the following morning, a strange sort of silence encompassed the fortress. For a Legionary Base that was normally bustling with soldiers to be so empty felt decidedly eerie. Only the bare minimum of troops remained to man the fortress. We watched Marcus depart with heavy hearts as he proudly flourished the standard of the First Cohort above his head.

Gorhambury Villa

Goddess Wall Stucco

Chapter Nine

AD 59 to AD 61

Verulamium,
Hertfordshire

'We're nearly there now,' Gaius remarked, bringing the horses to a halt. 'See, beyond those hills?' He pointed a finger indicating the direction. 'Verulamium.'

I peered ahead excitedly, just able to make out the first signs of town life; an odd couple of terracotta rooftops, and fine wisps of smoke curling high into the fresh spring air.

Moving off once again, we rounded a hill and then caught our first glimpse of the villa lying upon the slope. We had to continue a little way past the villa in order to turn onto the long track that led up to the house, taking us through a variety of fields, a couple of which had been sewn with crops of some sort. We passed a small round house and an aisled building with a sharply pitched straw roof, both part of the farm complex. Further along the track could be seen another, smaller, farm building, and an animal pen, and there, at the far end, lay the villa, its clean, white walls almost glistening in the afternoon sun.

I was speechless. Gaius reined the horses to a halt once again, and we sat there in silence, admiring it in all its glory.

'Are you sure we're at the right house?' I asked in disbelief as I finally thought of something to say. I stared wide-eyed at the sight that befell me, and Gaius laughed.

'Of course I'm sure.' He took my hand gently in his. 'This is our home now.'

'What, all of it?' I asked, gazing all around in wonderment at the adjoining fields.

'All of it,' Gaius confirmed with a smile.

We started off again, slowly drawing the cart up in front of the villa. As we scrambled down, we all stood for a moment, taking in the view that was laid out before us, the town of Verulamium just a half a mile to the east.

Leaving Goilladyn to tend to the horses and the mule, Gaius and I began to explore the house. The villa was of a single storey construction, being of a rectangular block and with a wing-room to one end. Below the *triclinium* lay a cellar. The entrance to the house was by way of an east-facing porch. Beyond the standard, plain, wooden doorway laid a feast for the eyes.

The room within had obviously been designed with the aim of impressing the casual visitor. All around, the walls had been decorated with painted plaster done into separate, individual panels depicting various scenes. These, in turn, were then surrounded by paintings of fruit, set amongst fresh, green foliage, bringing a feeling of summer to the entire room. The fruit had been drawn slightly larger than life-size, which had the effect of making it stand out even more.

Each room was furnished with items of quite good quality.

'It's already furnished?' I remarked in surprise.

'Of course,' Gaius replied. 'It would have been made ready should the governor, Suetonius in this case, have needed to stay here at any time. He'd have to have something to sit on, and sleep on.' He ran a hand along the length of the arm of one of the couches, feeling the quality of its workmanship beneath his fingertips. 'Not bad.'

Even the kitchen had plentiful of containers and cooking pots. Caitilin and Aine immediately began sorting out what was useful and what was not. We had brought most of ours with us, so we now had more than what we would ever use.

By the time we'd looked around and had partaken of some refreshments we were all ready for a good night's rest. Curled up together in one another's arms, Gaius and I made love, and then drifted off into a peaceful and contented sleep. It had been a long while since we had felt so relaxed and free.

Over the ensuing weeks, we became more familiar with our new surroundings, and with the town of Verulamium itself. This town, built on the banks of the River Ver, had been designed according to Roman standards, yet it was occupied mostly by native Britons.

There were many traders coming and going from foreign ports, some of whom stayed on in Verulamium to set up shop on a more permanent basis. The most notable thing about Verulamium, from my point of view at least, was the total lack of the strong military presence that I had become accustomed to. Of course, there were some soldiers around, stationed within the town to basically keep order amongst its citizens, but they were in the minority.

The fact that Verulamium was not a fortified town, nor did it contain any form of military base, unlike those established at Glevum and Viroconium, was the first thing that I observed. To amble along the streets or peruse the *macellum* without coming across groups of soldiers at every turn was quite pleasant for a change and I felt I could relax at last.

The amazing thing was the terrific sense of freedom about the town, and the villa, just half a mile distant, neither of which was enclosed by the high walls of the previous two military townships. There were no Legions stationed here, no barracks, only a very low-key military presence centred mostly on the *forum*.

From our new home, and indeed from the town itself, one could see the surrounding countryside for miles around, the many hills and dips. The grasslands seemed to go on forever, bringing with them a complete feeling of space and tranquillity, not unlike standing atop the Mendip.

The villa itself, as it turned out, stood on the site of the previous *oppidum* of the Catuvellauni, the aisled barn and outbuildings belonging to the original Catuvellauni settlement. The land had been handed over to Roman ownership upon their pledge of allegiance to Roman rule. Thus, it had become one of the properties of the Governor of Britannia.

Suetonius was the first governor to take an interest in the property for living purposes, and had the current house reconstructed to the design of a small, Roman villa upon his appointment as governor of these isles, yet he had never been given the chance to reside in it. Basically, what we had been given was a brand-new house.

The old hill-fort of the Catuvellauni was enclosed by a dyke system, connecting three main dykes, or ditches, which ran along the northern edge of the property and were quite steep, but provided an excellent view once one reached the summit. The villa itself was positioned towards the east, with views of the River Ver and the town beyond.

Soon after settling into our new abode we recognised the need to engage extra labour to assist with the farm, of which but a couple of fields were currently utilised for the growing of mainly corn and grapes. Immediately below the house lay a small orchard. Added to this was a limited amount of livestock that included a couple of goats and a small cat, the like of which I was not familiar with, domestic cats having arrived in Britannia along with the Romans. We were told that the cat's name was Nero, after the current emperor, and that it was there to keep down the rodents.

'You can pet it if you like,' Gaius had suggested, but when I reached out a hand tentatively to stroke it, Nero hissed and scratched at my arm.

'Ouch!' I complained, and I pulled my arm away swiftly.

'I can see why he is called Nero!' Gaius laughed. 'Never mind, he'll soon get used to us.'

Goilladyn was a blessing, quickly making himself known around the town, which was more like a large Celtic settlement than a Roman town, as it was only just beginning to grow, but he managed to find us plentiful supply of seasonal labour amongst the Britons residing there. Gaius' loyal old manservant also proved invaluable in helping Gaius to start his own business dealing in Roman Law.

Goilladyn had helped to spread the word throughout the town that Gaius was available to undertake any form of legal work, should anyone require assistance. Roman Lawyers were unpaid, but often received gratuities and favours in other ways for successfully won cases. It wasn't long before Gaius obtained his first clients, and from there on, his business prospered.

Word of mouth travelled fast, and with many people experiencing difficulty with the money-lenders, Gaius' reputation for his kindness and expertise soon spread. The people who consulted him were invariably deep in debt but were only too happy to help with work on the farm in appreciation of his assistance.

By the close of the first year, we were all enjoying the new lifestyle, being well settled into our Roman villa. After a while, we managed to find a little more time to ourselves, although Gaius was often occupied with legal work or with keeping the books for the farm. Everything had to be written down before it was sent off to market.

To ensure the health of the crops, Gaius commissioned a plaster wall mounting of the Roman goddess, and in a way, my namesake, Diana, to be placed in the *triclinium*. It was to have a double intention, as although Diana was well known as the "goddess of the hunt" she could also be beneficial for the fertility of crops and was the goddess of childbirth, and sadly we had not been blessed in this way.

The goddess was portrayed as if she was reclining, with her right arm laid back, the hand resting beside her head, while her other arm came across her stomach and held onto a babe in swaddling cloth that lay snuggled alongside her right breast. She had her knees together and twisted toward the right, while her feet pointed straight down.

The goddess was naked save for a red cape that covered her left shoulder to come across her midriff then down her right side almost to her feet, her legs remaining uncovered.

While life progressed well for us, Suetonius' push into Northern Cambria was beginning to heat up. Reports had been coming in throughout the year regarding some exceptionally heavy fighting, with many losses on both sides. It was also rumoured that the druids had banded together and had a network of communications that ran the length and breadth of the country. Some said that they were plotting and scheming and casting evil spells, calling upon ancient spirits to bring destruction upon us all. Gaius instantly discounted this as a lot of propaganda and superstitious nonsense.

We had heard how early in the January of AD 60, Prasutagus, King of the Iceni, had passed away of illness, his lands now forfeit to Rome, and how his wife, Boudicca, had protested against this resulting in herself and her two daughters being beaten and treated quite harshly. By the close of that year and with the onset of winter, the Legions were now entrenched well within the heart of the Cambrian Mountains, in readiness to strike once the spring thaws began. Their target was the very epicentre of the druid activity, on the Isle of Mona itself.

AD 61, and as the fighting in Northern Cambria intensified, the early summer heat urged us more and more to spend extra time relaxing at the baths in an attempt to keep cool, the distant fighting a world away and soon forgotten amongst the peace of Verulamium. It therefore came like a bolt out of the blue when one of our farm labourers arrived one morning with dire news.

The town of Camulodunum had been sacked and burnt to the ground. The Iceni, led by the vengeful Boudicca herself who had titled herself "queen", had banded together with the Trinovantes tribe. The rebels numbered in their thousands, and we had no idea where or when they would strike next. With Suetonius and his Legions now attacking Mona, some two-hundred and fifty miles away, there was little anyone could do but sit tight and pray.

Imagine our surprise when just three days later Suetonius arrived at the villa, riding wearily up to the house astride a magnificent dark grey stallion and with three of his favoured officers riding alongside. The remainder of the cavalry he had left to refresh themselves, and their horses, at the riverside where they were encamped. They must have ridden hard and fast to get here so quickly.

Nero scampered hastily out of the way the moment he registered their approach, his paws skittering across the freshly swept porch, grumbling and hissing as he went.

'Londinium may well be their next target,' Governor Suetonius rounded off having filled us in on the past few days' events. 'That isn't very far from here. It wouldn't be difficult to envisage Verulamium falling soon after that,' he added, disconsolate, 'and I've no hope of defending either town.'

He finished off the last of his refreshments that Aine had brought in and leaned back on the couch, exhausted.

The three officers had taken some wine outside and sat on the porch relaxing in the afternoon sun.

'You know, this is the first time I've actually been in this villa,' Suetonius added casually, looking around the *triclinium* in admiration. 'It's quite nice here. Do you like it Gaius?'

'Very much, sir, thank you.'

Suetonius arose for a moment and stood admiring the large plaster goddess and child, which being about a third life-sized tended to dominate the room.

'So, what should we do about this rebellion, do you think?' he asked, looking hopefully toward Gaius for an answer. 'What can we do?' he continued in desperation.

Gaius shrugged. 'No walls,' he responded simply. 'I always said we should have built walls around all the towns.'

He stroked his chin thoughtfully. 'There is little you can do. Without the remaining Legions…'

'I know, I know. I can't understand why the Second Augustan fails to respond.' Suetonius sighed heavily, sitting down upon the couch once more. 'The Ninth has already fallen into a trap. Stupid! Cerialis has only his cavalry left. We're in serious trouble this time, Gaius Julius.' He ran his hands over his already thinning hair. 'We're reconstructing the fort at Manduessedum, on a smaller scale,' he added hastily.

'Good idea,' Gaius responded. 'It might be useful having a few more forts scattered about.'

Suetonius raised a questioning eyebrow and gazed hopefully at Gaius. 'I could do with a good tactician?'

'No,' Gaius replied a little more sharply than he had intended.

'It is no exaggeration to say that this could mean the end of the province under Roman control,' Suetonius persisted.

'I said no,' he responded curtly. Gaius arose abruptly, turning his back on Suetonius. He walked over to the open doorway and gazed out across the rolling fields.

'Well, it is good to see you are both looking so well,' the governor continued, a little disconcerted by Gaius' cold response.

I offered him a little more wine and smiled apologetically.

'Thank you, Julia Dana, but I really must be going,' Suetonius responded as he stood up. 'We've very little time to spare.'

He made his way towards the doorway, pausing as he came alongside Gaius.

'If you don't want to come along with us, Gaius Julius, that's understandable,' he said. 'I don't blame you—it's very pleasant here—but if I were you I'd be leaving right now. Don't be so stubborn as to risk your lives here. Not because of me, nor the Army, and certainly not for Rome.' He looked meaningfully at Gaius, his expression grave. 'You're far to close here,' he added.

'We'll be fine, sir,' Gaius replied solemnly. 'We've the last of the crops to harvest soon lest they be ruined, but thank you for your concern.'

'Very well, I wish you luck.' He turned to leave. 'If you will not assist us, I would welcome some advice?'

Gaius remained silent. General Suetonius shrugged his shoulders in defeat.

'Farewell then, and take care.' They shook hands awkwardly. Suetonius gave me a weak smile. 'Julia Dana,' he added with a nod of his head.

Although he wanted no more to do with the Roman Army, his tactician's mind still worked perfectly well. Gaius stepped forward. He bit his lower lip in pensive thought, his mind obviously considering some plan.

'Perhaps...' Gaius remarked suddenly.

Suetonius paused. He looked expectantly at Gaius.

'Perhaps,' he began once more, 'you could draw the rebels off northwards. Lead them away from the towns, and...'

'And find a place to battle of our own choosing!' Suetonius completed enthusiastically. 'Perhaps too, they will follow us and leave the towns alone? Perhaps,' he sighed 'It's a long shot but it might just work! But where shall we lead them do you think?'

Gaius thought for a moment more. 'There's a field close to Manduessedum, with some woods adjacent.'

'I know the place,' Suetonius replied, his eyes displaying the first sign of hope since his arrival that day.

'If the men were to keep their backs to the trees, so that they cannot circle around behind them,' Gaius suggested. 'It's not numbers that win a battle at the end of the day, it's strategy.'

Suetonius nodded in agreement. He placed a hand on Gaius' shoulder. 'By the gods, we'll win this battle yet! Come with us?' he entreated once more in a last attempt to make Gaius see reason, but Gaius merely stepped aside, shaking himself free of Suetonius' grasp.

'No? Then I must leave without you,' Suetonius said despondent, and he stepped outside.

I looked upon this renowned Roman General and Governor of Britannia with nothing but admiration. He seemed so vulnerable, going off to fight against this barbarian horde, and yet his mind was a sharp as any younger man's—sharper even.

'Good luck, Governor Suetonius,' I said sincerely, and Suetonius nodded once more.

'Oh, by the way,' Suetonius remarked in afterthought, halting in his stride. 'I nearly forgot to tell you, what with everything else happening,' he paused a moment, as if trying to find the right words to say. 'We lost Marcus early on in the campaign,' he placed a sympathetic hand upon Gaius' shoulder. 'I'm sorry,' he added. 'I know he was your friend.'

We were both stunned.

Suetonius breathed a heavy sigh then continued on his way. The weight of the world seemed to be upon his shoulders. He and his officers mounted their horses and rode away slowly, leaving the villa in total silence. Neither one of us spoke for several moments.

Gaius then strolled outside, his gait heavy and tired, as he headed along the porch. He sat down wearily and placed his head in his hands, resting his elbows upon his knees. Gaius closed his eyes in silent prayer for a moment, brushing his golden locks back off his face as he then raised his head to gaze out across the fields once more and far into the distance towards Verulamium. The only sign of Suetonius' visit was the trail of dust left lingering in the air.

Gaius sighed, deep in thought. 'For the first time in my life, I don't know what to do,' he admitted helplessly.

I stepped out of the house and knelt down beside him, encircling his arm as I lay my chin upon his knee.

It seemed so peaceful here, the surrounding countryside looking as if it could go on forever, the only sound being that of the constant birdsong all around. It was difficult to imagine any form of fighting or rebellion ever taking place here.

I glanced up at Gaius, looking to him for guidance.

'Is Suetonius right?' I asked worriedly. 'Are we too close here?'

'I don't know,' he replied honestly, taking a deep breath. 'I really don't.' He paused for a moment, as he considered all options. 'Possibly.'

I laid my head back down on his knee, gazing mournfully into the distance. 'Poor Marcus,' I said sadly.

Gaius placed his hand on my head and stroked my hair gently, yet he remained silent. These past few years had taken a heavy toll on him, what with the trial and his sudden resignation from the Army, added to which he had never forgotten the loss of his cohort during the Silures campaign, then there was the loss of our baby and now, just when things were going so well for us, came this rebellion, and Marcus, dear Marcus. He was only thirty-eight.

When we had stood and watched him march off that morning, I had known, somehow, deep down, that we would never see him again. Not in this world. Perhaps, in the after-life, in what the Romans called *Elysium*, we would all meet up again.

'Marcus and I, we trained together, and when I learnt that he had been posted to the Fourteenth Legion's cavalry unit, I always swore I'd look out for him,' Gaius recounted fondly. 'We always watched each other's backs. One of us was never far away if the other ever needed help, even when I was in command of the Thracians.' He sighed, taking a deep breath. A tear ran down his cheek and he hastily brushed it aside. 'What now?' he asked in anguish. 'I have failed in my promise.'

'It's not your fault,' I responded swiftly. 'You did the right thing. You always have.' I placed my hand in his and he grasped it firmly.

'You know, we used to imagine that if we were to die in battle we would be standing side by side, facing the enemy in an honourable death,' he added, managing a half-smile. Gaius kissed the back of my hand, blinking away a further tear.

'His death was not in vain,' I stated firmly. 'I don't think I've ever met a more honourable man, except for you that is!'

Gaius laughed a little and allowed himself a further smile. 'He was carrying the Standard of the First Cohort, and that is an honour in itself.'

'Well, there you are then, he did have an honourable death at least,' I said earnestly. 'Something a Dobunni warrior would have been proud of!'

'I suppose,' Gaius agreed sadly.

'Listen, you've served your twenty-five years with the Army, and these past years you've accomplished so much more, helped so many people,' I reasoned, appealing to his logic. 'Poor people, with huge debts to the money-lenders, and yet they always find a way to repay you, one way or another, out of sheer gratitude.' I smiled up at him encouragingly. 'You've done what you always wanted to do, and you're good at it. Marcus would have been proud of you.'

'I know he would have,' Gaius replied warmly. He ran his fingertips tenderly down my cheek then leant forward to kiss me gently upon the forehead. 'As I am proud to have you as my wife,' he added. 'And, I am grateful to have the farm and the villa. Truly, I am.'

'Then perhaps you should mention that to Suetonius?' I suggested, knowing how strained their relationship had been since the trial, and Gaius smiled.

At the close of day, there came such a brilliant sunset, as if the sun was going down in a blaze of glory for the last time. It felt like the end of an era. For how long would this all be ours, I pondered, with the rebellion so close by?

As I looked at Gaius, I knew he had to be wondering the same thing. Before retiring to bed, we both entreated our favourite gods and goddesses, each of us saying a special prayer for Marcus.

That evening found us both deep within our own thoughts, and as we lay abed, curled up in one another's arms yet unable to find any peace in repose, I decided to voice my concerns.

'Gaius?'

'Mmm?'

'You know how I've always trusted your decisions,' I began tentatively.

'But?' he prompted, gazing down at me and gently pushing a stray hair back off my forehead.

'But, having survived one massacre and narrowly avoided a second,' I continued, pausing for a moment to gather my thoughts. 'Look, if you really think we should stay, then I'll stand by you. You know I will.' I swallowed hard, trying to quell my fear. 'And there are the crops to consider too I suppose.'

Gaius hugged me closer, tenderly caressing my hair as he peered across the darkened room. For all his tactical expertise, no doubt he couldn't help wondering whether, this time, he was making the right choice.

'We should let the servants go, if they choose to, and give the slaves their freedom,' he remarked thoughtfully. 'I'll not force anyone to stay against their will, not even you. I'll stay and get the last of the crops in by myself if necessary. There isn't much left to harvest now.'

'There will be two of us then,' I stated firmly.

With the loss of his own cohort almost ten years ago now, it nevertheless still haunted him, and Gaius must have realised that our very lives now hung upon his decision. "A good tactician never makes a move until he's considered all the angles". That statement had been impressed upon his memory during his early days of serving with the XIIII Gemina. Perhaps that was what he was trying to do now, consider all the angles?

'Dana, we don't even know if they will attack Londinium yet,' Gaius replied eventually, 'and I'm sure we shall hear once they do. With any luck, they should follow Suetonius northward,' he continued, trying to sound encouraging. 'If they do decide to attack Verulamium as well, we should have plenty of time to get away while they're looting the town. Meanwhile, we can keep a constant vigil from the top of the ridge,' he added logically. 'We should be able to see them coming for miles from there.'

'Hmm, but I'm still not convinced,' I said in reply.

Gaius smiled, a little wearily. 'I know,' he said. 'Neither am I.'

We put Gaius' proposition to the servants the next day. As it turned out, Goilladyn and Caitilin offered to stay, while Aine and all the farm workers chose to leave. So, it was just the four of us. It was mainly the orchard fruit that now awaited picking.

It was some days later when Goilladyn returned from the town with news of the expected attack on Londinium. He would go to the *macellum* every day on normal business, and during the course of conversation Goilladyn would pick up snippets of news. With something as major as the Iceni rebellion, word travelled fast.

All the inhabitants who had steadfastly refused to leave Londinium had been brutally slaughtered, the town ransacked and burnt to the ground. Boudicca's forces were now taking their time celebrating and collecting the booty. They were becoming greedy and were in no hurry to leave Londinium, taking their time over the spoils.

Gaius remarked that the Iceni's delay in pursuing Governor Suetonius would give him more time to deploy his troops at the chosen battlefield. He and his cavalry had now met up with the slower moving part of his Legion, the infantry, and those involved in moving the gigantic Roman war machines, and he would have the time now to construct more of the machines on site. Suetonius had hoped to be ready well before the rebel forces arrived.

Meanwhile, there had been no sign of the Second Augustan Legion who should have rendezvoused with the Twentieth and Fourteenth en-route down from Cambria.

A further few days had elapsed when the news came that we had all been hoping for. Boudicca's forces were on the move northward, bi-passing our town. It looked as if the plan had worked. The Iceni and Trinovantes had been lured northward and Verulamium would be spared. We all breathed a huge sigh of relief and gave thanks to the gods, praying for victory for Suetonius in this forthcoming battle.

Meanwhile, the town of Verulamium had been all but abandoned. Most of the townsfolk had considered it prudent to leave as soon as they heard the news of the attack on Londinium. They would probably wait until the battle was all over with before they returned to their homes.

It was late at night and well after we had retired abed when we were awakened by a noise near the porch that set my heart racing and struck the fear of the gods into both myself and Gaius. Someone was prowling around outside.

Gaius arose in an instant and reached for his *gladius*. In fear for his life, I grabbed hold of his arm. Had the Iceni hoard returned under the cover of darkness to attack us while we slept?

'No, Gaius!' I urged, pulling him back.

'Don't worry,' he replied, forcing a smile. 'Barbarian hoards tend not to come one by one.'

He made his way cautiously out of the bedroom and crept silently towards the front door, unfastening it as quietly as he could. Goilladyn was now up and right behind Gaius, a heavy cooking pot in his hand.

Gaius leapt through the doorway as soon as he'd flung it open, surprising the prowler. There was a loud crash as the man knocked over some empty pots.

'Oh, sorry my lord!' he babbled. 'We thought the place to be abandoned!'

'We?' Gaius lowered his sword a little and gazed around warily. The man's accomplice was already becoming a fleeting figure disappearing into the darkness. 'Be gone with you!' Gaius yelled angrily, waving his gladius for emphasis, and the man scrambled hastily to be off.

Relieved, but somewhat shaken, Gaius strolled back inside. 'Or,' he added, taking a deep breath, 'even two by two.'

With the rebels now a good twenty miles or so at least to the north of Verulamium, we all felt a lot safer. Nevertheless, Gaius and Goilladyn continued to patrol the boundaries at set intervals throughout the day. It was easy to become complacent, but with no news from the town we had no idea what was going on, and after the previous night's interruption we all felt a little on edge.

For all we knew, the final battle could be all over, although I was certain that Suetonius would have sent us some word, assuming he had been victorious of course.

It had been an exceptionally hot summer with very little rain. Caitilin and I were busily working in the field to the front of the villa, picking the last of the fruit. It looked like being yet another dry and sunny day with still no rain in sight, rain that we had desperately needed for our crops. Many a crop had been ruined this past year from the continual drought. The long grass that wafted gently in the welcome breeze remained brown and dry, the sky bright blue with not so much as a single cloud.

Almost a week had passed since we last had news of the Iceni. Gaius came out of the house, Goilladyn following close behind. They ambled across to where Caitilin and I were working happily. It was so pleasant and peaceful out in the field, with the sound of bird song, the swallows dipping and swooping overhead. As midday approached, however, the heat was becoming just a little too unbearable. I straightened myself up, wiping my brow and smiling as I saw Gaius approach.

'We're just off to check the boundaries once more,' he said, returning my smile.

'All right, my love,' I replied. 'Don't be too long though, will you? We'll have lunch when you return.'

Gaius took my hand gently in his and gave it an encouraging squeeze before strolling over to where Goilladyn was patiently waiting. I stood and watched them contentedly as they headed towards the north of the property.

Sweeping my hair back off my face I returned to my work. If we didn't finish getting the last of the crops in soon more would go to waste.

Caitilin had just taken another basketful back to the storeroom. I was alone. The only sound was the rustling of the long, dry grass. Not even the birds were singing now. The sudden silence was unerring and I shivered, despite the heat of the day.

Then, a noise. An unmistakeable sound coming from the west and I gazed up towards the villa, shading my eyes from the hot sun and the glare. And then I saw them. They came out of nowhere—thousands of them. A vast horde of fearsome-looking warriors appeared from behind our villa. I gazed on in horror as they converged upon the house. In an instant, they had the villa surrounded. Yelling out their battle-cries and brandishing their weapons, they began to ransack our home.

Unbeknownst to us, Boudicca's barbarian horde, having gorged themselves on the bounty of food from Londinium, and seen off all the wine, were now ravenous for more. They had decided in their drunken fury to circle around and pillage Verulamium for all it was worth, their previous success spurring them on to even greater glory, before heading off to confront Suetonius's Army in one, final, bloody battle.

While some warriors were plundering the villa, their compatriots remained on guard outside, and with even more warriors spilling over the hilltops beyond, like ants from out of an ant nest.

It was too late to find a place to hide. Dear Caitilin never stood a chance. I watched in horror as she emerged from the storeroom only to find herself completely surrounded. She dropped the basket and screamed in terror, starting to run towards me, but she was instantly intercepted by one of the brawny, male warriors who towered over her. With one swing of his enormous broadsword, her head went flying across the field. The victorious warrior then let out a shriek of triumph, running to retrieve Caitilin's severed head and holding it up aloft for the entire tribe to see.

I had no time to ponder about Gaius's whereabouts as I was soon to find myself in a similar situation. One powerfully built tribesman suddenly began to advance down the slope towards me. He was a giant of a man, well over six feet tall, with rippling muscles and wearing a thick, brown fur slung across his left shoulder. He too carried a broadsword which he waved menacingly above his head, letting out a blood curdling cry as he charged.

'Gaius!' I called in desperation.

I had no option but to reach for my sword, although the situation seemed hopeless. I stood my ground, wielding my own sword, as he brought the heavy Celtic sword down upon me. I managed to defend the blow using all my might and strength in an effort to merely hold onto my own sword as the larger weapon struck.

The man was massive, his face surrounded by long brown hair and a shaggy beard. Suddenly I was glad for all the sword lessons that I'd insisted Gaius give me, although inwardly I knew that I was fighting a losing battle. The barbarian's sheer strength would eventually prove too much for me. It was only a matter of time.

The warrior came at me again, and again, and I defended deftly as he forced me further and further down the slope away from the villa. He slashed at me once more and again I blocked the savage blow. Raising the sword up high, he then brought it down in one mighty sweep.

The length of his broadsword was at least twice as long as my own, and all I could do was to defend, and this I did valiantly once more, holding the mighty Celtic sword at bay as it dominated over me and my much shorter weapon.

I was grasping my sword firmly with both my hands as the warrior's sword pressed harder now against mine, locked together for a few moments in an impasse, when suddenly, unexpectedly, the barbarian slid his sword along and beneath my own. There was the grating sound of metal against metal, then a swift slash across.

I knew that I'd been cut, and cut deeply, although I felt no pain. The point of the broadsword had caught me across the midriff. I fell backwards, clutching my stomach and half sitting up as I gazed, petrified, at the enormous figure of a man now bearing down upon me.

The barbarian moved in for the kill. He raised his sword up high. It was obvious that he planned to take my head, just as his colleague had done to dear Caitilin. I looked up at him helplessly, wide-eyed and terror-stricken.

And then I heard Gaius. 'Dana!' he cried out as he came charging desperately across the field. 'No!'

He collided straight into the heavy-set warrior, shouldering him aside and knocking him off balance. The massive barbarian stumbled a little, but he remained on his feet. Before he had a chance to regain his stability, Gaius plunged his *gladius* into the big man's side. The mighty warrior fell to the ground with a heavy thud.

While this particular warrior was now no longer a threat, there were thousands upon thousands right behind him, and I had already received a fatal wound.

Abruptly, the barbarians who had been raiding the house had ceased at the sound of Gaius' cry. As if noticing us for the first time, preoccupied as they were with their looting of our property, one of them now began to draw his sword, stepping slowly off the porch and heading straight towards us.

It was then that I glimpsed the woman standing before him. Instantly she thrust out an arm, thereby blocking his path. She looked to be in command and the man immediately halted in his tracks, lowering his sword a little. The two of them just stood there, side by side, in front of our villa.

The man, like the majority of his tribe, wore his hair long and sported a shaggy beard. The woman's hair was left loose and flowing, and was of a brownish copper colour, the sun occasionally highlighting the auburn tones as it wafted gently in the breeze. Was this Boudicca herself? Whoever she was, at

251

least she seemed to understand the need for some honour in death.

Ignoring the hoard of onlookers, Gaius instantly ran to my side, focusing his attention upon me and me alone as he stabbed his *gladius* into the sun-baked ground upon which we sat. Gently, he cradled me in his arms as he knelt down beside me.

I looked up at him, my eyes full of tears for the years we would now not see together. 'I'm sorry,' I whispered. 'I didn't have any choice.' I knew how much Gaius disliked me fighting with the sword, or fighting at all for that matter. How often had he warned me against such an action? He had been constantly reminding me since the very first day we'd met. Yet this was self-defence, and I had failed to defend myself this time.

But Gaius wasn't angry. He merely smiled and stroked my hair tenderly. 'I know,' he said.

Removing his cloak swiftly, Gaius then rolled it up and pressed it against the wound in an attempt to staunch the bleeding. I think we both knew at this point, however, that it would be all to no avail. We had, both of us, seen far too many battles, but I expect he felt he had to try something.

Goilladyn was now kneeling on the other side of me, and he too tried in vain to help stop the bleeding. Instinctively, I knew how serious the wound was although I could not see it and had no wish to. I only had to look at Gaius's face. Somehow, I imagined that if I did not look at the wound I would, perhaps, recover but then suddenly I began to feel very weak yet still I felt no pain.

'Gaius, I'm frightened,' I whispered urgently. 'Give me your hand, quickly!'

Goilladyn instantly took over tending the wound as Gaius released the cape and took hold of my left hand firmly in his, resting my head gently upon his knee.

The mere touch of his hand seemed to revive my inner-strength as I fought with renewed effort and determination to remain conscious even though I knew that the end was near.

'I don't want to leave you,' I breathed tearfully.

Gaius was too distraught to speak. He simply kissed my hand and then tenderly held it against his cheek as he closed his eyes, just for a moment. When he gazed upon me once more I could see that he was crying, yet at the same time he gave me that warm smile of his that I had come to know and love. I smiled back at him, my heart so full of love, as my tears too began to roll slowly down my face.

I gazed upon his handsome face for the last time, committing to memory every last detail, every line, from those wonderfully high cheekbones to his soft, golden locks, the colour and warmth of his eyes, now welling with tears. Even now, despite the tears, he still retained the ability to smile with those eyes. One of his tears suddenly escaped and began to wend its way down his face, leaving behind a trail of silver that glistened in the late morning sun.

I had seen him cry but twice before; the first was when he had lost all his men to the Silures, and then, more recently, upon the news of Marcus' death.

As I reached out with my free hand, intent on brushing the errant tear aside, my strength suddenly failed me and everything went black. My arm went limp and fell back and I rolled onto my left side towards Gaius, who clung onto me tightly. I felt a sharp pain—just for an instant—then, crying out softly, I was gone.

My life in Roman Britain had now come to an end, and yet curiously, somehow, I was still aware and remained for a little while at least.

I found myself standing next to where I had fallen. I have no doubt in my mind that it was through sheer determination and force of will in my refusal to leave Gaius and the home that I loved, despite such a short existence there, which had caused me to linger. I stood, as it were, on the side-lines and watched, somewhat bewildered, no longer a player in this game of life and death.

Gaius gazed upwards to the heavens above as he cradled my lifeless body in his arms. 'No!' he screamed to the gods, his tears rolling down his face in endless streams. Abruptly, he gazed towards where the woman stood watching.

'She was the only bright thing in your grey world!' Gaius shouted out to her bitterly through his tears. He took in the steadily increasing number of warriors gathering around the villa and surrounding hills, and he knew what he must do. The woman too, I think, expected the same of him.

Slowly and gently, he laid my body down upon the ground, and then, with one eye on the barbarians, he leaned across and steadily retrieved his sword from out the earth. The woman was watching him with keen intensity.

Swiftly, Gaius turned the *gladius* about, aiming the blade directly at himself.

'No, master!' Goilladyn appealed, Gaius' intention now unmistakable. The faithful old servant took hold of Gaius' wrists.

Gaius gazed upon Goilladyn's face, his features weathered now with age. They had been through much together over the years, from early on in his career, all the way from Gaul, long before he had ever met me.

'Do me one, last service, my friend,' Gaius requested of him, placing an arm upon the older man's shoulder. 'See that we're buried together.'

Goilladyn nodded slowly and released his grip. 'If I can,' he replied sadly, looking around with some uncertainty at the barbarian audience.

Before committing this final act, Gaius paused for a moment, seeming to remember something important. He arose slowly, acutely aware of the thousands of eyes upon him as he took but a few steps then stopped to retrieve my fallen sword.

Returning to my side, he carefully laid the sword beside my lifeless form and placed my hand gently upon it before turning his own sword once more upon himself.

Gaius then fell upon his sword, thus achieving an "honourable death".

Author at Gorhambury Walk

Burrington Combe

Dolebury as seen from Burrington

Gorhambury Exhibit at Verulamium Museum

Site of death as seen from location of Villa

Site of Villa marked by trees with present day Manor in the
background

Worlebury from Sand Bay

Worlebury from Western Entrance of Dolebury

Epilogue

The Romans were quite late in moving into the Southern Dobunni territory, leaving the Dobunni tribe to continue more or less as they were before the invasion. Many of the Roman villas in the North Somerset area were not built until after AD 270. With the exception of the mining activities, the Roman influence was small in comparison to the rest of Britain.

Historians and archaeologists have failed to understand why this is, while my own personal memory tells me that this was part of the peace treaty made between my people, the Southern Dobunni, and the Romans.

It is also unclear as to why Suetonius became so hell bent on revenge after the Iceni attacks, as if he had received some personal injury. As my own story shows, he did, in fact, take it as such.

The reason I decided to write my account as a historical novel was not only to fill in the gaps not yet surfaced within my own memory, but also because I wanted to recreate the full flavour and feelings of life in Roman Britain, and to be able to take the reader back to those ancient times of our ancestors.

How long my soul remained at Gorhambury Villa, or wandered the grounds, I have no idea. There is the theory that cremation aids the soul in departing towards its "heaven", so perhaps we did not linger too long. My last memory is of my mortal body being laid out in state within the aisled barn, presumably in preparation for cremation. I could see the massive beams and rafters overhead which formed the "A" shape of the roof as I gazed upwards. I felt confused, unable to understand why it was that I couldn't arise. I seem to have re-entered my lifeless body in an attempt to reanimate it. I can only assume that Gaius' body was also laid out likewise within the barn.

Interestingly enough, "two almost complete vessels" were unearthed together with a "native jar" and an "imported terra rubra fine-ware cup", that were "possibly a burial", just across from the aisled barn at the eastern entrance to the property. Both had been carefully placed alongside one another with due ceremony.

The faithful manservant, Goilladyn, perhaps, carrying out his master's final request?

Afterward

The final battle between Boudicca's Army and that of Gaius Suetonius Paullinus took place as planned somewhere in the midlands. For some time now, the location of the battlefield is thought to have been close to Mancetter, the Roman Manduessedum, in Warwickshire, although it has yet to be proved.

While the rebel Britons vastly outnumbered the Roman troops, they were completely disorganised with their numbers being boosted by simple farmers and women. Added to this, indications are that the Iceni were further disadvantaged by the fact that many if not most of this tribe seem to have been left-handed. This theory may be further supported by the Iceni King, Scavo (AD 35-AD 45), as a name that could be connected to the Latin *scaeva*, "left" and *scaevola*, "left-handed". With their shields held in the right hand, and lacking in any form of body armour, an opponent could easily strike straight at the heart. Furthermore, they were no match for the well-disciplined and experienced Roman Army.

Tacitus tells us that almost eighty thousand Britons fell in this one mighty battle. At the first onslaught, the Roman legionaries held their ground without counter-attacking. Then, once the order was given, they hurled their javelins forth in a wedge formation, together with the infantry of the auxiliaries. The cavalry was to attack last, vanquishing all resistance. A glorious victory for Rome.

Queen Boudicca herself is said to have escaped from the battle, only to have taken her own life by use of poison shortly afterwards.

The victorious Suetonius Paullinus was then to wreak havoc across the country as he swore vengeance for what had occurred. Even tribes who were perhaps neutral or undecided and who had not participated in the rebellion, were "ravaged with fire and sword" until finally a new governor was sent. Suetonius was recalled to Rome, having been criticised for not terminating the war.

Peace now reigned within Britannia, which was to remain a Roman province for the next four hundred years.

The Origins of the Dobunni

(Originally Published in CBA South-West Journal #8, Winter 2002)

The *Dobunni* Tribe of the North Somerset/Gloucestershire region were originally of Iberian descent, coming from the Bell Beaker people of Spain and Portugal.

These people are also known to have travelled to Brittany, where a tribe known as the *Coriosolites* existed. It is my belief that some of this tribe may have sailed to the coastline of Somerset, thereby beginning the Dobunni. Indeed, the Dobunni are understood to have traded with the Coriosolites of ancient Armorica (Brittany), and the fact that the name "Corio" appears on some of the early Dobunnic coinage may be more than a mere coincidence. I should like to suggest that this is in fact stating the origins of the tribe itself. It may well be that the chief of that time did perhaps take the name of Corio from the name of their forefathers as a mark of respect, or as a way of remembering their ancestors.

While this group of Iberians had landed at Brittany and Somerset, further groups set sail towards Ireland and other parts of Southern England and Europe.

This brings us to the tribal name of "Dobunni", the meaning of which has never been explained. The spelling of the name "Dobunni" can no doubt be ascribed to the Roman Latinisation as to the pronunciation of the word. Now, if one was to sound each syllable out, then convert the same sound into the Irish Gaelic spelling we get the following;

'DUBH' pronounced "Doo" which means; *dark or black-haired.*

'BUNAITHE' pronounced "Boo-Nee" which means; *established*

OR

'BUNAICH' also pronounced "Boo-Nee" and which means; *establish, found, set (up), start.*

OR POSSIBLY

'BUNADH' pronounced "Boo-Na" and means; *people, inhabitants.*

OR EVEN

'BUNAIOCH' also pronounced "Boo-Na" and means simply; *primitive.*

Putting this simply, the name "Dobunni" means literally, either (The) **'DARK-HAIRED (ONES) ESTABLISHED (THIS PLACE)'** *or perhaps just* (The) **'DARK-HAIRED PEOPLE'.**

Such a tribe would have stood out against the fair-haired Celts who came along later. Indeed, one only has to look at the dark-haired Spanish and Portuguese, together with many of the Irish and long-term residents of Somerset who have lived there for generations and still retain the dark hair of the Dobunni to see the connection.

Meanwhile, the Iberian connection to the Dobunni is further supported by the Beaker pottery shards and vessels unearthed, and in the style of hill-forts which they left behind, in particular those at Worlebury and Dolebury which use stone in construction of the ramparts. Similar types of hill-forts which use stone for their defences can be found in Spain and Portugal and with some of likewise construction also to be found in Ireland.

Further to the meaning of the Dobunni name, I believe it is quite possible that the language of the Dobunni may well have been closer to the Irish Gaelic than to the Brythonic Welsh supposedly spoken by the Celtic/British Tribes. No doubt an amalgamation of these languages could have occurred over the centuries. The original Gallic spoken on the continent became extinct during the onset of Christianity and the eventual change over to Latin.

With the arrival of the Celtic tribes, there were bound to have been a few inter-tribal marriages between the already resident Dobunni and the incoming Celts once peace was established, or perhaps as a means of establishing peace between one or more Belgic groups. However, I believe that the Dobunni remained essentially;

'THE DARK-HAIRED PEOPLE'.

1908: "Earthworks of England", *Allcroft, A H;* MacMillan & Co Limited, London.

1977 "The Bell Beaker Cultures of Spain and Portugal", *Harrison, Richard J;* Harvard Univ., Cambridge, Mass.

1980 "Worlebury, The story of the Iron Age hill-fort at Weston-Super-Mare", Woodspring Museum.

1998 Wroxeter, "Life & Death of a Roman City", *White, Roger & Barker, Philip,* Tempus Limited, Gloucs.

1999 "Irish Dictionary", Harper Collins, G.B.

1999 "Irish First Names", Harper Collins, G.B.

FOOTNOTE

The reference to "Corio" has since been revealed to be of a common name amongst ancient peoples, with several meanings noted, one of which could simply mean "crown" or "beloved".

Author's Note

It began with a dream, or should I say a sequence of dreams, in which people, places and especially feelings were as real and as vivid as they are in this world that we call "reality". But more than this, I was not "myself" in these dreams, but "someone else".

The first dream inspired me the most and set me wondering as to whether or not this was "just a dream", or was it in fact a memory of a past-life? Within this particular dream, which I assume lasted only minutes, I spent an entire day of in-depth conversations and interactions, interspersed with some intensely emotional feelings; memories within memories.

A couple of months later, further dreams emerged, although not always in chronological order and with some continuing on where the first dream left off.

Using these dream memories as a basis, I began searching through texts, historical references and archaeological surveys for the period concerned, finding facts and events that tied in exactly with the events in the dreams. With the use of a good, although modern day map, providing surprisingly only a few possible locations, it was only the Mendip Hills of North Somerset that fitted precisely the geographical scenery I was searching for.

I had deduced it to be on the west coast as this was where the sun had set, towards the coastline, and that there were five hills, with a gap running between the most western hill upon which the hill-fort laid, and the previous hill upon which I had been running.

There was Dolebury Hill-fort, as described in my dream, sitting atop the Mendip on the western most hill, and close by, Burrington Combe, a steep escarpment of rock that runs between the two hills, and exactly as I had seen.

The first hill-fort had been destroyed by the Romans and supposedly lay on the coast nearby. Imagine my surprise when I came across such a massacre site just a short distance away at Weston-Super-Mare! There it was—Worlebury—the hill-fort by the coast that had been so thoroughly and utterly destroyed, and with the likelihood that it was the Romans that had been responsible for this, specifically the II Augustan Legion under the command of General Vespasian, who was later destined to become emperor (AD 69-AD 79). He had already been responsible for the attack on Maiden Castle, Dorset, Hod Hill being the only other site at the time of writing showing signs of such a vicious attack by the Romans, so they were not exactly plentiful.

Worlebury Hill-fort is an imposing *oppidum* sitting majestically above the seaside resort of Weston-Super-Mare, on the edge of the Weston Woods. Even today, it has a sense of awe about it; a silent sentinel, its inhabitants long gone.

The fort dates back to the Iron Age, although there is evidence of Stone Age occupation from about 3,500 BC. At some point it acquired the name of "Caesar's Camp", yet there is no evidence to date to suggest that Caesar did actually visit there.

It was only after locating my "massacre site" that I experienced the "prequel" dream. This lasted only an instant during which I saw myself and just six others making our way across the fenland. It was dark and cold and with just a full moon to light our way.

Dolebury commands fine views toward Worlebury from the western boundary, its defences possessing a natural steep slope and with enhanced fortifications where the approach is easier.

The most incredible thing was the lake that was there some two-thousand years ago and is not there now, although there are two man-made lakes quite nearby that very location today, those of Blagdon and Chew Valley. The lake was in the precise location that I had recalled, and this was mentioned in only one archaeological journal that I came across. The lake would come and go as the course of the river that fed it altered. It would sometimes disappear altogether during the summer months. Current maps of Roman Briton today now show the usual position of the lake, without flood or drought.

When I first began researching these memories, my entire knowledge of the Invasion of Roman Britain consisted of Gaius Julius Caesar and "Boadicea", both of whom I thought lived at the same time and not, as I was to discover later, about one hundred years apart! I certainly couldn't have quoted any dates, let alone how many soldiers there were in a Roman Legion.

I was astonished to discover therefore that my "dream" was correct with the numbers of some ten-thousand soldiers heading towards the Mendip, at about five-thousand soldiers per Legion, and that the Fourteenth and the Twentieth *did* in fact travel together during that time in Britain.

Furthermore, the Sixth Thracian Cohort *was* attached to the Fourteenth Legion, and the Fourteenth Gemina was stationed at Mainz, in Gaul, from AD 9 to immediately prior to the invasion—so yes, Gaius Julius did spend some time in Gaul since enlisting, as he had remarked.

Also, the two villages at Mainz were of the La Tene culture, so no doubt Gaius had recognised the craftsmanship of the sword I was carrying, for it was a La Tene style sword, of this I am certain. I wonder now what became of the sword, for none were found at the burial site. Had Boudicca's Army stolen it and the *gladius* as booty, or did Goilladyn return them to the gods by flinging them into the river Ver?

Perhaps he returned my sword to my people at Dolebury, telling them the sad tale of how our lives had ended? If it is not one of the many swords already to have been recovered elsewhere, perhaps one day it will be found, albeit rusted and corroded by time.

Although there are many ideas to the contrary that it was the Twentieth Legion only that was stationed at Glevum when the fortress was begun, and that it was not large enough to hold two Legions, there is evidence that the Sixth Thracian were stationed within their own fortress nearby and the fact that it was attached to the Fourteenth speaks for itself.

There are also many beliefs that the Fourteenth remained at Manduessedum, but there was no reason for them to stay on there as the *Pax Romana* had already been established in this area. The real problem lay along the Welsh borders, and as stated in the Tacitus, Annals XII 32 *"castris legionum premenda"*, interpreted literally as "suppressed by the camp of Legions". Tacitus also reports, Annals XII, 31, that *"cunctaque castris antonam et Sabrinam fluvios cohibere parat"* or "prepares to hold the line of the rivers Trent and Severn with forts".

I believe, and as my "memory" tells me, it was the Fourteenth that was stationed at Glevum, along with a detachment of the Twentieth, while the remainder of the Twentieth was to man these forts, plus a further detachment in later years had begun the fortress at Viroconium.

The Second Legion moved into Glevum when the Fourteenth and Twentieth departed. They had failed to respond to the call to assist during the battle against Boudicca. Their Commanding Officer later committed suicide by falling upon his sword.

The fact that centurions and officers were allowed to marry is another interesting detail, whereas the common legionary was not and had to wait until discharged after twenty-five years of service. This did not stop some having women and families outside their fort however.

I have found as I have been working on this project that I am now beginning to remember things during normal waking life, as well as through the occasional dream.

All places, events and most names in this novel are based on fact. In some instances, it was necessary to use "writer's imagination" in order to provide a continuous link or to incorporate particular people whom I know I have met at some point in the story. All the events and dialogue from Chapter One, and most from Chapter Two, are the result of this first, amazing "dream", and are all quoted word for word from memory.

The decision as to where to locate the Legionary fortress of Glevum alongside the Sabrina and with the VIth Thracian fortress being close by is also from memory, as are the battles and encounters with the war-like Silures tribe.

The actual details of the killing of Vecilius at the time of writing have evaded me but the memory of being pursued by the soldiers up to Marcus loaning me his horse is an exact recall, as was the cave and events at Tickenham rock shelter where I believe I hid.

The trial itself was based on how Roman trials were held, having but little memory of this event myself, other than the argument between Gaius Julius and Suetonius, a small part of Gaius' speech at the trial, and finally the offer of Suetonius' house at what is now called Gorhambury Villa. My memory of the events at Gorhambury begin on the morning of the attack by Boudicca's Iceni and Trinovante warriors.

The memory of the plaster "stucco" model of the goddess and child was inspired by the remains on display at the Verulamium Roman Museum, which my instinct tells me were for fertility. The archaeological description of the one hand being in a "fist" I recall as actually being quite relaxed, as shown in my sketch, and not in a fist at all, for it is not clenched tightly enough.

All my major characters and most of my secondary characters are taken from either past-life memory or historical texts. Some of the actual names were difficult to come by, with Anturiaethus, Eber, Broduil, and my own name of Danamanadera, basically my own invention, plucked from various "Celtic" dictionaries. I recall my full name as being approximately six syllables in length, and that it was shortened, but I cannot recollect exactly what it actually was!

Neither am I in any way certain that I was the daughter of the Dobunni Chieftain, but the fact that I was carrying a rather stylish La Tene sword would seem to indicate that its previous owner, "Dana's" father, would have been a man of some importance.

The names of Roisin and Dafydd came to me in dreams, while Sabina and Creag were basically invented characters, however I did experience a recall of "Vecilius" telling me that he had raped "my friend".

I must have come across Petulius Cerialis at some point in this past lifetime for I recalled exactly what he looked like and drew the sketch shown within this book immediately afterwards, long before I had access to a computer upon which one can now find images. Amazingly, the sketch I drew looks remarkably close to the Roman bust of him that can be found on the internet. The same is true of the Roman Governors, although I didn't complete a sketch of these.

The name of Gaius Julius was as I had recalled it, and with an inscription discovered in 1800 (RIB 346) that included the last name of Caecinianus, the cognomen, which tells us he came from Northern Italy. The inscribed stone was originally found at *Burrium* (Usk), close to the Roman Fort of *Isca* (Caerleon). Its whereabouts since sadly remain unknown.

His grandfather's grandfather had been a Gaul who was enlisted by Caesar and rewarded with Roman citizenship upon retirement for his loyalty and bravery.

A Monumental Arch still stands at Saintes (*Mediolanum Santonum*) today and was erected by a wealthy Gaul, one Gaius Julius Rufus, showing his family tree. Was he "my" Roman centurion's grandfather? Was the Gaius Julius born in AD 19 "my" centurion? Certainly, the age would match up correctly.

If this is not Gaius Julius Caecinianus' family tree, it would have looked something similar, and to be schooled in law and history and "bought" a commission into the Roman Army at centurion rank his father would have had to have been reasonably wealthy. Epotsorovidos, Gaius' grandfather's great grandfather, was an aristocratic Gaul, residing in Aquitaine just prior to Caesar's conquest.

EPOTSOROVIDUS (GAUL)

GAIUS JULIUS GEDOMO
(Rewarded by Caesar and received citizenship)

GAIUS JULIUS OTUANEUNUS

GAIUS JULIUS RUFUS
(Honorary ADC)
Became Priest of Rome, constructed Amphitheatre at Lyon, and Arch at Saintes in AD 19 where this inscription can be found

GAIUS JULIUS?

GAIUS JULIUS (Caecinianus?)
b. AD 19

Marcus Petronius' tombstone (RIB 294) was excavated at Wroxeter and proves that he died just prior to the Iceni revolt. It now resides at Shrewsbury Museum.

Ostorius Scapula I recalled to be a very brusque man, who enjoyed a laugh but often at someone else's expense. He had short, very dark hair, and was quite muscular. Didius Gallus, I pictured as small and wiry, an older man, balding on top, with a razor-sharp mind but who would often forget people's names. Quintus Veranius, an energetic leader, quite young with a muscular build and with some curl or wave to his hair which was perhaps a light brown in colour. And Suetonius Paullinus had a sallow, olive complexion with black, thinning hair, balding on top. He would often use more force than required to get his own way. The black rings under his eyes perhaps hinting that he had seen one too many battles.

While I cannot be sure of ever having met Cartimandua, I am certain of travelling on occasion with Gaius Julius at times when it was deemed safe to do so. I like to think that I had the chance to meet her, and my instinct seems to tell me that she was a woman who knew exactly what she wanted and how to achieve it. I feel she was attractive and had a liking for power and control, but also for the luxuries that Rome could bring her.

Whether or not one believes in reincarnation, the fact remains that somehow I have acquired the memories of this young native girl at a poignant time in British history. The thought occurs to me that had "Dana" not attacked the centurion, and had instead returned to warn the tribe, the warriors would most likely have attacked and killed him, and the Roman Army upon their arrival would have thus wiped out the entire tribe. History could have been quite different.

This "Past Life" memory was not in fact the first. Indeed, my first memory of being "someone else", living in another time, occurred when I was only twelve years of age, and this one too I have found to have been documented in historical texts.

Since writing this book, I have had other memories of other times emerge, and again, at a point in history of which I had very little prior knowledge, at least in this lifetime, but which can in many cases be verified.

It's as if I had managed to locate some universal history book, taking on the part of the person I was reading about. Was it "me", living in a past-time, or had the memories of these people somehow managed to attach themselves to me? Either way, it is encouraging to know that when we are gone, somehow, some way, our memories live on.

"… for the belief of Pythagoras prevails among them, that the souls of men are immortal and that after a prescribed number of years they commence upon a new life, the soul entering into another body."

Greek historian Diodorus Siculus
(V.28:56-6; 1st century BC)

"Caitilin"

Have you ever come across a complete stranger, yet one who seems so familiar, and that you have so much in common with that you feel as if you've known them all your life? And though you may never see them again, you find you have recounted each other's entire life stories in a very short space of time.

I had such an experience while travelling home on the train once. As I took my seat, a woman opposite me of about my age commented upon the socks I wore, noting that they were the same as hers. Thus, began a conversation that never stopped until my train pulled into my station. The socks were, in fact, RSPCA socks emblazoned with a multitude of cats. Our conversation lasted but 45 minutes, the time it took for my train to reach my station. "K" was to disembark the train one stop further on than me.

During those 45 minutes we discovered a mutual love of cats and horses, her favourite and mine, and indeed a fondness for all animals. In fact, we shared many of the same views on many things. We swapped information on our entire lives in that short space of time, as if "catching up" with an old friend after a very long absence.

"K" had fair hair and features that reminded me of Caitilin. Amazingly, as the train pulled into my station, and I arose from my seat, I noticed that she wore a pendant of the White Horse of Uffington that lay within the Catuvellauni territory. She commented that her sister had bought it for her during a trip to Britain, but it left me wondering had we met before? Caitilin was of the Catuvellauni. Was "K" actually Caitilin reborn?

Southern Dobunni

Dana

"Dana"

Interestingly enough, upon a recent visit to St Albans and my first visit to the Verulamium Museum, I noticed a lady working at a café nearby who looked exactly like Dana from the sketches I had drawn, even down to the shape of the eyes and eyebrows, and the habit of flicking her long hair over her right shoulder. The hair too was worn down and mostly loose—although more of a medium brown rather than the dark brownish black of the full Dobunni. I am left pondering this experience, having not plucked up the courage to speak to the woman, and yet wishing that I had, wondering of her ancestry. Could Dana's long-lost baby brother have survived, his descendants going forth and resulting in this lady? Perhaps he was adopted by some Roman couple who had resided close by? Or perhaps this lady has just a little Iberian DNA? I have no recall of "Dana" ever having children, but maybe more memories and events will surface as time goes by.

And so, the adventure continues.

Glossary

Aquae Sulis	Bath. The goddess Sulis was equated to the Roman goddess of wisdom, Minerva. This was amalgamated to become Sulis Minerva
Aquilifer	A Legion's Eagle Standard Bearer.
Armatura	Weapons Instructor
Atrebates	Thought to be originally a Belgic tribe, or one that has intermingled with Belgic tribes.
Atrebas	Singular form of Atrebates tribe
Atrium	Entry Hall. A central room in Ancient Roman homes open to the sky at the centre.
Auxiliary	Auxiliary troops of non-Roman soldiers.
Bagendon	Chief town of the Dobunni, under control of the Northern Dobunni.
Belgae	Group of Belgic tribes that originated in Gaul.
Ballistae	Catapult-type artillery that shoots rocks and boulders.
Basilica	Public Courts
Burrium	Usk.

Catapultae	Catapult-type artillery that shoots bolts akin to large arrows and javelin
Cambria	Wales.
Camulodunum	Colchester.
Canabae	Civilian settlement that grew up outside a Roman Legionary Fort, and often housed military families.
Centurion	Originally commanded a century (100) of men
Cohort	Six centuries of soldiers.
Corinium Dubunnorum	Cirencester. This was the chief Roman town in Northern Dobunni territory and close to their capital at Bagendon.
Decurio Princeps	Senior Decurion of the Cavalry.
Duplicarius	An Officer on double pay.
Eborcorum	York.
Elysium	The Roman equivalent of Heaven
Equitata	A Roman Cohort containing both cavalry and infantry
Gladius	A Roman short sword.
Glevum	Gloucester
Hibernia	Ireland.
Isca	Caerleon
Isca Dumnoniorum	Exeter.

La Tene	A style that originated with the Iron Age people of the archaeological site of La Tene, which sits on the northern side of Lake Neuchatel in Switzerland, where thousands of objects had been found deposited in the lake. The term refers to the later period of art of the ancient Celts, identifiable by its curved and "swirly" decoration.
Legion	A Legion contained 10 Cohorts of 6 Centuries each, which included some 4,280 soldiers, 60 centurions.
Legionary	An ordinary Roman soldier.
Legion VIIII	Legion IX (Nine) Hispana—originating in Spain. The Georgians changed the way some Roman numerals were written to what they thought was a more logical format; VIIII to IX; XIIII became XIV etc.
Legion XIIII	Legion XIV (Fourteen) Gemina, Martia Victrix. "The Legion of the Twin" was a Legion of the Imperial Roman Army that was levied by Gaius Julius Caesar in 57 BC. The addition of *Gemina* was added when the Legion was combined with another understrength Legion after the Battle of Actium. "Martial and victorious" (added by Augustus in AD 9) and again added after the defeat of Boudicca in AD 61.
Lindum	Lincoln. *Lindum Colonia* was the Ninth Legion's Base before their move up to York.
Londinium	London.

Macellum	The Market Place
Manduessedum	Mancetter
Militaris Peritus	Roman Army Tactician
Military Tribune	Those on the governor's personal staff. A rank above Centurion but below a Legate. They were capable of commanding a Legion, as second in command, but were often engaged in personal staff duties for the governor.
Mona	Anglesey, the power centre of the druids.
Oppidum	Fortified settlement.
Optio	Second in command of a Century
Pugio	A Roman dagger
Sabrina	The Briton's name for the River Severn
Signifier	A Standard Bearer for a Century who was responsible for carrying the Signum, a standard made up of silvered discs and symbols.
Triclinium	Roman dining room containing three couches, hence the word "tri" meaning three, positioned around a small serving table.
Vicus	Village or town that grew up outside a Legionary Fort.
Villa	Grand Roman home, most country villas incorporating a farm or orchard
Verulam	The Briton's name for St Albans

| *Verulamium* | St Albans |
| *Viroconium* | Wroxeter. |

The Terra Rubra Cup that was discovered on the grounds of Gorhambury Villa, along with a Native Jar, and is thought to have formed part of a burial. (Photo by David Thorold; Courtesy of the Roman Verulamium Museum)